I.B.TAURIS SHORT HISTORIES

I.B.Tauris Short Histories is an authoritative and elegantly written new series which puts a fresh perspective on the way history is taught and understood in the twenty-first century. Designed to have strong appeal to university students and their teachers, as well as to general readers and history enthusiasts, *I.B.Tauris Short Histories* comprises a novel attempt to bring informed interpretation, as well as factual reportage, to historical debate. Addressing key subjects and topics in the fields of history, the history of ideas, religion, classical studies, politics, philosophy and Middle East studies, the series seeks intentionally to move beyond the bland, neutral 'introduction' that so often serves as the primary undergraduate teaching tool. While always providing students and generalists with the core facts that they need to get to grips with the essentials of any particular subject, *I.B.Tauris Short Histories* goes further. It offers new insights into how a topic has been understood in the past, and what different social and cultural factors might have been at work. It brings original perspectives to bear on manner of its current interpretation. It raises questions and – in its extensive further reading lists – points to further study, even as it suggests answers. Addressing a variety of subjects in a greater degree of depth than is often found in comparable series, yet at the same time in concise and compact handbook form, *I.B.Tauris Short Histories* aims to be 'introductions with an edge'. In combining questioning and searching analysis with informed history writing, it brings history up-to-date for an increasingly complex and globalised digital age.

www.short-histories.com

'In his fresh and lively introduction to the New Testament, Halvor Moxnes covers a great deal of ground clearly, unpretentiously and with a lightly held erudition. His readers are introduced to the bread and butter issues but a good deal more besides - not least the changing landscape of interpretative engagement with the text. The New Testament is a small book which has had a huge impact, as Moxnes reminds us; but it is also one whose meaning and interpretation continue to be contested and debated as they have since the first century. Authoritatively, but not didactically, a master of the trade has helped show us why this might be the case and where the future may lie. This is a stimulating read, at once accessible and provocative.'

– James Carleton Paget, Senior Lecturer in New Testament Studies,
University of Cambridge, and Fellow and Tutor of Peterhouse

'Moxnes does an impressive job in conveying the nature and character of this enigmatic collection of texts, whose very title suggests that, like a will, it bequeaths something new as compared with the 'old testament' that preceded it. His book helps elucidate the contents, character and origins of the writings of 'The New Testament', their function in antiquity, their emerging authority, and the multitude of ways in which they have affected the lives of people through their interpretation and application. His thoughtful consideration of Galatians 3:28 in particular gives a rich flavour of the varieties of ways in which an influential Pauline text has been interpreted so diversely.'

– Christopher Rowland, Dean Ireland's
Professor of the Exegesis of Holy Scripture, University of Oxford

'Halvor Moxnes has been an innovative leader in New Testament scholarship for many decades, and here he provides for the student and the general reader a wealth of rich insights, written in an accessible and arresting style. With brevity and clarity he introduces us to the contents and original contexts of the New Testament, but also, via well-chosen examples, to its powerful impact on culture and society over the centuries. Finally, he makes us aware of our own role, as readers, in making sense of this text, and the social and political contexts of all reading-methods, both scholarly and popular. Up-to-date and masterful in its understanding of the issues, this book does not shy away from the problematic legacy of the New Testament in Christian attitudes to Jews, women and subordinate social groups. Readers of many kinds will be grateful for such a sure-footed guide, and none can come away without wanting to participate themselves in the long and enthralling history of engagement with the New Testament.'

– John M G Barclay, Lightfoot
Professor of Divinity, Durham University

A Short History of . . .

A SHORT HISTORY OF

THE NEW TESTAMENT

HALVOR MOXNES

I.B. TAURIS

LONDON · NEW YORK

To past and present students of the New Testament
at the Faculty of Theology, University of Oslo

Published in 2014 by I.B.Tauris & Co Ltd
6 Salem Road, London W2 4BU
175 Fifth Avenue, New York NY 10010
www.ibtauris.com

Distributed in the United States and Canada Exclusively by Palgrave
Macmillan, 175 Fifth Avenue, New York NY 10010

ISBN: 978 1 78076 607 2 (hb)
ISBN: 978 1 78076 608 9 (pb)
eISBN: 978 0 85773 552 2

A full CIP record for this book is available from the British Library
A full CIP record is available from the Library of Congress

Library of Congress Catalog Card Number: available

Typeset in Sabon by Ellipsis Digital Limited, Glasgow

Printed and bound in Great Britain by T. J. International, Padstow,
Cornwall

Contents

List of Maps and Illustrations

Preface

It is, of course, impossible to write a 'short history of the New Testament'. I knew that when Alex Wright asked me to write this volume in the I.B.Tauris Short Histories series; not just because so much is written on the New Testament, but because it required a new type of book combining material not found in any one existing volume. Traditional introductions provide an overview of the various writings of the New Testament and their content in their historical context, while others present ways of reading the New Testament by introducing various methods and perspectives. Then there are books that introduce the history of the Greek texts and translations of the New Testament, or the collections of the books into a canon. Recently, the history of interpretation of individual books of the Bible has become a focus of interest.

In order to introduce new readers to what they need to know to read the New Testament, even a short history must include these various perspectives, combining the origin, content and purpose of the writings; the use and influence of the New Testament through history; and the history of reading and interpreting these texts. Consequently, this book necessarily is an experiment – of course it does not claim to give a full picture. The lists of further reading, therefore, will aid the interested readers in their exploration of the history of the New Testament.

I am very grateful to Alex Wright who entrusted me with this task, and who has encouraged me throughout the process of writing. Colleagues who are specialists in various areas have read one or more of the chapters and given valuable advice: John M.G. Barclay, Troels Engberg-Pedersen, and my colleagues in Oslo: Vemund Blomkvist, Marianne Bjelland Kartzow, Hugo Lundhaug, Anders Martinsen, Ole Jakob Løland and Lance Jenott, as well as students from the Paul-class in the spring term of 2013. Designer Johanne Hjorthol has assisted me with the illustrations; where required, permission has been given by the artist or photographer. Christer Hellholm has assisted me with editing and indexing. The production team, especially Ricky Blue, Denise Cowle and Lisa Goodrum, have been very helpful and efficient. I owe my friend and young colleague, Jonathan C. P. Birch, PhD from Glasgow University, a debt of gratitude for a special partnership in writing this book. He has not only rewritten the manuscript into idiomatic English, but also read it with a sharp eye with regard to content and been an important discussion partner throughout the process. In the end, of course, the responsibility for the book remains mine.

Much of the book was written in the autumn of 2013 when I was a visiting fellow at the Divinity Faculty, University of Cambridge. Many thanks to professor Judith Lieu and the other colleagues in New Testament, to the staff of the Divinity Faculty Library, and to the staff and students at Ridley Hall for generous hospitality.

Since so much of what I know about the New Testament I have learned both with and from my students, this book is dedicated to the students of the New Testament with whom I have worked, over many years, at the University of Oslo.

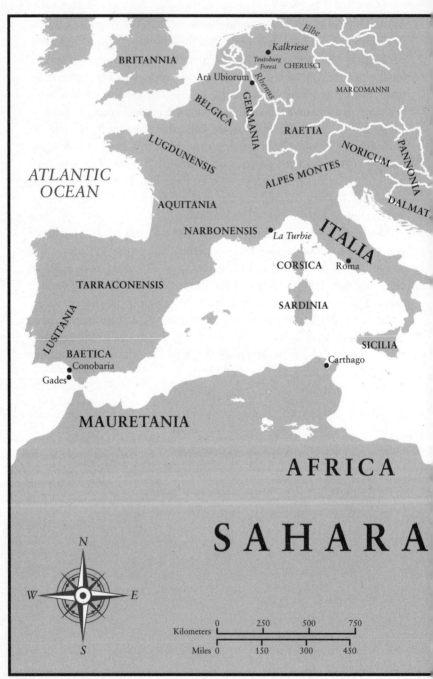

Map 1. The Mediterranean World at the time of Jesus.

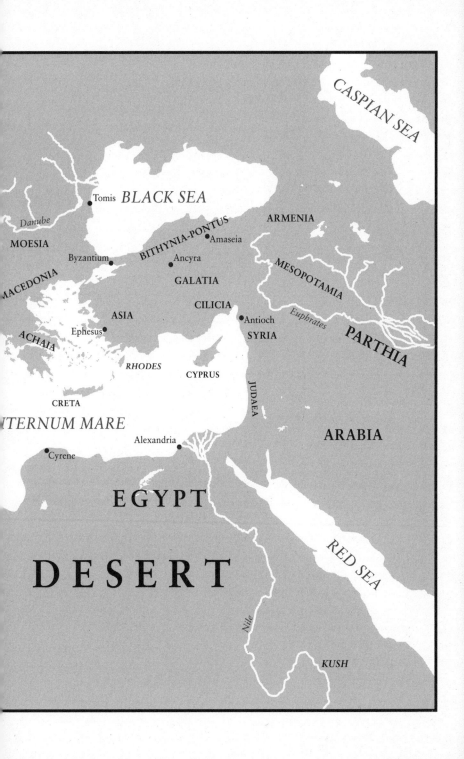

Introduction

WHAT IS A HISTORY OF
THE NEW TESTAMENT?

The New Testament is a small book that has changed the world. This may seem like a bold claim, but this volume on the history of the New Testament is an attempt to substantiate it. It is true that it is small; in a modern edition it covers only 250 pages, compared to the Old Testament's 815. Its success is curious in so much as there was little or no advantage to being 'new' in the ancient world when authority, especially religious authority, was so closely associated with the 'old'. In truth, the New Testament gained its authority because it was added to existing Jewish scriptures which were recognised as old. But the writings that became the New Testament did represent something new – the gradual growth of a Jewish sect into a new religion, Christianity, which was to spread over the known and unknown worlds, from Antiquity to the present modern age.

Since Jesus Christ, believed to be the Son of God and Saviour of humanity, was the centre of Christianity, the New Testament gained a unique position; it was not only the main source of knowledge about Jesus, but offered an interpretation of human existence, society and the future of the world in light of faith in Christ. Thus, the New Testament was at the beginning of what was to become Christendom – the gradual combination of Church, politics, culture and society, beginning in the Mediterranean world and the East before moving into Western and Northern Europe. After that followed the colonisation of North America, Latin America and Australia, and finally Africa (south of the Sahara) and new parts of Asia. The study of the New Testament eventually became a central plank in developments in the world of learning, from the first universities in the

Middle Ages to the establishment of modern academic disciplines in the eighteenth and nineteenth centuries, and their development (and in some cases transformation) in the twentieth century.

This history is no longer well known. In the secularised parts of the Western world, there is much less knowledge of the New Testament than even a generation ago, both of the actual content of the writings and of their larger historical and cultural context of transmission and influence. As a result, the relevance of the New Testament itself is sometimes called into question. A rewriting of the history of the New Testament is needed to address this changed environment. But where to begin? We have to go back to a period where the New Testament did not exist. The writings which became the New Testament were originally intended to be read by small groups, dedicated to following Christ, in their own time. Their authors could never have imagined that their work would one day constitute Scripture for the largest religion in the world, becoming a classic of world literature and a cultural cornerstone of Christian societies for millennia. They could have had no idea of the critical study, theory and literary method that these writings would have been subjected to in their ongoing interpretation over the last 200 years. All the considerations alluded to here need to be integrated into even a short history of the New Testament, thereby capturing something of the history which originally produced these texts, the history which witnessed their canonisation, and the history which was made, and continues to be made, through acts of interpretation and application in the lives of readers. This book therefore divides into three parts titled as follows: 1) Beginnings, 2) Shaping History and 3) Reading and Meaning-Making.

The first section, Beginnings, introduces the relevant writings from the first century after Christ, and therefore long before they became 'The New Testament'. I use this traditional term, 'after Christ' (usually AD), instead of the now standard Common Era (CE) to emphasise just what caused the production of these writings: the historical person of Jesus from Nazareth, and the faith his followers had in him as the Messiah (Christ). My guiding interpretative perspective, developed in the following chapters, is the view that the purpose of these writings, especially the gospels, was to tell the story of Jesus of Nazareth in such a way that they shaped the identity of their readers. Or, in the case of the letters, they presupposed knowledge about Jesus, while reminding their readers of the appropriate formative quality of that knowledge. These writings, I will stress, must be read within the context of the Greco–Roman world: they employed literary genres and conventions that reflect their Hellenistic and Jewish environment. The last chapter in this section discusses the process that led up to the formation of a fixed collection of texts called The New Testament.

The next section, Shaping History, discusses how the New Testament became such an important and influential document in so many parts of the world. We start with the material history of the New Testament: how it was produced, published and disseminated. The technological development of media is reflected in this history: from the handwritten codex via printed books to the electronic webpage. The spread of the New Testament is part of a history of translations and of geographical distribution through mission and colonisation. Based on this material history, the cultural impact of the New Testament can now be studied in a new perspective represented by reception history.

Reception, broadly understood, includes not only the interpretation of New Testament writings in a theological or academic setting, but also the dissemination of themes, topics and images – through art, music, literature and films, for example. This was not only an activity for the elite: 'ordinary' Christians participated in activities which made the memories of Jesus come alive. The New Testament also had a great impact upon discussions of pivotal moral and social causes – for example the liberation of slaves and gender equality. These discussions are illuminating examples of the importance of the New Testament since they had broader social and political implications in addition to being internal Church issues. However, the New Testament has been a double-edged sword in this respect: it has also been used to support slavery and discrimination on the basis of race, gender and sexuality.

Finally, the third section, Reading and Meaning-Making, includes the history of how the New Testament has been studied and the different methods and theories that have been applied in different ages. The Enlightenment and the subsequent establishment of modern universities in the nineteenth century had tremendous consequences for its study. This was the period of the so-called 'historical-critical' method in many disciplines, and the original, historical meaning was the goal of most biblical interpretation. This method became dominant in the study of the New Testament, until its hegemony was broken in the last part of the twentieth century. In the last generation, there has been greater diversity in methods and theories, and biblical interpreters have interacted with the social sciences and literary studies. But perhaps most significantly of all, there has been a turning away from the ideal of the 'objective reader' – personified in practice by a white, male scholar – to wider groups; for example women, Africans, Latin-Americans, Jews, Muslims and atheists. These readers brought with them new methods and perspectives, for example feminist, post-colonial, religious and secular liberation readings. The history of the New Testament shows that it has been a classic text, and the vitality of many modern readings suggests that it will continue to engage new readers, both within and outside the structures of the Christian churches.

Part 1

BEGINNINGS

FROM JESUS
TO THE GOSPELS

Jesus was before the gospels, but we only know Jesus through the gospels. That is the paradox we face when we speak of 'the historical Jesus'. By this we mean the person we can reconstruct using historical methods, evaluating and combining available sources, some of which are Jewish and Roman. The Jewish historian Josephus c. 90 tells that Jesus was crucified by Pontius Pilate, and that he still had followers. The Roman historian Tacitus writing about Nero, c. 115, observed that the Christians, who were accused of having started the fire that destroyed Rome, had their name from a certain Chrestus who was executed by Pontius Pilate. Thus, these sources tell us that Jesus was a historical person who was crucified, but they do not say much about who he was. For that we must use the gospels as sources and, by comparing and sifting through them, we can deduce some information that seems trustworthy: Jesus was a Jew who grew up and lived in Galilee (his birth in Bethlehem may be a later tradition). He was, at some point, a disciple of John the Baptist, but started his own group and activities that included preaching – the coming of the Kingdom of God was his main message. This message was associated with his activities as healer and exorcist, as well as with an inclusive meal praxis that included 'sinners'. Because his position was so counter-cultural, it seems likely that he left his own household and called at least some of his disciples to do the same, living a life as itinerant and homeless. His main activity was in Galilee where, although accepted by many, he faced criticism and resistance from synagogue leaders and scribes. At some point he decided to go to Jerusalem, where the conflicts with the Jewish leadership increased and the disturbances that he caused during a sensitive period (Easter was a celebration of the liberation of the Judeans from Egypt) led to the Roman authorities crucifying him, probably with some involvement from the Temple leadership.

Figure1. An early portrait of Jesus from the Comodilla catacomb, Rome, late fourth century.

For this information about Jesus to be meaningful, it must be placed within a geographical, political and religious context. Although not correct in historical details, the well-known introduction to the birth narrative in Luke's Gospel (2:1–4) provides this information. It tells that Jesus was born under Augustus' reign of the Roman Empire, in a landscape that administratively was part of Syria; his hometown was Nazareth in Galilee, but his father hailed from Judea. The next historical vignette in Luke 3:1–4, from a later date when Tiberius had become emperor, describes the political situation of the area in more detail. The areas that had been ruled by Herod, as a vassal king under the Romans, had now been divided – the southern part, Judea, was directly ruled by Rome with a governor, Pontius Pilate; Galilee was ruled by Herod Antipas (a son of the previous Herod) as a Roman vassal; and other regions to the east and south were ruled by his brothers. We must not imagine that these regions were nation-states in a modern sense; they were under personal rule, in this case divided up by the Romans, in other cases gathered through internal power struggles, conquest or marriage. The Judeans, descendants of the ancient Israelites with mem-

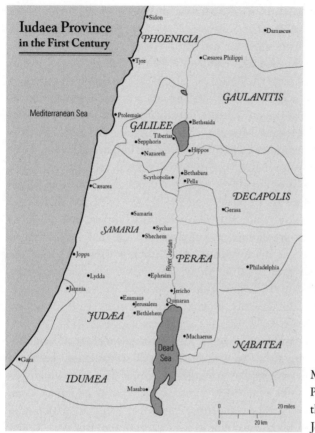

Iudaea Province in the First Century

•Sidon

PHOENICIA

•Damascus

•Tyre

•Cæsarea Philippi

GAULANITIS

Mediterranean Sea

•Ptolemais

GALILEE

•Bethsaida

Tiberias•

•Sepphoris

•Nazareth

•Hippos

Scythopolis•

•Bethabara

•Pella

•Cæsarea

DECAPOLIS

•Samaria

•Gerasa

SAMARIA

•Sychar

•Shechem

River Jordan

PERÆA

•Philadelphia

•Joppa

•Lydda

•Ephraim

•Jericho

•Jamnia

•Emmaus

Qumaran

•Jerusalem

JUDÆA

•Bethlehem

•Machaerus

NABATEA

Dead Sea

•Gaza

IDUMEA

Masaba•

0   20 miles

0   20 km

Map 2. Palestine at the time of Jesus.

ories of the great kingdoms of David and Salomon, had for generations been conquered and ruled by different empires, mostly through vassal rulers. In addition, when the Romans had direct rule, as in Judea, they let local forms of rule continue, as long as they kept peaceful control over people. In Jerusalem that meant that the high priests of the Temple (Luke 3:2), were also political rulers, the Temple being the central institution of power (a power that in modern days has been separated out in political, economic and religious sectors). The northern region, Galilee, that for many hundreds of years had a separate history, had some generations before the time of Jesus been re-populated by Judeans, but it was still a border area towards Hellenistic towns and pagan cities, such as Tyre and Sidon, to the North.

With this information we can better place Jesus in his context. That Jesus was known as a Galilean indicates that he was a Judean from a region outside the heartland of Judea. The tradition in Luke's Gospel that he was born in Bethlehem, the ancient town of David, linked him to the dreams of the times of the great king David and to the hopes of a new Messiah (that is, an anointed one; *Christos* in Greek) who would re-establish the Davidic kingdom. These expectations also form a backdrop to Jesus' central message of God's kingdom or empire, but this kingdom did not conform to expectations; it appeared to be both contrary to the expectations of the Judeans and critical of the rule of the Roman Empire. Instead, Jesus appears to have proclaimed a Kingdom of God that responded to the needs of people, with healings of the sick and exorcisms of the possessed, feeding of the poor, preaching a reversal of power structures and breaking traditional rules of purity. This is such a consistent picture in the gospels that it must go back to the earliest memories of Jesus.

Thus, it is possible to imagine Jesus as the leader of a 'kingdom movement' that, although peaceful, caused turbulence, gathered crowds around him, and created expectations that Jesus might be the Messiah. If this reached a climax in Jerusalem at Easter time, when the city was full of pilgrims, it is not difficult to understand the concern of both the Temple leaders and the Romans, under Pontius Pilate, and the Romans' decision to execute him.

The resurrection of Jesus cannot be verified as a historic event by normal historical criteria. But that the disciples and first followers of Jesus experienced encountering Jesus as risen may well be historical; there are many and diverse memories of such encounters both in the gospels and in Paul's letters. We cannot say anything about the character of these experiences, but they must have made it possible to overcome the trauma of the death of Jesus and the loss of the expectations that his disciples had in him. The result was a continuation of the Jesus movement, and now not just with the message about the Kingdom of God, as preached by him, but proclaiming Jesus as the Messiah (the Christ) as the central message of the Kingdom.

It was this message that seemed to rapidly convert the Jesus movement into a missionary movement; it spread from Jerusalem and Galilee to the Jewish Diaspora in the East, to Egypt in the South and to Asia Minor, Greece and even Rome within a few decades. We know about this mission towards Asia Minor and Greece primarily through Paul's letters and, at a later stage, through an idealised description by Luke in the Acts of the Apostles. Since Paul's letters are the earliest writings we have, we shall start with them. In the New Testament they follow the gospels (and Acts), in which we get a full picture of Jesus. Therefore we easily overlook that in his letters Paul tells next to nothing about Jesus' life: only that he was borne by a woman, under the Law (Gal 4:1–2), that he instituted the new meal of the Eucharist (1 Cor 11) and that he was crucified (1 Cor 1). This lack of information is so surprising that we are left to wonder what Paul had told them when he preached and gathered new Christ followers, and how they preserved and retold stories about Jesus.

At some point the Jesus followers must have felt the need to write down these stories and memories of him, but that is most likely to have happened a generation after Paul wrote his letters. And again we are in for a surprise: we have not just one collection of words and memories about Jesus, but four: Mark, Matthew, Luke and John, partly related and reworked, partly independent of each other. If anything, this shows that there must have been diversities and different emphases in the Jesus movement from its beginning.

In the last chapter in this section we shall see that these diversities among the Christ groups continued in the second century, with a proliferation of memories about Jesus, in many cases spoken of as 'gospels'. However, at the same time we see attempts to control the traditions; we encounter terms such as 'Apocrypha' and 'canon', reflecting the beginning of a process of the inclusion and exclusion of writings in the 'New Testament'.

1

BECOMING CHRISTIANS: LETTER WRITING AS COMMUNITY FORMATION

COMMUNICATION AND LETTERS IN FIRST-CENTURY MEDITERRANEAN CULTURES

In the New Testament we have a selection of early Christian letters (often called epistles) from the first century AD. At least seven of them were composed by the Apostle Paul, and they represent the earliest scriptures in the Christian tradition. Written by Paul and other missionaries to the first groups of Christ believers, in a formative period in the lives of these groups, these letters make up a unique collection. We only have one side of this dialogue: the correspondence sent *to* Paul and the other New Testament authors are lost to history. Even so, through the advice in the letters, we are afforded glimpses of these groups as they come into being: as they struggle to form as social units, organise worship, find ways to express what they believe and discuss moral issues. While community formation was an important purpose of the letters, they also reveal information about the relationship between the writers and their audience. The letters sometimes read like the kind one would expect of correspondence between friends, but there are similarities with official letters, too, as the authors attempt to establish their authority over the groups they address. What becomes obvious through these writings, whether one focuses on their personal or official dimensions, is the transformative nature of their faith in the risen Christ, and their struggles to live in their existing social world guided by the light of faith.

Paul's letters to the various newly founded communities are about giving shape to a life centred on faith in Christ. The letters address organisational issues, difficult relationships within the various communities and their interaction with the wider societies in which they lived. These issues of community formation and orientation will be foregrounded in this chapter – rather than the more traditional focus on the theological content of Paul's writings – as the basis for a future theological system.[1]

This is not to marginalise theology: there have been great changes in the interpretation of Paul and his theology in the last generation of scholarship, and these changes are discussed in Chapter 9. What I want to show in this chapter is how Paul's theology developed in the process of responding to practical situations which arose within the communities with which he corresponded. But before we explore the letters, we must ask: Who was this Paul?

WILL THE REAL PAUL PLEASE STAND UP?

Paul is the only New Testament author who can be securely identified, but to understand *who* he was we have to distinguish between at least four different pictures of him: the modern Paul, the Paul of the New Testament (of which there are two), and Paul as he actually was, as a historical figure.

The 'modern Paul' is Paul as he is understood today, although a plurality of modern perspectives on him exist. Just two will be summarised, both of which emphasise his historical influence, albeit for different reasons. For many people, especially in Protestant churches, he is the founder of Christian theology and one of the most important authorities for Church teaching. Others see him in a less favourable light, as a major source of religiously mandated prejudice and discrimination, especially towards women and homosexuals.

In the New Testament itself we find two presentations. One comes from the Acts of the Apostles, where the largest part, Chapters 13–28, tells the story of an evangelising mission 'from Jerusalem to the ends of the earth', in which Paul is the main protagonist. This narrative is strongly coloured by Luke's wish to place Paul in a

Figure 2. Icon of the Apostle Paul, *c.* 1550, The Ecclesiastical Archeological Museum of the Moscow Theological Academy.

positive light, and to portray him as a loyal Jew. In Acts we learn that he studied with Gamalial in Jerusalem, that he was a Roman citizen and that he started his mission in the synagogues. But this information comes from Acts alone; it is not verified in the sources for our third picture of Paul – his letters.

Paul's letters are the best sources we have for his life and character, but he does not give a systematic account, or even chronological outline, of his life. Nor can we assume that all the information Paul does provide is factual: like many writers, Paul constructs a picture of himself which corresponds to the persona he wanted to project. For instance, the biographical description in Galatians 1:11–24, which tells the story of how he was called by God in the same way as God called the prophets, supported his claim that he had the right to be an apostle, a term that many would restrict to the 12 disciples of Jesus. Paul's obvious interest in securing his apostolic authority raises the suspicion of modern historians as to whether this is indeed an autobiographical reflection, or an apologetic invention. To a considerable degree, the historical figure of Paul remains elusive; nevertheless, there is scholarly agreement on many aspects of Paul's life, and it is to these that we now turn.

PAUL'S LIFE AND LETTERS

With a great deal of certainty we can say that Paul was a Jew from the Diaspora, possibly Tarsus in Asia Minor (modern Turkey); that he self-identified as a pharisee; and that he partook in the persecution of members of the movement that was to become Christianity, before having a vision, or some experience, of the risen Christ that radically changed the course of his life, which henceforth was that of a fervent Christ believer (Gal 1:11–17, 1 Cor 15:8). We also know that he made long missionary journeys in the Eastern Mediterranean, through Asia Minor and Greece. In Chapter 15 of his letter to the Romans, he looked back upon his completed mission to the Eastern Mediterranean and looked forward to travelling to the West: to Rome, and further still to Spain. But first he planned to visit Jerusalem, where he intended to deliver a collection to the poor of the city as a sign of the unity between gentile followers of Christ and the Jewish part of the community in Jerusalem. This visit resulted in conflict, Paul's arrest and his deportation to Rome where he most likely was executed *c.* 64.

The chronology of Paul's life and letters cannot be established with any certainty, but a historically plausible sequence of the latter is as follows:

The First Letter to the Thessalonians, *c.* 50–1
The Letter to the Galatians, *c.* 54
The First Letter to the Corinthians, *c.* 53–5
The Second Letter to the Corinthians, *c.* 54–6
The Letter to the Romans, *c.* 57
The Letter to the Philippians, *c.* 56 or *c.* 62.[2]
The Letter to Philemon, *c.* 61–3.

THE FORM AND FUNCTION OF PAUL'S LETTERS

So why did Paul write letters, and what are the key characteristics of letters as a form of communication? A letter is different from a narrative text in that it is explicitly part of a communication between two parties: a letter is one half of a dialogue, and a substitute for personal presence. Hellenistic letter writing provides the closest model for Paul and other early Christian letters, and the study of Hellenistic letter writing has made it possible to study Paul's letters as the 'occasional writings' that they were, within their own historical context.[3]

In the Hellenistic world of the first century letters were a popular genre, and many letters from this period are preserved. They range from the personal to the official and business orientated, where we learn about daily life, family relations, friendships and financial dealings. The Roman Empire produced many letters, from the emperor himself to governors and administrators who, in turn, wrote back with necessary reports or to ask for advice. There were also official and open letters, where the emperor or governor wished to address an entire city. This type of letter was a way of keeping the Empire together and, with a good system of roads and horse messengers, they were an efficient mode of communication between the imperial powerbase and the more distant parts of the Empire. Another notable use of the open letter during Paul's time was that favoured by philosophers and other public intellectuals, who would offer reflections and advice about moral values, or comment on the social and political norms of a place, in order to create or solidify a school of thought, or to influence public opinion.

Letters composed in this era had several conventional forms, such as the formalised greetings that introduced the letters, with ways to express the authority of the author *vis-à-vis* the addressees, and good wishes and a gesture towards maintaining good relations. The body of the letter changed depending on the purpose, whether it offered admonishment, praise or advice, etc. In this main section of the letter, the writer used the form of rhetoric which was appropriate to the purpose of the correspondence: the art of letter writing and the study of rhetoric were interrelated during this period and required formal schooling, at least at the level of secondary education. When we know what these forms are, we can more easily see how Paul employed their conventions and requirements to develop specific issues that were relevant for each letter.

THE THREE CONTEXTS OF PAUL'S LETTERS

Literary form and communicative function clearly influenced Paul's letters, but they also reflect the socio-cultural and political contexts of Paul and of his addressees. We may identify three such contexts: first, the communities comprised of individuals and Paul's relations with them; second, the world in which these groups lived, the Greek *polis* with its Hellenistic social forms and culture; and finally, Paul's formative world of the Jewish Diaspora (living outside of the Land of Israel), and the forms of faith and tradition characteristic of that world.

Wayne Meeks famously described the addressees of Paul's letters as 'the first urban Christians',[4] pointing out that, in contrast to the Palestinian followers of Jesus, Paul established groups of Christ believers in Hellenistic cities. The Hellenistic *polis* was therefore their immediate context, where they lived with families and neighbours, participated in its economic and social life and experienced a tense relationship with the local religious culture, with its pagan activities and obligations. The *polis* was a political entity with clear expectations of its inhabitants when it came to participation in the city's cultic practices. The *polis* was made up of households, with 'housefathers' and 'families' consisting of wives, children, other dependants, slaves and possibly clients. The *polis* was built on a hierarchical structure, with marked class and gender differences. These structures and hierarchies were supported by Greek and Roman religious myths, and popular philosophies, such as Stoicism. These elements made up the social and ideological world in which the Christ believers lived. Many of the issues that Paul addresses in his letters concern how the Christ believers should relate to this world: a world which was their given and familiar social context but which, in the light of their new faith in Christ, had also come to be encountered as 'the Other'.

Relationship with the Jewish world was always crucial for Paul.

13

He identified himself as a Jew (Phil 3:5–6) and he preached the message about Jesus Christ, raised from the dead by the God of Israel. In his letters to the Corinthians, Thessalonians, Philippians and Philemon, however, there is no discussion of the internal relations between Jews and Gentiles, few references to the Jewish scriptures and no discussion of whether the Gentile believers should take on a Jewish identity through circumcision. All of that changes dramatically in Paul's letters to the Galatians and Romans. Probably because of the presence of Jews and Jewish missionaries of Christ, the question of circumcision for Gentile Christ believers, and the relationship between Jews and Gentiles more generally, is a prominent issue. In these letters Paul's argumentation reveals his grounding in Rabbinic discussion and interpretation, although his conclusions reached with such methods were controversial.

Two important issues are apparent in all Paul's letters. The first is his own relationship to his addressees, the other his concern for the unity and concord of the newly established communities. They feature prominently in all of his the letters because they are part of a communication process to shape the identities and social practices of early Christian communities. Having these issues in mind will provide us with the necessary focus for the reading of Paul's letters which follows, and will make it easier to register similarities and differences between the letters on these crucial issues.

PAUL'S RELATIONS WITH THE COMMUNITIES

If we see Paul's letters as being concerned with internal relations, social structures and the faith of the communities he was writing to, it becomes clear that he himself was very much part of this communication process. How the communities perceived his role, his credibility and authority would determine how they would receive his letters and advice. The matter of Paul's relationship with the communities he addressed takes up a large part of his correspondence, a fact which is easily overlooked if one reads them merely with a view to identifying his theological positions. The best place to start an investigation of this relationship is the introduction to his letters where, according to the conventions of letter writing, both the sender and the recipients were introduced. Take, as an initial example, 1 Thessalonians, which is the oldest of Paul's preserved letters and illustrates how he employed the conventions of Hellenistic letter writing. Paul used these common epistolary forms in all his letters, with modifications that serve to emphasise the purpose or character of each individual letter.

1 Thessalonians starts with a greeting, introducing the senders, 'Paul, Silvanus and Timothy', and the recipients, 'To the church of the Thessalonians in God the Father and the Lord Jesus Christ', followed by the greeting itself, where Paul has substituted the Greek 'greeting' (*chairein*) with Jewish formulae from worship: 'Grace (*charis*) to you and peace' (1:1). The use of formulae from Jewish worship, such as benedictions and prayers, is a characteristic element in early Christian letters – specifically Christian parts, such as hymns to Christ, are also included. The introduction in 1 Thessalonians is very simple and unassuming, whereas in other letters Paul presents himself in a way that emphasises his authority: he reminds the community in Corinth that he is 'called to be an apostle' (1 Cor 1:1). In his letter to the Romans, Paul presents himself to a group he had not established (Romans 1:1–5), over which he had no authority, and there is a more deferential attitude towards the recipients, who are addressed as those that are 'called' and 'holy' (Rom 1:7; 1 Cor 1:2).

This greeting is followed by another common formal feature, the thanksgiving, the purpose of which is to establish good relations between sender and recipient(s):

We always give thanks to God for all of you and mention you in our prayers, constantly remembering before our God and Father your work of faith and labour of love and steadfastness of hope in our Lord Jesus Christ. (1 Thess 1:2–3).

It reflects Paul's good relations with the Thessalonians that this section is very long (1:2–3:13), relating their common history when Paul came to Thessalonica and updating them on what had happened after he had left. Other letters also have thanksgiving sections, both for the support that Paul has personally received from the recipients, and more generally for their faith and the good example it sets for others (Phil 1:3–11; 1 Cor 1: 4–9). It is therefore a bad sign when, in his letter to the Galatians, he drops the thanksgiving for the community and starts with direct criticisms and strict exhortations (Gal 1:6).

The body of the letter contains the main message, tailored to each community's situation: Paul often used this part of the letter to deal with any issues arising in his relationship with the group which may intersect with the central theological or liturgical arguments presented. At the end of the letter there are also fixed epistolary forms with a final greeting and good wishes. In 1 Thessalonians this conclusion is rather brief, a greeting with a 'holy kiss', and a demand that the letter be read to 'all the brothers' (5:23–8). Other letters expand this section; for example, when Paul mentions the group of people accompanying him at the time of writing and sends greetings to specific members of the receiving community (1 Cor 16: 19–24; Rom 16:1–27). Paul's instructions as to how his letter should be read signals its function: it should be read in a gathering of the community, often by the messenger who brought the letter, who could fill out the information and explain Paul's intentions. In an oral culture, a written letter was only part of the communication – it was re-enacted and contextualised through direct oral exchange (see Acts 15:23–7).

The extended address and the thanksgiving served to establish good relations between Paul and the communities he was addressing, and there were several ways in which he could further strengthen them. One common motif is a shared memory. Paul reminds them of their common history, how he first came to them, and how they received him and came to faith in God and Jesus Christ (1 Thess 2:1–3:13, 1 Cor 1:14–17). Paul may also mimic the roles common to family letters – a popular epistolary form – with relations between, say, father and son (1 Cor 3:5–9;1 Thess 4:15). In 1 Thessalonians 2:7 he even uses female metaphors: he describes himself as 'gentle … like a nurse'. Paul's sustained contact with the communities was crucial to his mission, and this is manifest in his letters: his previous visits established or built on existing trust, while planned visits showed that he was serious about his ongoing relationship with them (2 Cor 1:15–23; Rom 1:13–15; 15:18–35). There are tensions, however, between Paul's expressions of friendship and equality and his emphasis on authority and power. Paul can also use himself and his situation – for example, his suffering for the gospel – to strengthen his apostolic credibility and defend himself against unfavourable comparisons with competitors in the Christ movement who may have seemed more successful (1 Cor 2:1–5; 2 Cor 1:8–11; Phil 1:12–18; 2 Cor 10–12). The long, apologetic section in Gal 1:10–2:16, emphasising that he received his gospel directly from God, would also serve as a defence against such criticisms.

Paul's letters have tended to be studied with his theology at the forefront of the reader's interests, and yet so much of the content concerns his relations with the communities with whom he was corresponding: these aspects of his correspondence make Paul a more rounded and human figure. Rhetorically, they show how he used a literary form of communication, designed to be performed in public, to impress his authority upon his addressees, but they also show how much he himself wanted and needed those relationships.

PAUL'S GOAL FOR HIS LETTERS: THE UNITY OF THE COMMUNITIES

In Pauline studies there has been a persistent quest for the heart of Paul's theology. Leading candidates include 'justification by faith in Christ Jesus' and 'participation in Christ'.[5] But if we take as our starting point the view, outlined above, that Paul's letters are primarily concerned with relationships within and between newly founded religious communities, the question should be posed differently: What was the purpose, or what was at the heart, of his letters? When conflicts arose within a community, in most cases Paul did not argue for any specific position. Instead, he argued that the two parties should be reconciled and be of one mind. This, therefore, is the recurring theme in all his letters: avoid conflict, live in harmony and be of the same mind. This desire is not, in itself, original or distinctive.

In Paul's Jewish world the most immediate basis for unity was faith in one God, in contrast to the many gods of the pagans which left the latter scattered and divided. For Paul, unity was a sign of the new community in Christ. He comes back to this point many times in his letters, conceptualising this unity in terms of a spiritual, at times even a physical, union with the object of their faith: Jesus Christ. It is especially important in his First Letter to the Corinthians, a community with many factions, where he says, 'For by one

Spirit we were all baptised into one body – Jews or Greeks, slaves or free – and all were made to drink of one Spirit' (1 Cor 12:13). Paul points to baptism as the source of unity, where the baptised received the one Spirit, and where people of different ethnic backgrounds, and different social status (and in Gal 3:28 also of different gender) were united into 'one body'. Paul wanted to unite the members of the community of the baptised and at the same time to embody them 'in Christ'. To be a Christian meant to become a member of Christ's body, and co-member with other Christians.

From this metaphor of the body, Paul draws conclusions about unity in the community, that 'there may be no dissension within the body, but the members may have the same care for one another' (1 Cor 12:25). He interprets the communal meal of the Eucharist in the same way: the bread of the Eucharist is 'participation in the body of Christ', and he concludes with the thought that, 'because there is one bread, we who are many are one body' (1 Cor 10:17). It is difficult to know how widespread this understanding of baptism and Eucharist was among Paul's addressees, but Paul effectively interpreted them as physical expressions of the unity of the members of the Christ community, with social responsibilities to follow.

There was a strong Christ-centred argument for unity, but members from Hellenistic cities would also be familiar with moral philosophers and how they too argued in its favour. Unity in the *polis* was part of the social imaginary of what society should be like in the Greco-Roman world, and the theme of *homonoia* ('concord' or 'harmony') was a common feature in the public speeches and writings of politicians and moral philosophers.[6] Paul must have been familiar with the popular morality of such philosophers; indeed, many of their concepts are reflected in passages on morality in his letters (Rom 12:3–18). But even if Paul shared the common Hellenistic ideals of concord and harmony, his strategy was different from that of the philosophers in his Hellenistic context. Speeches and narratives about discord and strife in societies in the Greek and Roman world were often given from the perspective of the elite. From their position, unity and concord were preserved when those of lower status accepted their place within society's hierarchical structure. A well-known speech by the Roman consul Menenius Agrippa (*c.* 500 BC) illustrates this attitude. He told a fable about the disastrous effects of conflict between various members of the body where, using the body as a symbol of hierarchy, his purpose was to make the plebeians refrain from mutiny against the senators.[7]

When Paul uses the body as a metaphor in his discussion of spiritual gifts in 1 Corinthians 12, he turns this image around and uses the body as an image not of hierarchy, but of equality in the matter of spiritual gifts. He does this by applying the image of the body to Christ. The contrast between 'the body of Christ' and the elitist Hellenistic image of the body is striking: Paul argues that through baptism all have become part of the body of Christ (12:13), and in the body of Christ all members must show consideration for one another, and accord most honour to the weakest and least honourable members (1 Cor 12:12–26). Paul shared with the Greek and Roman world the concern for unity and harmony in the *polis*, but he reshaped the 'body politique' of the city into 'the body of Christ', characterised by a reversal of the then-dominant social structures. Pauline rhetoric of *homonoia* was directed at shaping a distinctive identity among the Christ believers.

PAUL'S LETTERS TO HELLENISTIC AUDIENCES

Paul's letters to the Thessalonians, the Philippians, the Corinthians and Philemon address both issues internal to each community as well as their relationship to the wider society in which they lived and continued to be a part, even in their new state of faith. In these letters it is the Hellenistic city life that makes up 'the wider society'.

1 Thessalonians: Distance from the 'others' 'who have no hope'

In his letter to the Christ-believing community in Thessaloniki, Paul addresses them as 'Gentiles' and does not introduce any of the special identity markers of Jewish communities: his hope is that they shall be transformed as Gentiles. Their demonstrations of love suggested that the process of transformation was already underway, which helps to explain Paul's positive attitude towards them, but he encourages them to go further. Paul speaks of the large majority of their fellow members of the *polis* as 'others'; indeed, he describes their relationship to their fellow Thessalonians as one of suffering at the hands of 'your own compatriots' (2:14). This language of contrast between peoples is repeated throughout the letter when he describes the community of Christ believers in relation to 'outsiders'; those 'who have no hope' (4:12–13).

One way to describe the special character of Christ-believing groups was to call them 'holy': a term indicating separation, and one Paul often used in his introductory remarks to address the recipients of his letters (1 Cor 1:2; 2 Cor 1:1; Rom 1:7). In 1 Thessalonians 4:3–8, holiness is directly linked to control of sexuality and passion, in contrast to the Gentiles – that is, their neighbours in Thessaloniki. Paul sets up a contrast between their fornication (*porneia*) and Christian men who shall take a wife 'in holiness and honour'; in practical terms, that meant that a man should not try to lure away the wife of another member of the community (4:6). Paul encourages men of the community to break with their customs as Gentiles; changing marriage customs will mark them as holy.

This contrast to the 'others' also becomes visible when Paul describes the 'rapture' – the apocalyptic events when Christ will return (5:13–18). Belief that Jesus would soon come back to judge the world and rescue the believers must have been very strong. Therefore, when some of them died before this happened, believers among the Thessalonians became anxious about what would happen to them. Paul reassures them that both the dead and the living would be included in the rapture up to heaven, for those in Christ, in contrast to those others 'who have no hope'(4:13). This contrast is repeated when Paul speaks of the Christ believers, in what would become a traditional formulation, as 'children of light, children of the day', and whom he contrasted with those who were 'of the night or of the darkness' (5:5). He thereby defines the community by drawing boundaries between the Christ community and the others.

Philippians means friendship

The Letter to the Philippians presents a better relationship between Paul and this community than any of the others he founded. It is built around thanks for the partnership between the Philippians and Paul in service of the Gospel, expressions of friendship and exhortations for unity. All this contributes to making this a very personal letter, where Paul's reflections on his own situation play a large role. Paul repeats his main message twice in this letter (1:12–2:18; 3:2–4:9). He warns against evil-doers and then presents his own situation: first as a prisoner (1:12–14) then as a Jew (3:4–6). In both cases these are subordinate to what really counts: being 'in Christ'. Paul urges the Philippians to imitate him so that they can reach full unity and concord.

In a section where he encourages increased unity, he uses Greek language of friendship to illustrate how it can happen. A quote from Plato, 'friends have all things in common'[8], illustrates how Greeks saw friendship as an expression of unity. Paul uses these familiar ideas when he urges the Philippians be of the same mind, to show humility and to be concerned about the interests of others, not only one's own (2:1–5). Paul's main example of this unity in the service of others is Christ Jesus. In 2:6–11, Paul quotes a hymn – probably used in worship – about Christ, who was in the form of God and yet 'emptied himself' and became a slave, until death on the cross, when God reversed his downward trajectory, exalted him and gave him 'the name that is above every name'.

The letter ends with Paul's thanks to the Philippians for their material support of him and his mission (4:10–20), both recently and earlier, when he first came to Macedonia. Paul expresses his gratitude, though one senses that this was a sensitive matter. Support from a community might indicate that Paul was dependent upon them, whereas in other instances Paul insists that he is independent (1 Cor 9:13–18), so that he should not be reliant on anybody. This issue of dependence versus independence reveals the inherent tensions in these relationships. On the one hand, good relations were important if Paul was to continue to have an impact on the emerging communities of Christ. On the other, Paul obviously also felt the need to protect his authority and calling as an apostle, which may have been compromised by too cosy or dependent a relationship with a community.

Conflicts in Corinth

1 Corinthians provides the best illustration of the importance of unity in Paul's letters. The term for 'concord' (*homonoia*) was used for a genre of speeches, and 1 Corinthians has been called a *homonoia* letter, since Paul uses so many of the genre's common elements. Although relations to the *polis* and its cults are clearly problematic, the key dividing lines appear to be within the community. Thus, internal conflicts and disunity are the primary issues dealt with in this letter.

Were some of these internal conflicts caused in part by the social diversity of the community, reflecting its position in the multicultural city of Corinth? Corinth was strategically located at Peloponnese, a crossroad for trade and travel routes. It was a Roman colony, so many Roman soldiers had settled there, and it was a city with people from many parts of the Mediterranean and from many ethnic groups. This may have been reflected among the Christ believers, along with diversity in social status, with a majority of people being from the

Figure 3. Ancient Corinth, the Fountain of Peirene (photo by Ploync)

lower classes or even slaves. But there must also have been people of higher social standing; indeed, some of them are mentioned as patrons gathering groups of Christ believers in their houses. This multi-layered ethnic, social and cultural context may have been one of the reasons for the divisions and factions within the Corinthian community.

There must have been sustained correspondence between Paul and the Corinthians; although no letters from the Corinthian side are preserved, Paul refers to at least one (7:1), and most of their contacts with him may have been oral reports via messengers (11:11; 5:1; 8:1; 12:1). Paul starts his letter with the report of conflicts between groups with different leaders (1:12–13) with each staking a claim for superiority. His strategy is clear: Paul undercuts the competition between groups and leaders by introducing 'Christ crucified' as the expression of God's power. Thus, the demonstration of power through displays of wisdom and the performance of miracles (by Greeks and Jews respectively) is contrasted, negatively, with the weakness of Christ crucified, through whom God shows his

paradoxical power (1:18–25). It was, above all, the powerful who had to give up their claim to superiority above others: the crucified Christ was the only basis for this community.

When Paul has established this basis, he goes on to address the problems that have been reported to him by members of the community in Corinth. These issues are many and varied, but Paul responds with an overriding concern for unity, and how it was constituted by their being 'the body of Christ'. Since the Christ believers in Corinth were 'in Christ', they had become 'new creations' (2 Cor 5:17). To Paul this meant that the lives and social relations of the Corinthians must be reshaped in order to express this new identity. This 'being in Christ' was his response to the question of whether a man who was a believer in Christ might go to a prostitute, probably a female slave (1 Cor 6:12–20). In the Hellenistic society it was widely accepted that a free man, a citizen, had the right to use a woman (or, in some cases, a man) for the purpose of sexual gratification as long as their sexual partner was lower down the social scale – slaves being the most obvious example. It is likely, then, that some men in the community of Christ believers continued to follow this practice. Paul condemned this behaviour, however, arguing that if a man was in union with Christ his body belonged to Christ, and therefore it was unacceptable to enter into union with another body by having sex with a prostitute (6:15–17). Today, we may find Paul's moral reasoning strange: it only makes sense if we realise that for Paul, sexual relationships, like all relationships formed by believers, affected the 'body of Christ' to which they were joined.

The issue of female modesty at worship also became a matter of identity (11:2–16). Apparently Paul accepted that women might pray or prophesy during community worship (but see 14:34–5), but he demanded that they wear a head covering to show women's subordination to men. His arguments were based on the presupposition that men and women had an unequal relation to God, with only the man being made in God's image. No doubt this passage in 1 Corinthians 11 has contributed towards Paul's negative reputation among feminists. This criticism may be reading Paul from a modern position of equality which simply did not exist as a possibility in his day, but his inclusion of non-Jews without circumcision showed that he sometimes did break with strong social and symbolic structures. However when it came to women, although Paul appeared to accept them as collaborators and leaders in groups of Christ believers, he kept to traditional gender roles with regard to relations between men and women.

Another problem to be dealt with was disunity among members at the weekly common meal (11:17–34). Paul attempts to solve this by referring the Corinthians to Jesus' words at the foundation of the Eucharist (11:23–4). The purpose of this quotation is not to give a theological teaching about the Eucharist, but to encourage the participants to be imitators of Christ (11:1). To Paul, the body of Christ is not just the blessed bread that they are eating; it is also the social body of the community where the strong must show concern for the weak.

The recognition that the Corinthians belong to the body of Christ underpins Paul's concluding vision in Chapter 15. Paul describes the resurrection of Christ not as an individual miracle, but as the beginning of a new spiritual world where God will become all in all. Paul's detailed discussion of how the bodies of those who belong to Christ will be transformed into spiritual bodies at the resurrection shows the influence of Stoic cosmology. This is the final stage in Paul's building a new identity in Christ. It is not just a new creation of the individual or of the communal body; it is a new cosmic world created at the resurrection.

2 Corinthians

2 Corinthians has not been studied as much as 1 Corinthians. The unity of the text is disputed, with many scholars thinking it is a compilation of different letters. One section gives a fascinating insight into Paul's bitter fight for his authority *vis-à-vis* accusations from the Corinthian community (2 Cor 10–13). In his conflict with competing missionaries, Paul is fighting with all available means including a highly ironic self-presentation and boastful rhetorical posture. His travelogue of dangers, from robbers at sea and on rivers, provides a glimpse into the life of a travelling missionary (11:25–7). One section of the letter shows him as a missionary strategist: an important part of his project to unify the Christ-believing Gentiles in Asia Minor and Greece on the one hand and their Jewish counterparts

in Jerusalem on the other, was a collection offered by the former to the poor within the holy city of Jerusalem (2 Cor 8–9). This particular strategy failed: to have accepted the gift would have implied fellowship with the Gentiles – the Jerusalem community did not recognise this fellowship, and so rejected the collection.

Philemon and the problem of slavery

The letter to Philemon is the shortest of Paul's letters but still presents many problems of interpretation. It is a letter of recommendation written on behalf of a slave, Onesimus, to his owner, Philemon, in Colossae. While Paul was imprisoned in Ephesus, Onesimus, a runaway slave, joined him in prison and became a Christ believer. Paul sends him back to Philemon with a letter that balances Paul's authoritative sympathy for Onesimus with his respect for Philemon's final decision concerning how to receive 'a brother in Christ' on his return, given their pre-existing master–servant relationship. Whether Paul was actually asking Philemon to manumit Onesimus (that is, give him his freedom) is a matter of dispute. Paul is as ambiguous on this as he is in 1 Cor 7: 21–2. It is most likely he did not argue for the manumission of slaves.

CREATING UNITY BETWEEN JEWS AND GENTILES 'IN CHRIST'

The letters to the Galatians and to the Romans

Although Paul introduces himself in both these letters as an apostle to the gentiles, there are no letters where he is as consistently engaged in discussions of Jewish Scripture and the relationship between the gospel and the people of Israel. It was obviously necessary for Paul to defend a mission which did not, as he understood it, demand circumcision for converts. But this was just one major controversy within the context of the more general question of how Gentile members of the community of Christ related to Jewish Scripture and traditions. Once again, he is arguing for unity among the communities, but the issues were more complex than in the previous letters. Other Jewish missionaries of Christ seem to have claimed that unity between

Jewish and Gentile followers of Christ depended upon the latter becoming circumcised: in order to become a true believer in Christ, one first had to become a Jew. Paul rejected this and suggested an alternative way to unity between Jews and Gentiles based on faith in Christ. I will take this argument as my starting point for both letters.

The letter to the Galatians

This letter was written to several groups of Christ believers in Galatia, a central and northern region of Asia Minor.[9] The opening to the letter is exceptional in that Paul omits the usual thanksgiving for the addressees, and starts directly with a severe criticism: 'I am astonished that you are so quickly deserting the one who called you in the grace of Christ and are turning to a different gospel' (1:6). From his polemics,we may make a guess at what had happened in Galatia. It is likely that, after Paul's visit, other missionaries had come from Jerusalem and challenged his teaching. They may have felt entitled to question Paul's authority because he was not recognised as an apostle by the Jerusalem community. More importantly, they held that the followers of Christ among the Galatians ought to be circumcised in order to be full members of a movement born within Judaism.

This hypothesis would explain the way that Paul structures his letter. He uses the first part of the letter to defend his apostolic authority (1:10–2:15). He points out that he was called by God alone with no intervention from the Jerusalem authorities – who eventually recognised his mission to non-Jews without the requirement of circumcision – and fellowship between non-Jews and Jews should be based on a shared 'faith in Jesus Christ', not on circumcision that symbolised the requirement of Jewish law (2:16).

Central to this argument is Paul's appeal to the figure of Abraham, who was the forefather *par excellence* for Jews and a prototype of what it meant to be an Israelite. In Galatians 3–4, Paul reinterpreted the history of Abraham so as to exclude circumcision. He made Genesis 15:6 his proof text: 'Abraham believed God, and it was reckoned to him as righteousness' (Gal 3:6). In the exposition of this and other texts Paul showed himself to be well trained in methods of Rabbinic interpretation, although in this case he uses them to turn sacred texts against traditional Jewish interpretation. For instance, by pointing out that the Law on Sinai came 430 years later than the story of Gods' promise to Abraham, he 'proved' that faith takes precedence over the law (3:17). Moreover, in the promise to Abraham and his offspring, the word 'offspring' was singular, not plural, and therefore pointed to one man, Christ (3:16). Therefore, those baptised 'into Christ' – regardless of whether they were Jews or Greeks, slaves or free, male or female – belonged to Abraham's offspring (Gal 3:16, 26–9, see Chapter 7). This was a drastic reinterpretation of the story of Abraham as forefather of the Jews, and Paul came very close to excluding Jews from belonging to the offspring of Abraham, in so far as they did not share faith in Christ.

The Letter to the Romans

The Letter to the Romans has done more than any other text of the New Testament to shape the image of Paul and his theology for later generations (see Chapter 9). It has been treated as a theological treatise by generations of Christian interpreters, with the doctrine of 'justification by faith' at its centre (especially 1:16–17; 3:21–4:25). In keeping with Paul's other letters, however, scholars are increasingly concerned with the text as correspondence: more specifically, as communication directed at issues among emerging Christian groups in Rome (especially 14–15:13).[10] This refocusing on the historical occasion for the letter does not solve all the theological questions raised by the text, however. Paul addresses the recipients of his letter as gentiles (1:1–6), so why, then, does he discuss issues relating to Jewish Scripture and tradition so extensively (especially Chapters 1-4, 9–11)? His frequent use of the ethnic categories 'Jew and Greek/Gentile' when he speaks of God who shows no partiality and is the same for Jews and Greeks (Rom 2:1, 3:29–30), may indicate an answer.

In this letter, Paul's concern for unity is linked to his missionary strategy of including Gentiles in the community of Christ believers without circumcision. There may well have been tensions between Jewish and Gentile Christ believers in Rome, and if so it is possible that, once again, Paul's primary purpose with a letter was to promote unity between Gentile and Jewish followers of Christ.[11] He links this unity to a grand scheme of world history, told from the point of view of how God had now revealed himself, in the gospel that Paul proclaimed: God's righteousness in Christ to those who have faith, 'to the Jew first, and also to the Greek' (1:16–17). Just as this was part of Paul's introduction of the main theme of the letter, so it reoccurs in the conclusion (15:5–13). In light of this equal access to salvation that was now revealed, it was also possible to look back and see that in the past, when sin reigned, there was also no distinction between Jews and Greeks either: they were equally sinful (1:18–3:20). It is against this background of equality in sin that Paul explains how God's righteousness is universal, including Jews and Greeks/Gentiles.

For Paul this universal salvation was a Jewish concept. It was Abraham, the ancestor and the prototype for Jews as a model of obedience to God (and to the Law), who, in Paul's reinterpretation, became the ancestor for Gentiles and a prototype for faith without Law observance. This was a remarkable re-imagination of Jewish tradition: Jewish ethnicity was no longer exclusive, but inclusive and universal; at the same time, it was stripped of its former characteristics of 'Law' and instead linked with 'faith' (3:21–4:25). No sooner had the gesture against exclusivity been made, however, that a new dividing line was drawn: this time constituted by 'faith in Christ'.

After rewriting the scriptural history of the Jewish people in Chapters 1 to 4, from Chapter 5 Paul speaks directly about Jesus Christ, the source of life over death (Chapters 5–8). And those who believed in Christ, who were baptised into him, experienced this new power that transformed the world: the Spirit that overcame death and sin. Paul looked towards the cosmological future for all of creation, where the 'children of God' had a special role: 'For the creation waits with eager longing for the revealing of the children of God' (8:19). Thus, Paul placed the believers in Christ into his rewriting of world history, with a hope for the world to come that provided comfort amidst the present struggles.

But there was one problem with this reconstruction of history, and that was the question of the future of the Jews and their covenant with God. Most of them had not accepted Paul's claim that God had now revealed himself through Christ; as such, they were not part of this new history. So what would their future be? Had

God failed in his promises to Israel (9:6)? Had God rejected his people (11:1)? In Chapters 9–11 Paul struggles with these issues and attempts to resolve them in two ways. First, he accepts that only a few Jews (Paul among them) had accepted the gospel, but he argued that this was in line with the previous history of Israel's lack of faith in God. But second, Paul expected a mystery to be revealed at the end of the world so that 'all of Israel' should be saved (11:26).

Paul did not subordinate his letter to the narrative structure of his theology: the God-ordained end-of-world history alluded to in Romans 11 is not the end of the letter. Paul returns to present matters, giving advice to the faithful of Rome about their communal life (12:1–15:13). The starting point for this advice is consistent with Paul's previous re-imagining of world history and proclamation of the radical change brought about by the revelation of God in Christ: he urges the Christ believers in Rome to be transformed and their minds renewed (12:2). In practical terms, however, many of the examples on community living were based on advice probably drawn from Roman moral philosophers, who were also concerned with unity in their respective cities. He speaks, for instance, of showing concern for one another and warns against seeking one's own honour over that of others (12:3–21).

Paul established a new image of the world based on the revelation of Christ. But his addressees in Rome also lived in the present world, ruled by the emperor who demanded taxes and obedience (13:1–7). Romans 13 addressed this 'present world' situation – it is a chapter that has played an enormously important role in subsequent political theology. There is a long tradition of reading this part of the letter as a distillation of Paul's political theology of the state and divinely authorised power. Given the occasional nature of these letters, however, Paul's remarks are more plausibly read as a pragmatic attitude to the personal power of the emperor, rather than as the basis for future political theorising. The tremendous influence that Romans 13 has exerted in reception history (providing support for the absolute rule of kings and furnishing arguments against democracy) is one of many examples where Paul has been accorded a level of authority far in excess of anything he enjoyed in his own time.

PAUL AFTER PAUL: PAULINE LETTERS BY HIS DISCIPLES

There are 13 letters in the New Testament attributed to Paul, but only seven are generally recognised as having been authored by Paul himself. A majority of scholars hold that Colossians, Ephesians and 2 Thessalonians were written by disciples of Paul, perhaps in the generation after him. This position is based on differences in style and vocabulary from the genuine letters and some differences in theology. There is an even larger majority who think that the so-called Pastoral Epistles (1 and 2 Timothy, Titus) were written much later than Paul, towards the end of the first century or even later. Many of the other epistolary writings of the New Testament are letters in name only. Stylistically they may have preserved some epistolary forms, but they are general addresses without local specificities and some (Hebrews, 1 John) are more like sermons or theological treatises, retaining almost nothing of the epistolary form.

What shall we say about the use of Paul's name in the letters that are attributed to him but were probably written by disciples or later followers? The writers obviously intended to bring Paul's authority to issues in their own day and to present what they believed Paul would have said. Pseudonymity was a common literary strategy in Antiquity, so the modern tendency to use the term 'forgery' may be misplaced; some scholars would prefer to speak of these letters as belonging to a 'school' – the continuation of a tradition of thought after the departure of its founding figure – and comparable to philosophical schools of the same period.[12] However, the authors may consciously claim Paul's authority for positions that were against that of Paul in his original letters – for instance in models of the church and the role of women – and when it comes to a collection of letters written in Latin in the third century, purporting to be correspondence between Paul and the Roman philosopher Seneca, we may speak, with confidence, of forgeries.[13]

Colossians and Ephesians

These letters are both concerned with developing the identity of their respective communities. Colossians, probably written before Ephesians, presents Christ as the basis for the identity of the community as they transfer from 'darkness' to 'light'. This is expressed

31

through a hymn to Christ as 'the image of the invisible God', the 'first-born of all creation' and 'all things have been created through him' (Col 1:15–20). This is further developed in Ephesians, which speaks of the mystery of how Christ united Gentiles and Israel into 'one body through the cross' (Eph 2: 11–22). That they are said to be 'in Christ' seems consistent with Paul's theological refrain, but these letters go further: where Paul says that those who are baptised receive the hope of future salvation, Colossians and Ephesians say they are already resurrected with Christ (Eph 2:4–6).

This mystery of their new existence 'in Christ' separates the Christ believers from their old social context but, when it comes to everyday morality, the advice is compliant with societal norms. The primary examples are the so-called 'household codes'. These were adapted from the orders of household management, popular in the Greek and Roman world, which described the relations between different household members: husband and wives, parents (mainly fathers) and children, and house masters and slaves. The system was based on hierarchy, so relationships were always unequal, with the husband, father and house master having most authority and power. Thus, even if these household management orders also had rules for the husband, father or master to show care or even love, the exhortation to the subordinate in the relationship was to submit, show obedience, etc. This system was taken over and adapted in the so-called 'household codes' in Colossians, Ephesians and 1 Peter (Col 3:18–4:1; Eph 5:21–6:9; 1 Pet 2:18–3:8) and thoroughly integrated into the exhortations of the Pastoral Epistles (1 Tim 2:8–15). There were some modifications that can be ascribed to a more specifically Christian sensibility – for instance, emphasising the responsibilities of the husband, father and master. On the other hand, this hierarchical structure of subordination was given divine justification; for example in Ephesians when wives are told to submit to their husbands as 'to Christ himself' (Eph 5:22).

1 and 2 Timothy and Titus

These are presented as letters from Paul to two of his disciples who had responsibility for leading Christian communities. These letters reflect a situation where the Christ-centred communities had a much more developed organisation than at the time of Paul, with names for various offices of authority, such as overseer (bishop), presbyter, deacon and widow. Moreover, the very model for these groups differs considerably from that of Paul's letters. We noticed that Paul used the 'democratic' city gathering – the *ecclesia* – to designate the communities of Christ (1 Cor 1:12; 1 Thess 1:1). In the Pastoral Epistles, the model is the *household,* and this is the term used for the groups addressed (1 Tim 3:1–13). The most important qualification for a man who shall have an office is that he is married (but only once), and that he is able to govern his own household and have obedient children (1 Tim 3:1–5). This is the model of the Roman household with the *pater familias* at its head, and the authors of the Pastoral Epistles evidently felt that the Christian community should be organised as a household with the same patriarchal leadership.

This combination of leadership structure and the ideal household model reflects an adaptation to the patriarchal structures in the social environment of the early communities of Christ, placing women in thoroughly subordinate positions. In the Pastoral Epistles, women are not mentioned in leadership roles and the male author attempts to suppress women's groups, called 'widows' (1 Tim 5:3–16). It is possible that these were groups of unmarried women who were independent of men's authority and thus presented a challenge to patriarchal rule.[14] There is reason, therefore, to be sceptical about the historicity of the leadership models suggested by these letters: they should not be read as descriptions of the situation in these communities, but as prescriptions for how some male leaders wanted their Christian communities to be structured. They reveal a wish to be integrated into Roman society and a mentality that is very different from Paul's message in an earlier generation, as in his letters he mentions many women in leadership roles. [15]

DIVERSITY IN EARLY CHRISTIANITY

The Letter of James

If the Pastoral Epistles are written from the perspective of householders –that is, from a situation of some economic means and social status and a position worth defending – The Letter of James has a different concern: it attacks the well-to-do in the community for not showing concern for the poor. In this letter the author develops the Jewish wisdom tradition that spoke of a God who protected the poor. The text begins in the manner of a letter but it is, in fact, a general moral exhortation written in the name of James, the brother of Jesus – a pseudonymous reference. James' criticism of Paul's position on justification by faith appears to be based on a popular adaptation of Paul's theology, not Paul himself. He invokes the example of Abraham 'who believed God' (Gen 15:6, Jas 2:20–4) that Paul used in Galatians and Romans, but his conclusion is not so much theological as moral: if a man says that he has faith but 'a brother or sister is naked and lacks daily food' his faith cannot help him (2:15–16). The Letter of James represents what may be called a form of Jewish Christianity, although it is peculiar among New Testament writings in that it has no references to Christ beyond the first verse.

1 Peter

Another pseudonymous letter written more in the Pauline tradition, 1 Peter is perhaps from Rome – a city associated with the tradition of both Paul and Peter. The letter addresses 'the exiles of the Dispersion in Pontus, Galatia, Cappadocia, Asia and Bithynia', and speaks of them as 'foreigners' and 'aliens' (2:11). Is 1 Peter speaking to Christians who were actually 'resident aliens', or is it a metaphor for being 'foreigners' in this world? The first alternative provides a plausible social context for the message of the letter: God provides a home for the homeless[16] – those who were 'no people' have now become God's people. At the same time as the contrast to the world is emphasised, the letter (as with Colossians and Ephesians) has a household code that urges submissiveness to the established order of society; slaves towards their master, women towards their husbands (1 Pet 2:18–3:8). Moreover, the household code is prefaced with the obligation to obey the emperor. There is no protest against the Empire – in a contrast to the apocalypse that sets up the conflict between God and the Roman Empire –1 Peter says, 'Fear God. Honour the emperor.' (1 Pet 2:17).

2 Peter

Scholars agree that 2 Peter was written by a different author to that of 1 Peter and even further removed from the Peter of the Gospels and Acts; indeed, this may be the latest writing in the New Testament, probably from the first part of second century. One of its most notable features is the interesting information it reveals about the reception of Paul's letters: in a section on eschatology it says that Paul speaks of this, 'as he does in all his letters' (2 Pet 3:16), which may indicate that at the beginning of the second century there was already a collection of Paul's letters circulating among Christian communities.

The Letter to the Hebrews

Ironically, this is neither a letter nor is it sent to the Hebrews (Jews), but rather it is a long sermon (13 chapters) lacking an epistolary introduction, although it does close with an epistolary greeting (cf. Hebrews 13:22–5). It probably dates from the last part of the first century and gives a fascinating glimpse into the theological laboratory of the earliest Christians and how some of them interpreted Jewish Scriptures. We saw how Paul argued that faith in Christ was in continuity with Jewish faith in God, and that Gentile believers in Christ were heirs to the promise to Abraham. Hebrews represents a very different interpretation. Its introduction sets up a contrast between what God said through the prophets, and what he has now said through Jesus (Heb 1:1–2): the first is like a shadow of the present reality. Jesus is compared to figures from Israel's history, especially the High Priest and his sacrifices, and his sacrifice of himself makes the old sacrifices superfluous (10:1–17). Thus, Hebrews represents the beginning of an understanding of salvation in Christ as superseding Jewish faith.

1, 2 and 3 John

The letters 1, 2 and 3 John belong to the same theological tradition as John's Gospel, and give an interesting view into the development of the Johannine communities, their conflicts and splits. 1 John is not a letter but a theological treatise concerned with two main topics from the Gospel of John: on the one hand, Christology, on the other hand, mutual love among members of the group. It is a warning against some who have a false view – who deny that Jesus was from God and also human (4:2) – those who confess that Jesus is the son of God shall also love their brothers (4:21), that is, with a love that is restricted to their brothers.

The sectarian tendencies that were present in the Gospel appear to have increased; 1 and 2 John were written by an anonymous elder who reveals conflicts and the breaking up of communities. In 2 John he warns a community *not* to receive messengers who do not preach the correct teaching about Christ. In 3 John the situation is reversed: the elder writes to a member of a church advising him to accept these messengers after the church leader had refused to welcome them. These letters reflect the diversities and conflicts within the early Christian communities: the formation of communities occurring alongside splits and exclusions.

Coming at the end of this review of the early Christian letters that were eventually gathered into the New Testament, 2 and 3 John give insights into the social and practical side of communication by letter. Letters were sent by messengers, Christian emissaries, who often travelled over longer distances, needed lodging overnight and depended upon hospitality from local church members, and they therefore needed letters of recommendation as an introduction and proof that they were 'true' messengers. The letter and the messenger belonged together, as the written message was read aloud in the gathering of the community, and the living voice brought the author of the letter alive; his presence was invoked by stories and greetings through the messenger. So we can see that, in the context of early Christianity, it was rather more than 'just' a letter.

2

MEMORY AND IDENTITY: THE GOSPELS AS JESUS-BIOGRAPHIES

What was the media culture in the world of the early Christians like?[1] When the gospels were written down in the latter part of the first century, they appeared in a world totally different to ours - the world of the early Christians was not dominated by texts and the printed word.[2] This was before Gutenberg and before mass literacy: orality was the dominant mode of communication and, at most, ten per cent of the population could read.[3] The written word therefore had a different function from that in our world: in an oral culture texts were written to be performed, not simply to be read.

ORAL GOSPELS

In many societies today orality remains the principle medium of communication, and storytelling the way to transmit the history and traditions of communities. Studies of such communities past and present, for instance in Africa, suggest parallels with those of the early followers of Christ: sayings of Jesus and stories about him were told, retold and handed down to new listeners. Stories of the history of a group, of important events or founding figures, serve to shape and strengthen the group's identity in its present situation and inevitably bear its mark. In the same manner, we must imagine that, in stories about Jesus and his teachings, the memories of Jesus were fused with the concerns of the early Christian communities as those stories were reiterated. Memories of Jesus, narrated and shaped by individuals, became part of the social memory of the group as a whole.

For about the first 40 years after the death of Jesus, oral transmission in the form of storytelling and preaching was the way in
which his memory was preserved and spread. Over time, individual
stories and sayings were gathered, probably in collections of similar
stories, for example those concerned with healing. The narratives of
Jesus' last week in Jerusalem, his suffering, death and resurrection
were gathered into a long passion narrative. Clusters of his sayings
were also gathered early on in the tradition he inspired, such as
those in the Q source and the *Gospel of Thomas*.

The transition from oral tradition to written documents was a
significant step, and there were two reasons behind the move: to
secure and stabilise the tradition after the death of the first generation of disciples, and to meet the needs of a movement spread
throughout the Greco-Roman world. This new, literary medium
required a different skill set for producers and consumers, not least
a working knowledge of Greek – the lingua franca of the Empire
– and the ability to compose a written document. In short, it required
people with some education, at least to secondary level, that included
the teaching of grammar and literature.[4]

The writing down of the gospels, integrating the sayings of Jesus
into a narrative, did not put an end to the oral tradition of storytelling. We can therefore imagine three different 'media channels' of
Jesus traditions in the late first century: 1) orality, 2) at least one
written collection of sayings, and 3) the narrative gospels. Even if
the written gospels were read and performed orally in gatherings of
the earliest Christians, that they existed in writing made a difference.
Studies of the introduction of writing practises into oral cultures
have found that whereas oral communication is an event, shaped
and changed through interaction with the audience, written communication 'fixes' the meaning of a story, giving it a certain independence from the audience receiving it. Writing is therefore a way
of defining a tradition and a form of controlling meaning. If we
apply this insight to the gospels, we can see that written preservations
of once-spoken memories of Jesus would have the capacity to shape
the identity of the audiences in particular directions and introduce
community ideals. The purpose of this chapter is to investigate the
ways in which the gospels do this; by how they tell the story of

Jesus, how they describe him and the other characters, and also how they relate to their audiences.

GOSPELS AS BIOGRAPHIES

First we must clarify what type of writings the gospels were in their historical setting. To what genre did they belong? A generation ago, many scholars held that the gospels could not be compared to other forms of literature: the stories of Jesus were considered a unique literary form, to be studied as a genre in their own right. For most scholars today this position is no longer tenable, and it is standard practice to look for other literary genres of the time that may have served as models for the gospels. Among plausible candidates, ancient biographies appear to be the closest models.[5] This was a well-known genre at the time, commonly referred to as *Lives* (Greek *bioi,* or Latin *vitae*). For example, the Greek author Plutarch (*c.* AD 45–120) wrote a series of *Lives* of celebrated Romans, and the Jewish author Philo of Alexandria, working in the middle of the first century, wrote *Lives* of Jewish heroes such as Moses and Abraham. Ancient biographies differed from modern biographies, which are often informed by notions of self-conscious personhood and the development of character. Ancient biographies described character not through analysis of personality development, but through deeds and words. Biography was a type of writing that was often used by people who had gathered round a teacher or leader and were seeking to perpetuate his ideas. As such, biographies often had a community-building function. A comparison of the gospels and Greco-Roman biographies shows many similarities. For example, in keeping with the formal structure of those ancient biographies, the gospels give a chronological development of a life, with an emphasis on the last days and death. On the other hand, the genre of biography was sufficiently flexible to be adapted to the distinctive features of individual lives: for instance by blending the preserved teachings of Jesus into a narrative framework.

One of the purposes of writing a biography of a person was to present him as an ideal, as an example to be followed.[6] The gospels did this by focusing on the relationship between Jesus and his disciples in such a way that the readers, or listeners, were included in the stories. By writing the gospels down, the emerging communities of Christ preserved stories about Jesus and his sayings around which their new identities were formed, while regular readings and performances of them reminded these Christians of their new identity.

In what follows, I will introduce the gospels with a focus on their presentations of who Jesus was, how he related to his contemporaries and how this image shaped the identity of his followers. Of the reading methods outlined in Chapter 8, this chapter adopts a narrative reading of the gospels. The main purpose of this strategy is to read them as literary universes in their own right; examining how the characters function within that universe, how the story of which they are a part unfolds and how the audience becomes incorporated into those universes. This method requires us to read the gospels in the same way we might read and analyse other narrative texts, and it is a type of reading many will be familiar with through participation in various humanities programmes at university or even from school. I hope to present a plausible reading, the success of which is something the readers can best judge for themselves by reading my interpretation alongside the gospel texts.

At the end of my analysis of the gospels I will raise some historical questions which present themselves to modern readers of these texts. One such question posed by this exercise has already informed my approach: Where might the picture of Jesus and his followers in each of the gospels fit with the historical development of early Christian communities? It is with this question in mind that I have chosen not to consider the gospels in their canonical order, but to attempt to sketch a possible sequence of the narrative gospels from Mark, as the earliest, to John, as the latest. I will, moreover, include the Q source in my reconstruction, since it contains most of the sayings material common to Matthew and Luke.

MARK: THE SUFFERING JESUS AND DISCIPLES WITHOUT UNDERSTANDING

Mark introduces the public ministry of Jesus with his declaration: 'the time is fulfilled, and the Kingdom of God has come near, repent, and believe in the good news' (1:15). Jesus immediately starts calling disciples: 'Follow me and I will make you fish for people.' This was a call for the disciples to leave their households and their boats, that is, their primary places of socialisation. The call to follow Jesus represents an introduction to what, in sociological terms, is described as re-socialisation, that is, a transfer into a new social context and communal identity. The story of Jesus and that of his disciples are intertwined: Mark shows how Jesus attempts to form the lives of the disciples by beckoning them into a new identity by following him. Thus, the scene is set: the story shall be heard as the coming of the Kingdom, and the record of how those who are called to imitate the life of Jesus will respond to that call.

So who is this Jesus? Mark provides little information about his central subject – his birth and family background is of no interest at the start of the gospel[7] – and he is only introduced as Jesus who came from Nazareth of Galilee (1:9). But even if Jesus appears unknown at the outset of Mark's Gospel, readers (or listeners) are left in no doubt as to who the author considers Jesus to be, with the opening statement: 'The beginning of the good news of Jesus Christ, the Son of God.' 'Christ' is the Greek form of the Hebrew Messiah – the anointed one – a figure in Jewish tradition who was expected to bring in God's rule. And 'Son of God' was an honorary designation used of the King of Israel in the Psalms. So these titles immediately place Jesus within the matrix of Jewish history, presenting the reader (or listener) with familiar religious motifs and arousing expectations in them that they will be fulfilled in the course of the narrative.

But are they? At important points in the story Mark repeats that Jesus is the Son of God: for example, through God's voice at Jesus' baptism (1:11), at the transfiguration (9:7) and through the voice of the Roman soldier at Jesus' death (15:39). Mark has chosen the three most important events in the life of Jesus to affirm his claim that Jesus is the Christ, the Son of God. And yet these bold statements clash with consistent features of the narrative. When, for instance, Jesus performs healings which the sick recognise as miracles caused by the power of God, Jesus forbids them to speak of it. In the history of scholarly interpretations of Mark's Gospel, this came to be known as the 'Messianic secret'. Why did Jesus, as represented by Mark, want to keep his identity a secret? Many answers have been suggested by scholars, but I propose that it has to do with Mark's unease about some of the traditional meanings of the term Messiah, and so he reinterprets Messiah-ship and what it means to be a follower of the Messiah, a reinterpretation which slowly comes into view following repeated misunderstandings. So, for example, when Jesus asks his disciples: 'Who do you say that I am?' (Mark 8:27–30), Peter gives the 'correct' answer: 'the Messiah'. But when Jesus goes on to predict his suffering and death in Jerusalem, Peter's protest shows that he has still not understood the type of Messiah Jesus is.

In terms of self-definition, instead of Messiah, Jesus uses the designation 'Son of Man'. The precise meaning of 'Son of Man' is a long standing controversy: some have suggested a mythic and apocalyptic figure in the Book of Daniel, but it had also been pointed out that it could simply be an idiomatic reference to 'man': a human being. What is clear, however, is that a figure associated with suffering represents a dramatic reversal of traditional expectations of a Messiah. The importance Mark places on this transformation of traditional expectations of the Messiah is emphasised by the triple prophecy of Jesus' suffering and death (8:34–8; 9:30–5; 10:32–45); each time combined with a demand that the disciples follow him in his suffering.

These three prophecies of Jesus' suffering point towards the passion story, which is the centrepiece of Mark's Gospel (Chapters 11–16). But here, too, the disciples fail him: when Jesus suffers during his prayers in Gethsemane, his disciples fail to stay awake with him; when he is arrested they all leave him and run away; and when Jesus is interrogated by the Sanhedrin, Peter denies any knowledge of him. At the crucifixion scene only some women are in attendance, watching at a distance.

There are multiple meanings to Jesus' suffering and the events surrounding it. Jesus was crucified, accused of claiming to be 'King of the Jews', and mocked because he could not save himself (15:31–2), but Mark's readers will remember a previous saying of Jesus: 'For the Son of man came not to be served but to serve, and to give his life a ransom for many' (10:45). Thus, the suffering and shame of crucifixion has a purpose. Moreover, it was the death of the suffering Jesus that made the Roman officer in charge of the crucifixion exclaim: 'Truly this man was God's son'(15:39). Jesus' death was also accompanied by a sign: the curtain that separated off the holiest part of the Jerusalem Temple was torn in two. Within this cultural context, such narrative events might have been understood to mean that Jesus was now recognised as the Son of God by non-Jews, and that access to God in his Temple was open to all.

Figure 4. The crucifixion of Jesus, from the famous illustrated edition of the Bible by Gustave Doré, 1866.

The resurrection narrative in Mark is not as triumphant as one might expect. The women travelled to Jesus' tomb to anoint his body for burial, but met a young man who proclaimed that Jesus was risen (16:1–8). Here, during one of the cruxes of the whole gospel, we read that, 'they said nothing to anyone, for they were afraid' (16:8). Is this the final verdict of Jesus' disciples, who did not understand, and who did not know how to follow him? And did this ending imply that when the good news had reached the listeners or readers of Mark's Gospel it was not because of the disciples, but only by the power of God?

To conclude, at the micro level Mark tells a story of Jesus' interactions with disciples, opponents and the wider public. As a metanarrative, however, it is a story of how Israel's traditions about the Messiah and the Son of God are transformed and given new meanings. It is a different title, Son of Man, that Jesus adopts to combine the present reality of suffering and death with the hope of his glorious resurrection, and this becomes the model for his disciples to follow. The disciples did not understand, but Mark's Gospel challenges the audience to follow the suffering Son of Man through their own suffering and to wait for his coming in glory.

The Gospel of Mark is now generally recognised as the first gospel to be written, most likely c. AD 70. For a long time scholars held that Mark's Gospel was the most historical. It appeared to be more 'down to earth': less literary and more factual. But even if this gospel does contain significant historical data, it is Mark's construction which marks it out: drawing a dramatic picture of Jesus as he moved from crowd-pleasing miracle worker and teacher in Galilee to his suffering and death in Jerusalem, all within a period of one year. Most scholars seem to have accepted this structure in their historical reconstructions of the life of Jesus, but we need only look at John's Gospel to find a quite different narrative (see below).

THE SAYINGS GOSPEL Q AND THE HOMELESS SON OF MAN

The now-dominant view that Mark was the oldest gospel and the main source for Matthew and Luke was the result of a long discussion that took place in the nineteenth century (see Chapter 8). It was also recognised, however, that Matthew and Luke probably had another common source containing their shared sayings material not found in Mark. The best example of where such a source becomes a plausible hypothesis is with the sayings that Matthew collected in his long 'Sermon on the Mount' (Matt 5–7), many of which Luke gathered in a much shorter 'Sermon on the Plain' (Luke 6:20–49). Since this discussion of literary sources for the gospels was an exercise in German scholarship, the name for this hypothetical document (Q) is simply taken from the German word for 'source': *Quelle*. This general hypothesis is still widely accepted today, but there is less agreement on the question of whether it must have been a written source. The theory that it was a written document has proved especially popular among North American and British scholars, who have even published a Greek text of Q – reconstructed from Matthew and Luke – and who speak of it as a gospel in its own right.[8] While it was once thought unlikely that there would be a gospel consisting only of sayings of Jesus, the *Gospel of Thomas*, found among the Nag Hammadi codices, provides an example of just such a gospel. Many of the sayings in the *Gospel of Thomas* that parallel the so-called 'Q sayings' may belong to an earlier tradition than the synoptic gospels, but the final collection is generally agreed to be later, so we will defer detailed discussion of the Gospel of Thomas until Chapter 4.

Compared to the narrative gospels, Q and the *Gospel of Thomas* contain Jesus' sayings but without a narrative framework. The major difference is that these saying gospels did not include the passion story or the resurrection narratives. In the narrative gospels, the death of Jesus played a determining role in their picture of him, and his resurrection was the catalyst for the faith that Jesus was still present in the communities of those who recognised him as the Christ. Q may reflect knowledge of the death of Jesus, but it is interpreted differently. For instance, the saying in Q 14:27[9]: 'Whoever does not carry the cross and follow me cannot be my disciple', seems to imply knowledge of the death of Jesus and a warning that the disciples must be willing to follow him into suffering. A similar theme is the demand to give up everything to follow Jesus. Just as he himself was homeless, the disciples must leave household and property to follow him (Q 9:57–62) and to depend on support from sympathisers (10:1–16). Many of the sayings that are collected in the Sermon on the Mount emphasise the demand for total discipleship and obedience to God, and at the same time the disciples shall show complete trust in God (Q 12:2–31).

If we construct our image of Jesus on the basis of his sayings in Q, he does not seem to be the Saviour as depicted in the narrative gospels or the letters Paul but, rather, a wisdom teacher; a man who lived his life in total dependence on God; and a man to be imitated. The genre of wisdom literature was widespread in many cultures in the Ancient Mediterranean and Near East. However, while much of wisdom literature involved the transmission of conventional wisdom – common sense relative to social context – many of the sayings of Jesus were socially radical. And the radical character of these sayings becomes particularly apparent when they are taken out of the domesticating narrative context of the canonical gospels. One (controversial) suggestion is that a group of Hellenistic philosophers, known as Cynics, may have provided a model for this type of itinerant, ascetic lifestyle with a subversive social message. This suggestion has met with heavy criticism since it seems to imply a non-Jewish influence on the formation and outlook of Jesus without any direct evidence of contact between Cynics and Galilean Jews during the relevant period. On the other hand, Galilee was surrounded by Hellenistic cities, where there were at least some philosophical schools, so the case for making serious comparisons of lifestyle and teaching between Jesus and these figures cannot be dismissed out of hand.[10]

MATTHEW: JESUS – A TEACHER LIKE MOSES?

The Gospel of Matthew follows Mark in so far as Jesus' public ministry begins with his proclamation: 'Repent, for the kingdom of heaven has come near'(4:17). This call, and the call of his first disciples, is immediately followed by the Sermon on the Mount (Chapters 5–7), which portrays Jesus working fully within Jewish law: 'I have come not to abolish [the law and the prophets], but to fulfil' (5:17). And his followers are called to do the same: 'unless your righteousness exceeds that of the scribes and Pharisees, you will never enter the kingdom of heaven' (5:20). Jesus' proclamation of the Kingdom is obviously meant to represent a new beginning, but the explanation which follows seems to present this as a better way of keeping the law and the way of the prophets: that is, being faithful to the traditions of Israel. This tension between the new and old is one of the distinctive underlying themes of this gospel, and it raises the question of how its recipients will understand their identity in relation to Jewish traditions.

It is the beginning of Matthew, however, and the story of the conception and birth of Jesus (Chapters 1–2) that immediately sets this gospel apart from that of Mark. Stories of birth and childhood were often part of Greco-Roman biographies; however, they were not part of the original oral preaching that focused on Jesus' death and resurrection but were added to the Gospels of Matthew and Luke.[11] One purpose behind the introduction of such narratives was to emphasise Jesus' relationship to God and to the history of Israel, but there was also a more general element of curiosity and a desire to know as much as possible about Jesus: his place of origin, the identity of his parents and what he was like as a child. With their focus on two significant features of the biographies of great men that were popular at the time – a miraculous birth and an illustrious genealogy – the birth and infancy stories in Matthew and Luke stand at the beginning of a tradition that flourished in later apocryphal gospels (see Chapter 4).

There was no single common source for these stories. Although they share some elements, Matthew 1–2 and Luke 1–2 give very different accounts of Jesus' birth, accounts which make sense within their respective gospels. For instance, Matthew tells the story with Joseph as the protagonist while Mary plays only a minor role. Matthew introduces Jesus as the one who 'will save his people from their sins' (1:21), and as 'the King of the Jews' (2:2). From the very start he is the target of assassination plots by unjust rulers; the flight to Egypt to escape King Herod connects the story of Jesus to that of Moses, who suffered a similar fate (Exodus 2:1–10). Matthew's many references to Scripture as fulfilled in the history of Jesus (1:22; 2:5; 2:17; 2:23), place the author as a scribe within Jewish tradition.

The structure of the Sermon on the Mount, with Jesus speaking

Figure 5. *The Adoration of the Magi* (Matt 2:11) by Abraham Bloemart, 1624, Centraal Museum, Utrecht.

to the disciples from the mountain, suggests another similarity to Moses, coming down from the mountain with the Law tablets (Ex 19–20). The Beatitudes promise the Kingdom of Heaven to 'the poor in Spirit' (5:3–11), most likely speaking to the community of Jesus followers. The phrase 'Kingdom of Heaven' (Matthew prefers this formulation to 'Kingdom of God', which is found frequently in Mark and Luke) is used 50 times in Matthew, placing it at the centre of Jesus' message: at the heart of the 'new' age he proclaims. However, in the Sermon on the Mount Matthew presents Jesus as discussing this new dawn within a Jewish context, redefining and clarifying Jewish teachings but not denying that the Torah remained valid. Consider the so-called antitheses in 5:21–48, with their well-known contrasts: 'You have heard that it was said … But I say to you' (5:21, 27, 33, 38, 43). These contrasts have often been taken as evidence that Jesus rejected the law, but they are actually indicative of Jesus' demand for true fulfilment of the law. With 'But I say to you' Matthew presents Jesus as a teacher of the law with authority.

Jesus does not advocate leaving the law, but his sayings are placed within a context of conflict with other Jewish authority figures.

Matthew can be read as having two principal concerns, requiring his audience to understand the text on two levels. The first is that of the narrative, with Jesus interacting with his disciples and engaging with the crowds he attracts – with supporters and adversaries alike. At another level, however, Matthew addresses the concerns of followers of Christ in his own time, *c.* 50 years after the death of Jesus. The structure of the gospel is constituted by a combination of speeches and stories about Jesus, often healing and miracle stories (8–9, 10–12), which conform to the biographical model of characterising a person through words and acts. Both the speeches and the stories have a community-building function, portraying Jesus as a model for others to follow. Chapter 10 narrates Jesus' speech to the disciples prior to sending them on their mission of healing and exorcism, at the heart of which is the instruction to imitate Jesus. Like Jesus, they shall proclaim the Gospel, heal the sick, cast out unclean sprits and expect to be treated like their master. In Chapter 11 they are encouraged to learn from his humility and meekness, and Chapter 13 presents 'parables of growth', emphasising that growth comes from God but also that it requires holding on to the word ('the seed'). In the rules for the community in Chapter 18, Jesus is particularly concerned with the little children and the treatment of 'the little ones' within the community (18:6, 10, 14). There is, Matthew wants to suggest, a special unity between Jesus and these followers.

The concluding apocalyptic speech and parables (24–5) warn the Christ believers of persecutions because of their faith in him; they urge watchfulness and a life characterised by care for the poor and the imprisoned – once again, 'the little ones' represent Jesus (25:31–46). Throughout the Gospel, the exhortation to follow the law and show righteousness is exemplified by Jesus' words and actions, and this righteousness is to be imitated by his disciples.

Death and resurrection

In Matthew, as in Mark, the passion narrative is where the true identity of Jesus is revealed, and also through his encounters with adversaries and the suffering they inflict upon him. The high priest charges Jesus with blasphemy and challenges him to say if he is 'the Messiah, the Son of God'. Jesus responds not by using these terms but, as with the Gospel of Mark, Jesus speaks of himself as 'the Son of Man' (26:63–4). At the cross, however, the political dimension is in focus, with the accusation that Jesus was, or claimed to be, 'the King of the Jews' (27:37). Again, it is through the accusations and mockery that the truth is revealed. A historical observation is in order here: most scholars will now say that the blasphemy charges against Jesus were later additions by the Gospel writers, reflecting conflicts with Jewish leaders in their own time. But there is one very problematic text which deserves further comment. There are references in Matthew to the Jewish 'crowds' who, on the whole, Matthew portrays as positive towards Jesus (21:8, 9, 11, 26, 46). The one exception occurs in the scene when Jesus is accused before Pilate in front of the crowd and Pilate declares himself innocent with respect to Jesus' fate. Instead of 'crowd' Matthew here uses the term 'the people as a whole' that responds: 'His blood be upon us and our children' (27:25). This saying has had a dark and fateful history; throughout the history of Christian political and religious supremacy in Europe, it was used to brand the Jewish people as a whole as 'Christ-killers' and to support anti-Jewish policies. Matthew cannot avoid the moral criticism that he seems to imply that the mob in Jerusalem represented the people as a whole, throughout all generations – a conclusion that modern readers will find unacceptable.

While Matthew appears to have been concerned with parochial infighting between Jewish Christian groups, the conclusion to his gospel shows he had larger ambitions. Once again, the setting for a crucial scene is a mountain where the risen Christ again speaks with authority, indeed, with all the power in heaven and earth, proclaiming a worldwide mission (28:18–20). It is the words of Jesus, more than the Law, that are the authority here: his followers will share in this mission to all nations, and Jesus promises that he will be with them 'always to the end of the age'. This is the ultimate promise of union between Jesus and his followers.

Matthew and his Jewish context

The relationship between the community of Matthew and the Jewish synagogue is one of the most difficult historical questions concerning the Gospel. Were Matthew and his associates still part of the synagogue towards the end of the first century, or had they left it and formed a new community? Scholars hold different opinions on this issue. For instance, Graham Stanton holds that Matthew was writing to communities who had 'separated painfully' from Judaism, whereas Anthony J. Saldarini argues that Matthew writes to a 'reformist Jewish sect' within the larger Jewish community.[12] The traditional way of thinking of Matthew's community, that it was fully separated from Judaism and had established a new religion, is obviously anachronistic. It is only at a much later stage that one can justifiably speak of two different religions. We notice that the Matthean Jesus did not establish an alternative to the Jewish law. He was concerned to give a true interpretation of that law, and his followers were urged to be more righteous in observing the law than the scribes and the Pharisees. On the other hand, the worldwide mission that Jesus proclaims (Matt 28:18–20) may indicate that Matthew was attempting to shape a new community that included both Jews and Gentiles. Such a combination would fit well with the suggestion that Matthew's Gospel was written in Antioch in Syria, but this can be no more than a plausible hypothesis.

LUKE: JESUS AND THE ECONOMY OF THE KINGDOM

Luke's Gospel introduces Jesus and his public ministry quite differently from either Mark or Matthew. The calling of the first disciples is relegated to a later place in the Gospel and, instead of a single call to repent because the Kingdom is near, Luke introduces the mission of Jesus through the latter's programmatic speech in the synagogue in Nazareth (4:14–22). Jesus identifies himself with a message from the prophet Isaiah: the Lord has anointed him with the Spirit to preach 'a good message' for the poor, the blind, the captives and the oppressed. This is the centre of Jesus' preaching, repeated throughout the gospel. I propose to call this Jesus' 'economy of the Kingdom', as an alternative to the present conditions under the rulers of 'this world'; the world as it is presently constituted and governed. This economy of the Kingdom provides the model for the followers of Jesus: they are called to implement this economy *now*, in stark contrast to the existing structures of the Hellenistic world.

That Luke is concerned with the identity of the emerging Christian community within a Hellenistic world becomes clear from the start of the gospel. Luke is the only author who presents himself as a Hellenistic historian: he collects material, sifts his sources and organises data using a clear structure to show the trustworthiness of his writings (1:1–4). Moreover, he uses the common scribal convention of dedicating his book to an individual, in this case a man called Theophilus (probably the patron who supported the publication). Like Matthew, Luke follows the genre of the Greco-Roman biography by introducing Jesus with stories of his birth and boyhood (1–2); he also includes a genealogy (3:23–38). Apart from the same birthplace, Bethlehem, Luke's story is very different from that found in Matthew 1–2. Luke uses the story to introduce important themes in his gospel: God's power and Jesus' prophetic significance is demonstrated through the latter's miraculous birth and the relationship between Jesus and John the Baptist; Jesus is Lord and Saviour of the world, not the Roman emperor Augustus, and the temple in Jerusalem is Jesus' spiritual home. Although the themes of birth and childhood correspond to Greco-Roman biography, the style of the infancy story in Luke is first and foremost biblical, built on the Septuagint and with biblical hymns (1:46–55; 1:69–79): Luke clearly wants his writings to cohere with Israel's traditions. In contrast to Matthew, the story of the birth of Jesus is told from the perspective of Mary, his mother. This is a perspective that is followed up by many stories of women in this gospel.

LUKE'S JOURNEY: FOLLOWING JESUS IN A PILGRIMAGE LANDSCAPE

In the first part of the gospel, Luke follows Mark's structure but introduces sayings from the common Q source. In contrast to Matthew, however, he has a shorter Sermon on the Plain (6:20–38) and spreads Jesus' sayings more evenly throughout the Gospel. The main structuring element where Luke departs from Mark's outline is the long 'travel narrative' of Jesus' journey from his activity in Galilee to the passion in Jerusalem. In Mark this journey takes one chapter (10:17–11:1); in Luke it takes ten (9:51–19:28), two-fifths of the whole gospel story. The purpose is obviously not only to describe a geographical journey: the journey is a pilgrimage to Jerusalem (9: 51, 53), and Luke transforms the geographical landscape into a moral or spiritual landscape with the purpose of creating a new community dedicated to following Jesus. This travel narrative is also where we find many of the parables in Luke's Gospel; indeed, they might be said to contain 'the gospel in parable'[13], illustrating the main points of Luke's distinctive message. Luke uses parables as a storytelling technique and a device for Jesus to answer his critics; for instance, if Jesus is involved in a discussion or is challenged he breaks off from a straightforward counter-argument by telling a parable. When a scribe tests Jesus by asking, 'Who is my neighbour?', Jesus responds by telling the parable of the Good Samaritan (10:25–37). Another much-loved parable, concerning the Prodigal Son, is part of a collection of three parables centring on the theme of things 'lost and found', told in response to criticism of Jesus that he had table fellowship with sinners and tax collectors (15:1–2, 3–32).

In this section Luke also includes some of the sayings material from Q, on trusting in God to provide for the disciples (11:2–13; 12: 22–34). At critical points throughout the journey the readers or listeners are reminded that Jesus and his disciples are on their way to Jerusalem (13:22; 17:11; 19:11). Thus, Jerusalem determines the horizon of the landscape; at issue is the response of Jesus and his disciples to the challenge that Jerusalem represents. Jerusalem starts out as the place of power that represents judgement (9:22, 31, 44), and the narrative presents Jesus and his disciples as travelling towards destruction. But, by representing what it means to follow Jesus, in service and suffering, Luke creates a moral landscape that subverts the hegemony of Jerusalem.

When Jesus comes near to Jerusalem the landscape is dominated by the hope of a new realm, the 'Kingdom of God' (19:11). This kingdom is also the central spatial metaphor in the last meal Jesus has with his disciples (22:15–18 and 28–30) and reappears at the crucifixion (23:42). In the midst of Jerusalem, cast as a landscape of terror, an alternative landscape emerges with a vision of a kingdom characterised by service and suffering (22:14–27). Throughout his suffering in the passion story Jesus remains in charge, responding with strength and dignity to the chief priests, to Pilate and to the women wailing over him on the way to the cross. And only in Luke, on the cross, does Jesus promise Paradise to the repentant robber (23:39–43).

The passion and resurrection stories in Luke are told in such a way that they address the reader or listener directly. During the last supper Luke makes Jesus address those who encounter the gospel with the instruction: 'do this in memory of me' (22:19). Thus the text, repeated at community meals, takes on a performative character: its function is to create fellowship with Jesus. The story about the two disciples who encounter Jesus on their way to Emmaus, after his death, also served as a model for Luke's audience (24:13–25). The way Jesus spoke to them of how his suffering and resurrection were foretold by Moses and the prophets informs the collective memory of the early community. That the two recognised their fellow traveller as Jesus when he broke the bread and gave it to them identifies the eucharistic meal as the place where Jesus became present among them as the resurrected one. Thus, 'following' and 'remembering' are at the forefront of the message Luke is trying to impress upon his readers and listeners, and are key words in the community he is trying to forge or sustain.

The political message

There are two social and political issues in Luke's Gospel that need special attention. The first, introduced at the beginning of the gospel, is Jesus' message to the poor; the second concerns the role of women in the gospel. Luke uses economic and social terminology to characterise people and communities: the way a person uses his or her resources reflects their personality. Many of the parables and sayings about rich and poor, although about individuals, have a wider relevance: they signal the structure of society. Luke lived in a society where structures were personal in nature: the emperor, his representatives, kings and their retainers who claimed authority and respect. His terminology reflects his world, a Hellenistic society with a Hellenistic economy, based on patronage and reciprocities: giving and receiving. Luke presents Jesus as absolutely opposed to this structure. He actually retains the technical terminology of reciprocities, giving and receiving among social equals, but presents an alternative structure: giving without expecting a return, inviting the poor and the disadvantaged who cannot repay (Luke 6:34–6; 14:12–14). Likewise, Jesus introduces a reversal of the authority structures of Greco-Roman society, where kings and rulers claim authority and bind their subjects to a patron–client relationship. In the community of Jesus' followers, this shall be reversed: the leader shall serve (Luke 22:25–6). These sayings represent what Luke sees as the ideal community, one that reflects 'the economy of the Kingdom', the world that God will create. Speaking of God's Kingdom in the Hellenistic world would always have a political meaning: it would be understood in contrast to the present rulers.

Men and women

Who were the followers of Jesus? If we look at Luke's vocabulary, it has a strong male bias. From the beginning of the Gospel those who are called to 'leave' and 'to follow' him to become his disciples are all men (5:27–8; 9:57–62; 18:28–30). Luke's is actually the gospel which speaks most about women, but they are never called to 'leave' and 'to follow', and he is very traditional in the roles he ascribes to them. Women who were healed by Jesus continue their traditional roles of 'serving' (4:38–9; 8:2–3). Women may serve as ideal figures in this regard: Mary, the mother of Jesus, is described as an ideal disciple who listens and keeps the word of Jesus (2:19, 51). Other women in the gospel are also held up as ideals – widows, for example (18:1–7; 21:1–4), and Mary, the sister of Martha, who sits listening at the feet of Jesus (10:38–42) – but they do not take on a preaching role nor, on the whole, share leadership responsibilities: that is the privilege of men. There is, however, a significant change in the portrayal of women in the last period in Jerusalem. The women who are witnesses to his death and burial are described as 'women who had followed him from Galilee' (23:49, 55). At the empty tomb they are encouraged to 'remember' the words of Jesus 'while he was still in Galilee' (24:6, 8). As witnesses to Jesus' death and resurrection, they are transformed to followers and witnesses to what Jesus said in Galilee. Luke's position on women has been much discussed. Many scholars will see him as a champion of women's rights since he pays much attention to them. However, there is a great ambivalence in his presentation of women: they represent ideals of discipleship but at the same time they are not fully equal with men.[14]

Luke and history

Probably written in the last part of the first century, most scholars see Luke's Gospel and Acts as texts written for a Gentile audience, but any such judgement must account for the way that the gospel,

Figure 6. *Jesus in the house of Martha and Mary* (Luke 10:38-42). Etching by Jan Luyken (1649-1712) in the Phillip Medhurst Collection of Bible illustrations, Belgrave Hall, Leicester, England.

from the outset, is deeply rooted in Jewish scripture. On the surface this may suggest a Jewish audience, but Jewish scriptures were already familiar to Gentiles who associated with the synagogues around the Mediterranean. In addition, as a Hellenistic historian Luke well knew the need for religious movements to have ancient credentials.

Luke's position with regard to rich and poor and to the Roman Empire has been much discussed. Some see him as an advocate for the poor, others as protecting the rich; the same conflict of opinion is evident among scholars on the question of his attitude to the Roman Empire, especially when Acts is brought into the picture (see Chapter 3). My own view, based on the outline above, is that Luke probably belonged to a well-to-do group (suggested by his literary skills), but his picture of Jesus advocated a society which included the poor and that was critical of the political powers and economic aggression of Hellenistic cities.

JOHN: THE SON FROM HEAVEN AND HIS COMMUNITY

The plot of John's Gospel

John's Gospel is much more of a theological biography than the others: the author's reflections on Jesus' relationship to God merge with the narrative of the life of Jesus himself. The prologue in 1:1–18 introduces this theological perspective on Jesus and on the community of believers. Where Matthew and Luke added the birth of Jesus to Mark's biography of the adult Jesus, John goes back all the way to creation, to the Word (*logos*) that was with God 'in the beginning', and participated in the creation of the world. It becomes clear that the 'Word' (*logos*) was a person who came into the world as the true light, became 'flesh', and revealed God, as the Son who makes his Father known (1:1–18). Previously, many scholars believed that John's prologue was based on Hellenistic cosmology; now, however, it seems more likely that the influence might come from Jewish wisdom tradition.

The prologue sets up the plot for the following narrative.[15] 'Plot' is, of course, a key term in a narrative analysis. It has several features:

sequence of events; a chain of causality that moves the story from one event to another; a unity of purpose that emerged at completion; and, finally, its affective power, moving readers to response. The goal of Jesus in John's Gospel is to create a community of believers (cf. the conclusion in 20:31: 'that you come to believe that Jesus is the Messiah, the Son of God, and that through believing you may have life in his name'). This is the project, then, and it is the attempt by Jesus' adversaries to frustrate and ultimately destroy this mission that moves the plot forward in John's Gospel. In the prologue these adversaries are characterised as 'the world' (1:10), a cosmic category; in the following gospel they are 'the Jews', stereotypical characters representing the Jewish leaders who oppose Jesus and are associated with the devil (see below). The human conflict between Jesus and his opponents symbolises the cosmic dichotomies which run throughout the Gospel: personalising the contrast between good and evil, heaven and earth, light and darkness, life and death.

The structure of John's Gospel

The biographical storyline in John's Gospel is markedly different from that of the synoptic gospels. The synoptics present Jesus as a Galilean preacher and healer, and Galilee is his homeland until his journey to Jerusalem for the fateful Passover. It is a cycle that can fit easily within a period of one year. In John's Gospel, Galilee is not the main scene for Jesus' ministry – he travels frequently between Jerusalem or Judea and Galilee. He goes to Jerusalem not just for his final Passover: John reports three Passovers (2:14–3:21; 6:5–65; 13:1–19:42) in addition to other feasts. This means that, according to John's Gospel, Jesus' public life could span three years. Jewish festivals are structuring elements in John's narrative, and most of the key events in Jesus' life take place in Jerusalem (2:13–3:22; 5:1–47; 7:10–10:21; 10:22–40; 12:12–20:29). On the other hand, the larger structure of the biography is similar to the synoptic gospels; after the prologue, John describes the public ministry of Jesus (Chapters 2–12), and it ends with Jesus' death and resurrection (Chapters 18–20).

Recognising Jesus

One distinctive feature of the plot is its power to affect the listener or reader. Notable examples are the stories of Jesus' encounters with people which challenge them to understand who he is. Similar stories are known from classical Greek drama and are called 'recognition scenes'.[16] People in such dramas are led from a state of ignorance to one of knowledge with respect to the central figure, while the audience already shares in this knowledge. Here we also find John's characteristic use of misunderstanding and double meaning. The dialogue between Jesus and Nicodemus in Chapter 3 turns on the idea of being 'born anew' (3:3); for Nicodemus this is impossible since he does not grasp that it means to be 'born from above' by the Spirit. Thus Nicodemus does not reach full recognition of Jesus. The Samaritan woman in Chapter 4 does not understand that the 'living water' that Jesus will give does not come from the village well. In Chapter 9, the blind man who was healed by Jesus shows gradual recognition of who Jesus is, while the Pharisees, although they have physical eyesight, remain spiritually blind.

'I am' the water, the bread, life, the way

A typical feature of John's Gospel is the way in which he develops stories of Jesus' miracles – similar to those in the synoptic gospels – into extended discourses and conflict dialogues, perhaps based on a separate source. When Jesus is accused of healing a man on a Sabbath (5:2–16), the story is followed by a discourse on how Jesus does the work of creation like his Father (5: 17–29). The story of the feeding of the five thousand (6:1–14) initiates a conflict dialogue on Jesus' statement: 'I am the bread of life' (6:25–65). The main point in these discussions or monologues by Jesus is always the same: Jesus does the work of his Father; he does nothing of himself, but is sent by his Father. Although John also applies traditional Jewish concepts to Jesus (Messiah, Son of God, King of Israel 1:35–50), the relationship between Jesus and God is characteristically expressed as a father–son relationship. The unity of the Father and the Son is a recurring theme throughout the Gospel, repeated with many variations.

'I have called you friends' – John's community according to 13–17

Chapters 13–17 represent a unique feature in John's account of Jesus' ministry: Jesus' extended farewell discourses to his disciples. At the level of the narrative, Jesus' speech reassures the disciples of his presence among them after his death. At the level of the reader this discourse provides the comfort that Jesus, although invisible, is present among them. In the synoptic gospels Jesus' continued presence is expressed in his institution of the Eucharist at the farewell meal with the disciples. John's Gospel contains the farewell meal but not the Eucharist. Instead, Jesus performs a foot washing of his disciples, taking on the role of a household slave, as an example for them and for future believers to follow (13:4–17). The disciples are portrayed as lacking in understanding, and Jesus continues with a long farewell address and final prayer for them (14–17). The main question is: How can Jesus be present among the disciples when he has gone to his Father? It is through the Spirit that Jesus promises them that he will continue to be present, but also by their abiding in Jesus – that is, in his words and commandments, and above all in his love. This marks their transition from being 'slaves', to being 'friends' of Jesus (15:14–15). And the final goal, which is the theme of Jesus' 'high priest prayer' in Chapter 17, is unity in love between the Father and Son. This unity between the Father and the Son has its correlation in the unity between Jesus and his disciples. The affective power of this discourse is considerable, with its insistence upon shaping the community in the image of the relationship between the Father and the Son. At the same time, there is something claustrophobic about the picture that emerges: it is love between insiders, not directed to others, to outsiders; it is a community that distances itself from 'the world' (15:18–25).

Jesus is 'lifted up' on the cross

After the long farewell discourse and prayer, the narrative comes back to the passion story, a narrative with a common structure in all the Gospels. However, John has a more political focus, which manifests itself both in the discussion between Jesus and Pilate on the nature of the Kingdom, and in the charge of the Jewish mob that 'everyone who claims to be a king sets himself against the Emperor' (19:12). More than in the other gospels, Jesus behaves like a king: he is in control, the principal actor in the drama, with others reacting to him (18:4–9, 11, 21–3, 33–8; 19:10–11). His final word on the cross is, 'It is fulfilled' [17] (19:30). In addition to being a violent and dramatic conclusion to a life, the crucifixion represents the completion of a plot constructed by John, both in terms of Jesus' mission among the people and his return to the Father. Indeed, the crucifixion scene brings to mind a saying by Jesus earlier in the gospel about the Son of Man, who must 'be lifted up, that whoever believes in him may have eternal life' (3:14–15; 12:32–3).

The resurrection narratives are also developed in a unique way by John, with Jesus' appearance to Mary Magdalene (20:11–18) giving rise to a fertile tradition centring on the idea that Mary, although a woman, was chosen to receive vital revelations from the risen Lord (see the *Gospel of Mary*, Chapter 4). The story of the doubting Thomas is also a distinctive feature of John's post-resurrection narrative, probably addressed to members of John's own community: 'Blessed are those who have not seen and yet have come to believe' (20:29).

John and the Jews

The portrayal of the Jews in John's Gospels has proved to be a headache for interpreters. The Jews are the main adversaries of Jesus in the Gospel, with their rejection of him as a revelation of God. John mentions 'Jews' 70 times in his gospel, negatively in most instances. But who exactly are 'the Jews' in John's account?[18] First and foremost, 'the Jews' are a stereotype – a personalised symbol of negativity and opposition to God – in the same way as 'the world' functions as a natural symbol of negativity and opposition to God. The term obviously does not apply to all Jews, as this would have included Jesus' disciples (13:33). 'The world' is also said to hate Jesus and his disciples, indicative as it is of unbelief in Jesus (15:18–21). Thus, 'the Jews' and 'the world' blend together. The gospel has many episodes in the form of 'challenge and riposte' between Jesus

Figure 7. 'The Jews took up rocks to stone Jesus' (John 10:31), from *The Life of Christ*, James Tissot, between 1886-1896, Brooklyn Museum, New York.

and 'the Jews', and Jesus does not shirk the challenge. Rhetorically, the exchanges are at their harshest where the Jews claim that they have Abraham and God as their fathers, and Jesus counters, 'You are from your father the devil, and you choose to do your father's desires' (8:44). The conflict comes to a climax in the judgement scene in 18:28–40, where 'the Jews' pressure Pilate into crucifying Jesus.

At a narrative level it is possible to study the function of 'the Jews' as a stereotype in John's Gospel, but this is an instance where a narrative reading is insufficient. It is impossible not to consider the reception history of 'the Jews' as the opponents of Jesus, and how this stereotype has contributed to pogroms, persecutions and legitimised anti-Semitism. John's negative stereotyping can be explained by pointing to a crisis in relations between his community and the dominant Jewish synagogue at the time,[19] but with the hindsight of history it cannot be excused. Since many aspects of the gospel are considered a positive influence – for instance its emphasis on love and unity – negative stereotyping must be rejected as an unacceptable form of communication.

CONCLUSION

Using the model of a biography to read the gospels has resulted in five different pictures of Jesus, the disciples and the communities that the gospels intended to shape: a suffering Jesus; a Jesus who revealed himself through his words; a Jesus who gave the true interpretation of the law and righteousness; a Jesus who introduced a new 'economy of the Kingdom' for the poor; and a Jesus as the heaven-sent Son of the Father. These different images of Jesus were also reflected in the way the disciples were described, with implications for the ideals of the communities the Gospels addressed, although historic constructions of such communities can only ever be educated, conjectural hypotheses.

A final and summary observation to make here is that the gospels reflect diversity both in their images of Jesus and in the ideals of the communities in which these images functioned. Contrary to one popular way of conceiving the history of early Christianity, diversity was not something that came later as a deviation from a supposed unity: diversity was there from the beginning.

3

ACTS AND APOCALYPSE: AMBIVALENT LIVING UNDER THE ROMAN EMPIRE

The Acts of the Apostles and the Apocalypse (or Book of Revelation) are usually taken to be very different New Testament texts, and with good reason. Acts is a detailed history of the early mission of the apostles, beginning with the activities of those disciples who actually followed Jesus in his lifetime, before shifting focus to the story of Paul as he takes the gospel to towns and cities throughout the eastern part of the Roman Empire. The Apocalypse is an ancient Gothic vision of cosmic conflicts between devilish beasts and dragons on the one side and God and his angels on the other. Apart from the fact that neither of them fits into the genres of the epistles or Gospels, what is it that makes it plausible to discuss them together? I suggest that the common denominator is that they are both responses by the second (or third) generation of Christ believers to the challenges of living under the power of the Roman Empire.

The Roman Empire was the given context for the first Christians, a setting that they could simply not avoid, but that does not mean that it always came to the fore in their writings. In the canonical gospels it is only towards the end, with the execution of Jesus at the hands of Pilate, that imperial politics come centre stage. And in Paul's letters, addressing communities in various cities within the Empire, Romans 13 stands out as exceptional in its explicit discussion of how the addressees should relate to the emperor and his representatives (see Chapter 9 on recent research on this matter). However, in the Acts of the Apostles and the Apocalypse, the Roman Empire is clearly visible as a force to be reckoned with, present in the institutions of law and order, taxation and the imperial cult.

Both writings were probably produced in Asia Minor in the last decades of the first century, but they offer different responses to the challenges of living in the Roman Empire as followers of Christ.

ACTS – EVANGELISING THE ROMAN EMPIRE

Acts is the second part of Luke's two-volume work, written in the genre of a Greco-Roman history. The goal of the story is introduced at the outset, when Jesus appears to his disciples after the resurrection and presents them with their task: 'you shall be my witnesses in Jerusalem and in all Judea and Samaria and *to the end of the world*' (1:8). This is an extremely ambitious goal, similar to his aim of making 'disciples of all nations' at the end of Matthew (28:19), and it forms a central plot line in Acts. Luke writes from a position where he clearly looks back upon the mission of Jesus' disciples as a success story. By this time, probably in the AD 80s, there were Christ believers, albeit only small groups, spread over a large area of the eastern parts of the Roman Empire, in Rome itself and other regions of what we would now call Italy. So how had this happened? Luke's answer is that it was by the power of God, through the Holy Spirit; in fact, Luke's narrative in Acts is permeated with the power of God and of the Spirit. It is introduced by Jesus who, from the outset, promises that the disciples will receive the Holy Spirit (1:5), and sets the scene for the signal event in Acts when the disciples receive the Holy Spirit through tongues of fire, giving them the capacity to speak in all the languages needed for their mission (2:1–13).

The first part of Acts, 2–12, narrates the story of the early witness of the disciples, to 'Jerusalem and in all Judea and Samaria'. They are, at all times, driven by the Spirit, not only to Jews but also outsiders such as the Ethiopian eunuch (8:26–40) and the Roman centurion, Cornelius (10). So, on Luke's account, the mission to the Gentiles had been initiated by the Jerusalem disciples of Jesus but, from the second part of Acts, it is Paul who becomes the protagonist (13–28). The narrative becomes a travelogue, with the plot structured around Paul's travels through Asia Minor and Greece, and to Rome. Again, it is the Spirit which drives him westward and into the centre of the Roman Empire. This focus on Paul's trajectory towards Rome

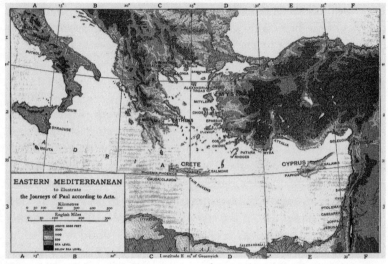

Map 3. The Eastern Mediterranean was the scene of Paul's journeys

must be a conscious decision by Luke. He leaves behind traces that point to the mission to Africa and to the East (8:26–40; 9:20–2); regions where missions must have reached as early as those on the western route taken by Paul. But the focus on Paul's activities in Acts marks the beginning of a hegemony of Western Christian storytelling.

The main story in Acts, then, is that, through the power of the Spirit, Paul's proclamation – of Jesus as God's son who would come as the judge of the world (17:31) – is one that has conquered the Roman Empire. Luke shows how this happened with stories of Paul's visits to various cities, some of them Roman colonies, the resistance he encountered there and how, in the end, he overcame it (Acts 14:6–23; 16:11–40; 19:23–41). The recurring pattern of these stories is that Paul started his mission by preaching in the synagogues with mixed results: some Jews followed him while others turned against him, even accusing him of wrong doing in front of the authorities. These authorities represent, or at least rule with the permission of, the Roman Empire, so the question is whether Paul – and, by extension, the contemporaries of Luke – has a place in the public life of cities in the Roman Empire. The answer, at times, seems affirmative: on some occasions Paul uses his status as a Roman citizen to escape from prison or punishment; in other instances the Roman or city authorities protect him against a Jewish mob (16:16–40; 18:12–17; 19:31–41; 22:22–9).

In the final test in Jerusalem and Caesarea (21:15–26:32), Paul's story begins to parallel Jesus' passion: he is accused by Jewish leaders but Roman proconsuls who know that he is not guilty are too weak to set him free. Unlike Jesus, however, Paul can still play his 'Roman card': as a Roman citizen he appeals to Caesar as his rightful judge and is despatched to Rome to face justice. After a dramatic journey, marked by a shipwreck, the climactic scene in Acts is strangely inconclusive: Luke does not end the story with the most historically plausible outcome, namely, Paul's execution at the hand of Rome. Instead, he concludes Acts by telling a story of Paul living under house arrest, able to receive visitors and 'preaching the Kingdom of God and teaching about the Lord Jesus Christ quite openly and unhindered' (Acts 28:31). This is a definite success story: the witness of the Kingdom of God and of the Lord Jesus Christ had reached the centre of the Empire almost 'unhindered'.

The terminology in this last statement in Acts is worth attention: 'Kingdom' is a translation of the Greek *basileia*, which could also be translated as 'empire'. The noun *basilievs* is used for the emperor, while the 'Lord' applied to Jesus Christ is also a term for the power of a ruler. So the terminology is parallel to that of Empire and emperor: the travelogue of Paul's mission in Acts is symbolically the expansion of the Empire of God and Jesus Christ into imperial Rome. Luke has a similar presentation of Jesus in the birth narrative of his Gospel: Jesus was born when Augustus was Caesar, and the birth of Jesus was acclaimed as bringing 'on earth peace' (Luke 2:14), a reference to (and contrast with) the *pax Romana* of the Roman emperor.

Using a post-colonial perspective we may say that Luke mimics the thoughts and language of empire: the power of God and the narrative of Jesus are certainly described in terms similar to those found in odes to imperial Rome. Paul's travels to Rome from the East are a counter-movement to the ambitions of the Empire, which sought to travel *from* Rome to the 'ends of the world': led by the Spirit, Paul carries the Gospel *to* Rome, resisting opposition from Roman and Jewish authorities and negotiating the anger of hostile mobs. The outcome of these controversies is that Paul and his followers can be present in city space: Paul has blazed a trail for later Christ believers to occupy a place in the Empire.

I have now read Acts as a story directed primarily at Luke's audience of committed followers of Christ and not, as some prefer, as an apologetic text directed at a Roman audience assuring them that Christianity did not pose a threat to their Empire.[1] I think Luke's story of how God's power conquers the Roman Empire is his main point in Acts, while simultaneously acknowledging Roman power as a presently enduring reality which has to be negotiated. He has a realistic evaluation of Roman power and authorities: in his descriptions of both Pilate in the Gospel and Roman power holders in Acts he exposes their weaknesses and shows how they are willing to let Jesus and Paul suffer to protect their own interests. Acts takes what appears to be an accepting but not uncritical stance towards Rome. Therefore it can be seen that Luke does not idealise the Roman Empire, nor does he demonize it. For this, we must turn to the Apocalypse.

APOCALYPSE AS EARLY CHRISTIAN WORLDVIEW

Before we examine the very different perspective of the Apocalypse, we should take note of some similarities between Acts and the Book of Revelation: similarities which, in truth, seem to have been a discernable feature of the worldview of all early Christian writers. In Acts, this feature is introduced by Peter's speech in Chapter 2. He sees the pouring out of the Spirit on the disciples of Jesus as a fulfilment of the promise of the Spirit in the prophet Joel. But there is another prophecy fulfilled by the resurrected Jesus: the prophecy of 'the Day of the Lord', with judgement and salvation, preceded by wonders in heaven and signs on the earth of 'blood, and fire, and vapour of smoke' (Joel 2:28–32 in Acts 2:17–21). This expectation of God's judgement over the world with drastic events was evidently widespread at the time, both in Jewish scriptures and among the early Christ believers. It is the main message of Paul's speech to the Greeks in Athens (17:31–2), while 1 Thessalonians 1:9–10 provides further evidence of this motif in typical missionary preaching: Jesus was sent by God as Saviour from an impending judgement of the human race. We find this type of preaching in sermons attributed to Jesus in the gospels (the so-called small apocalypses in Mark 13; Matthew 24; Luke 21). These discourses extensively develop the descriptions of the horrors that will happen before 'the Son of Man comes': wars, earthquakes, famines and persecutions of the Christ followers (Mark 13: 8–12). These images were common in apocalypses, a well-known literary form which, in the case of the Gospels, may have been inspired by the apocalyptic Book of Daniel, a text which was most likely written towards the end of the second century. In contrast to the Maccabeans, who rebelled against the Hellenistic rulers of Judea, Daniel proclaimed that it was the place of God, not men, to save Israel, through the miraculous intervention of a Messiah who would come and destroy her enemies. This type of end-of-the-world scenarios – expectations of 'Apocalypse NOW' – were obviously common among Jews and Christ followers in the first century: they were now directed at Roman rule.

APOCALYPSE NOW

Images of violent oppression of the believers and a dramatic fight against the powers of evil has led some scholars to suggest that the Apocalypse was written as a response to persecutions of Christians at the end of the first century.[2] This idea has had to be tempered, however, since there is no evidence that Roman authorities had initiated large-scale persecutions in this early period. Another suggestion, and one I take to be the more plausible, is that, written from a position that saw the Roman Empire as usurping God's power, the Apocalypse was a warning against followers of Christ who were tempted by the trappings of the Empire, with its pagan cults, sacrifices, social institutions and interactions. This view is supported by a reading of the first part of the Apocalypse or, as it is more commonly called, the Revelation to John. 'Apocalypse', it should be noted, simply means 'uncovering' and refers to secrets that are revealed (by God) in visions or dreams. It was part of the broader genre of prophecy and focused especially on the end of time and the coming judgement of God. In this book a man named John, of whom nothing more is known, informs readers that he received a revelation on the island of Patmos in Asia Minor (Rev 1:9–11). Before the details of these revelations are made known, he writes seven letters to seven emerging Christian communities in Asia Minor (Rev 2–3). A central theme in his criticism of these communities (apparently addressing only male members) is that they participate in idolatry and fornication. These criticisms seems to be aimed at pagan cults in the cities, including the cult of the emperor and the practice whereby free males had licence to engage in sex with whomever was dependent on them: women and slaves of both sexes.

Chapters 4–22 portray the destruction of Rome and its world in vivid and gruesome detail. The Apocalypse presents the contrasts to Rome in spatial categories set on three levels: heaven, earth and the underworld. The main events take place in heaven where the throne of God and the Lamb (an image of Christ) is the centre and where true worship takes place – in contrast to the Empire and imperial cult on earth. It is announced from heaven that devastation will sweep the earth.

This devastation unfolds in three waves: the first announced by the breaking of seven seals (6:1–8:1); the second at the soundings of seven trumpets by seven angels (8:2–11:15); and the third by the sending of seven plagues by seven angels. (16:2–21). Each of the seals, trumpet blasts and plagues signal the onset of disasters symbolised by figures that will be instantly recognisable to many even today. For example, the first four seals trigger the release of four horses and their riders, representing conquest, war, famine and death (6:1–8). The trumpets announce an array of cosmic disasters and the slaughter of humankind; the plagues sent down from the bowls of angels are worse than those God cursed the Egyptians with when Pharaoh refused to let the Israelites go (Ex 6–11). But the series of disasters is broken: there are moments when the picture moves to the souls of the martyrs or to the 144,000 righteous who worshipped the Lamb (7:4–8). Between the second and third cycles there is a narrative section, with a story of a woman and her child (Jesus) and a fight between the Archangel Michael and the dragon (Rev 12). Other sinister interludes focus on the two beasts from the sea and the earth (polemical images of Rome and the Emperor Nero, Rev

Figure 8. *The Four Riders of the Apocalypse* (*Revelation 6*) (1497-98), Albrecht Dürer, Staatliche Kunsthalle Karlsruhe

13), before the scene shifts to the sharp contrast between heavenly worship and worship of the beast (Rev 14).

The destruction of Rome is clothed in mythical descriptions of Babylon, 'the great whore', but the results are described in political and economic terms: the kings of the earth and the merchants will weep over the loss of power and wealth (Rev 18). The counterpoint to the fall of Rome is the celebration in heaven of God, with His power and just judgement over 'the great harlot' (19:1–10), before he leads the final battle between the cosmic powers of good and evil (19:11–20:15). At last, after all the battles and power struggles, the scene shifts once last time and we have the vision of 'a new heaven and a new earth', the new Jerusalem; a city of peace and comfort, where God is no longer a warrior, but is light (21–2).

What shall we make of this incredible work of rhetoric and vivid symbolism –a work which leaves this reader, at least, exhausted and grasping for understanding? The most common way to understand Revelation is to read it as presenting the ultimate protest against, and rejection of, the Roman Empire. There is nothing of the accommodation (albeit with a critical edge) into the public spaces of empire that one finds in Acts and Paul's letters. Revelation belongs to a literature of resistance. The Empire is not to be pacified: its true character must be revealed and repudiated. Emperor worship is the opposite of the worship of God, therefore the conflict is one between evil and good, darkness and light, destruction and salvation; it is of cosmic dimensions. Revelation is a 'hyper-dualistic cosmos', where worship of God, and the life of a Christian, is the absolute opposite to the Roman emperor, his cult and his culture. Therefore, the triumph at the end is nothing less than the victory of God: 'The kingdom of the world has become the kingdom of our Lord and of his Messiah, and he will reign for ever and ever' (11:15). This seems to be the way that the visionary seer, John, wants his readers to understand what he has written. But can we take him at face value? Does he realise what he has written? Is the *kingdom* referred to in 'the kingdom of our Lord and of his Christ' really so different from the *kingdom* referred to in 'the kingdom of the world'? Are they not both characterised by the same imagery of power, violence and the destruction of enemies?

These questions in the interpretation of Revelation have been prompted by studies of post-colonialism (see Chapter 9). One insight from these studies is that the relationship between coloniser and colonised is characterised by ambivalence: by attraction and repulsion at the same time. This can mean that the colonised may be lured into internalising parts of the culture of the coloniser. The result is mimicry: copying the coloniser's ideology and terminology. In the Apocalypse, God appears to be modelled on the Roman emperor. One could say that to speak of God as king, and of God's Kingdom, goes back to the Hebrew Bible, but that only brings us back to a God modelled on ancient Near Eastern rulers. Who is modelled on whom? Which way does the influence go? These questions become even more pressing in late Antiquity, when Christianity became the state religion of Rome, and a common representation of Christ in the churches was as the emperor, on his throne, ruling over his subjects. The Apocalypse clearly wants to reject the Roman Empire, and it exposes Rome and its emperors to mockery with its reference to 'Babylon' and 'the great whore'. But at the same time there is imitation at work; elements of imperial thinking had actually penetrated primitive Christian thought so that imperial ideology and terminology was combined with a theology of God the Father and Son, even when it was used as an attack upon the pagan Roman Empire.

The positions of Acts and the Apocalypse Rome and the Roman Empire are, in many respects, different. But, taken together, they reflect the tensions and ambiguities of living in the Roman Empire for the first generations of Christ believers. Luke's historiography in Acts points forward to Eusebius' *Church History* at the time of Constantine (see Chapter 4) with the Christian Church integrated with the Empire. The Apocalypse was considered so radical that it took a long time before it was generally accepted as a proper part of the New Testament and, if it was not a direct result of persecutions at the time of writing, it pointed towards periods of persecution in the second and third centuries.

4

INCLUDED OR EXCLUDED: WHEN WAS THE NEW TESTAMENT CREATED?

MYTHS OF THE CREATION OF THE NEW TESTAMENT

When did the various writings we have discussed in the previous chapters become the New Testament? That is, when were they gathered together in one collection that was considered canonical, as the uniquely authoritative Scripture of the Church? There are no unanimous or unambiguous answers to these questions. In the bestseller *The Da Vinci Code*, Dan Brown gives one answer which has proven popular with many readers.[1] According to Brown, as far as the Gospels were concerned, the decision was taken by the Emperor Constantine in a great conspiracy with the Roman Catholic Church at the Council of Nicaea in 325. The four gospels that we now have in the New Testament were selected from 80 gospels, many just as valuable as the four which were eventually included. Constantine had political motives: he wanted gospels which declared that Jesus was God so as to secure divine protection for the power of the Roman Empire. He therefore included only those gospels which described Jesus as divine and excluded those which treated Jesus as a human being.

The reason to start with Dan Brown's theory – which is, after all, the plot of a historical thriller – is that I think Brown's story chimed with similar ideas already held by a great many people. There are also a number of respectable scholars who emphasise the competition between Christian groups with different gospels and go on to argue that the New Testament canon was a political decision by the dominant group that became the Roman Catholic Church.[2] This scholarly view is an alternative to a more traditional view that, in its original form, Christianity was a unified movement and that 'heretical' groups with their own gospels were a later development as the apostolic age receded into history.

The question of when the New Testament canon was established is more than just a historical question: in contemporary discourse it is linked to questions of ideology and faith. The traditional view of a unified early Church can, of course, be taken to support the authority of the New Testament for today. The opposite view – that other equally valid gospels could have been chosen – serves to challenge the authority of the New Testament canon and offers support for alternative forms of Christianity. My own position is that, early on in its history, Christianity was constituted by diverse groups in so far as they were located in different geographical, cultural and religious contexts. There were indeed many different writings that were called gospels, although most were not as widespread as some would think, and they often served as supplements to the four (later canonical) gospels, rather than alternatives to them.

I will attempt to present the story of how the New Testament came into being in three steps: first, I will consider how the growth of the New Testament documents took shape within an early Christian context; second, I will profile some of the 'other' gospels read by Christians that did not make it into the New Testament; and third, I will sketch the historical process which culminated in the creation of a 'canon'.

THE DIVERSITY OF EARLY CHRISTIANITY

The traditional picture of early Christianity was one of unity, only later threatened by those identified as heretics by the orthodox consensus. This view found support in the Acts of the Apostles, but was more fully developed by the very influential *Church History* by Eusebius of Caesarea (*c.* 325).[3] Eusebius wrote at the time of Constantine, and also penned a panegyric biography of the emperor. His *Church History* is a large work, ten volumes, which describes the history of Christianity from its beginnings until his own time. Eusebius' starting position is that true Christian teaching existed from the very beginning. 'Heresies' then arose to threaten this truth, but they were overcome by the faith of the majority of orthodox Christians. Much of what we know of the conflicts between various groups in the early Church come to us through the extensive quotations in Eusebius' *Church History*. However, his version of history is written from the singular perspective of 'the great Church', which preserved the original unity and truth of the religion in the face of heretical enemies. This vast work of scholarship therefore lent intellectual support to Constantine in his wish for a unified Church to support the unified Empire.

Eusebius' work was quickly established as the model for writing church history, and it has exercised considerable influence ever since. Although there had been many criticisms from the Enlightenment onwards, a major challenge to the paradigm forged by Eusebius was Walter Bauer's *Orthodoxy and Heresy*, published in German in 1934 (see Further Reading). When the book was translated into English almost 40 years later, it made a significant impact on subsequent British and North American scholarship, initiating a new way of thinking about early Christianity. Bauer's main point was that there was no orthodoxy at the beginning of Christianity and therefore no consensus to be threatened by later deviations; rather, diversity was there at the very beginning. In fact, many manifestations of religion that were later judged to be heresies were among the earliest forms of Christianity. Bauer exemplified this diversity by studying Christianity in different geographical areas, such as Edessa, Egypt and Asia Minor. His survey of these divergent forms of Christian belief and practise enabled him to show that 'orthodoxy', conceived as a representation of the majority view of a unified groups of Christians, defined by apostolic teaching, simply did not exist in the second and third centuries. It was a later development, which Bauer attributed to the growing influence of the Church in Rome.

The impact of Bauer's arguments was considerable. Although he was criticised for failing to provide sufficient evidence to substantiate some of his proposals, his main thesis about early Christian diversity was supported by the discovery of the Nag Hammadi codices in Egypt in 1945.[4] These codices, from the fourth and fifth centuries, contained documents which proved diversity in early Christianity beyond any reasonable doubt. In some instance they were texts that had previously been known only through the accusations of heresy which have come down to us from orthodox writers. One very familiar group of heretics from Christian history who have come to be closely associated with these texts are the so-called 'gnostics'; indeed, some of the Nag Hammadi codices are often loosely referred to as the 'Gnostic gospels'. In more recent scholarship, however, greater caution has been urged when it comes to describing these texts and their readerships, with some scholars questioning how secure our knowledge actually is concerning the phenomenon of gnosticism.[5] One particular concern is whether the influence of ancient accusations of heresy attached to people labelled gnostics may have misled modern historians into treating them as a clearly defined group (or groups) who would have had their own distinctive texts, and who could be easily distinguished from orthodox Christians and their proto-canonical texts.

Gnosticism has often been described as a protest against the values

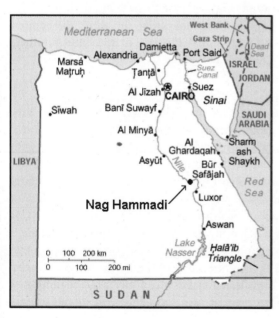

Map 4. Nag Hammadi in Upper Egypt

and norms of orthodox Christianity: rejecting the material world and the body, resulting in either asceticism or libertinism; and believing in determinism when it came to salvation. But critics have pointed out that, when the different writings are studied, they do not conform to such stereotypes but show a large variety of attitudes. Instead of lumping together many different text under a general category of gnosticism, they argue that it may be more useful to bring together texts that come from the 'school' of one particular teacher or tradition: for instance, the Valentinian or Sethian traditions. Moreover, in terms of understanding social-group dynamics, the charge of heresy by early Christian writers should not be taken at face value. These rhetorical boundaries may not have existed at the level of local realities: so-called gnostics may have been members of the same church as orthodox believers, inhabiting a shared Christian community.

The collection of diverse texts found in Nag Hammadi may also indicate that, in the fourth and fifth centuries, the fault lines between orthodox and heretics were not clear-cut. These manuscripts were probably owned and used by a group of monasteries in close proximity to the site where the jar container was found, and this diversity among the manuscripts may indicate that the monks represented a form of Christianity that did not draw the same distinctions between orthodox and heretical that some of the church fathers (and some modern scholars) have done.

WHAT IS A GOSPEL?

Is it possible to go behind what we know as the New Testament today, and to imagine a historical situation where collective terms for Christian texts such as 'Scripture', and even 'gospel', did not exist? Let us begin with 'gospel' (*evangellion*); where does that term come from? The earliest mention of it is in Paul's letters, where it means the message about salvation in Jesus Christ (Rom 1:1; 1 Cor 15:1); as such, it was an oral message. So when did it become a designation for a written description of the life of Jesus? The introduction in Mark 1:1 – 'The beginning of the gospel of Jesus Christ' – is suggestive of a transitional stage: it can mean the beginning of the message about Jesus but it also links the term to the written narrative that follows. The other gospels in the New Testament do not have such descriptions: the headings 'the Gospel according to Matthew', etc. are later additions from a time when it had become desirable to add names of the author to strengthen the authority of the text. From the middle of the second century there is evidence that gospel had come to be used to refer to written texts. Especially illuminating in this regard are the writings of Justin Martyr (*c.* 150), who speaks of 'the apostles in the memoirs which have come from them, which are also called gospels' (*First Apology* 66.3). Some of the Nag Hammadi codices are explicitly titled gospels; for instance the *Gospel of Thomas* and the *Gospel of Philip*.

Should we call these other writings gospels? It rather depends on how broadly or narrowly we define the term. If we make the gospels in the New Testament models for a literary form called gospel, we could describe it as a biography-like narrative of Jesus' life, death and resurrection, inclusive of his actions and sayings. In that case, few if any of the apocryphal texts found at Nag Hammadi and elsewhere would qualify. These other gospels are of a very different literary character. Only a few are narratives of Jesus' life: some focus on Jesus' death and resurrection; some are collections of Jesus words; and several are dialogues between Jesus and his disciples after the resurrection. Most of them are only preserved in fragments, or referred to in ancient writings, so it is not possible to have full knowledge of their content. Some of these texts have material that may be very old; for instance some sayings of Jesus that may have been part of oral traditions. Others develop forms found in the canonical gospels, especially the dialogue where Jesus reveals secrets to his disciples (cf. John 14–16). Other gospels are clearly legendary in character: they presuppose the four (later canonical) gospels but are responsive to human curiosity about those parts of Jesus' life that these gospels did not give sufficient information about, particularly Jesus' childhood and the life of his mother, Mary.

The Harvard professor Helmut Koester suggests a criterion for Gospel that is not based on literary form and structure but on their central concern: 'all those writings which are constituted by the transmission, use and interpretation of materials and traditions from and about Jesus of Nazareth'.[6] But even if we adopt this broad definition of gospel, there never were (as Dan Brown claimed) 80 different gospels in early Christianity. These 'other' writings didn't ever constitute a defined group in Antiquity. Collections of apocryphal gospels are published by modern scholars who have used different criteria and therefore give different numbers; one suggestion is around 20 gospels.[7]

The name 'apocrypha' for these texts – meaning hidden or secret – may have a double meaning. For the groups that produced and used these scriptures they represented a wisdom that was hidden from ordinary Christians and revealed only to those who had higher knowledge. From the point of view of their critics, these were books that should remain hidden and not be used in church. Many of these texts were known only through polemics by the influential bishop Irenaeus in *Against Heresies* (*c.* 175–85), and in similar books by other church leaders. Sometimes only the names or the authors of heretical books were transmitted: the texts themselves were lost. This was the situation for several gospels for Jewish Christians and also for the *Gospel of Thomas*, the most famous of the texts from the Nag Hammadi collection.

APOCRYPHAL GOSPELS

The discovery of the Nag Hammadi codices and other early Christian manuscripts contributed to the growing interest in apocryphal literature. It is impossible to give a full account of the apocryphal gospels (see the literature listed under Further Reading). Here I will briefly introduce examples drawn from three types of gospel: a sayings gospel, a dialogue gospel and a narrative infancy gospel.[8]

The *Gospel of Thomas* is the best known among the apocryphal gospels. It was known from references in ancient literature but was considered lost to history before it was discovered among the Nag Hammadi collection in 1945. *Thomas* is an example of a sayings gospel: a collection of 114 sayings of Jesus, but with no narrative framework and no mention of Jesus' death or resurrection. In that respect it is similar to the hypothetical sayings source, Q, and thus proves beyond doubt that there existed independent collections of Jesus' sayings. Half of the sayings in *Thomas* have parallels in the

Gospels of Matthew and Luke, while the other half are independent sayings. This composition has been explained in two different ways. Some scholars think that the author of *Thomas* has used Matthew and Luke as sources, and concluded that it must be later than these gospels, probably written in the second century. Other scholars hold that the wisdom sayings in the *Gospel of Thomas* belong to the same genre as Q and are equally as early as that source.[9] However, even if there was primitive material it seems safe to conclude that more material was added later; material which represents a type of Christianity later than, and quite different from, that represented by Matthew and Luke.

If we try to identify the social milieu in which *Thomas* was composed, the introduction may give an indication: 'These are the secret sayings that the living Jesus spoke and Didymos Judas Thomas wrote down.'[10] The name means Judas the Twin – both Didymos (Greek) and Thomas (Semitic) mean twin – and in early Syriac tradition this figure was venerated as the twin of Jesus but also identified with the

Figure 9. The Gospel of Thomas and The Secret Book of John (Apocryphon of John), Codex II, The Nag Hammadi manuscripts

apostle Thomas. The name was probably a pseudonym for the author. It is also remarkable that Jewish traditions play so little role in *Thomas*; for instance, it does not use any of the Jewish titles for Jesus – Messiah, Son of Man, etc. Instead, Jesus is portrayed as a teacher of wisdom, and especially of secret wisdom. Those who understand this wisdom will not taste death and, therefore, they must be 'seekers' who do not stop until they find, and what they find is the 'kingdom': this kingdom is 'inside of you, and it is outside of you' (3). The kingdom is both transcendent and immanent. Another saying (49) reads, 'For you are from it, and to it you will return'; this terminology is based on the idea that the addressees have their origin with God and will return to the heavenly sphere.

To be seekers of the kingdom required a special lifestyle, indicated by Jesus when he said, 'If you do not fast as regards the world, you will not find the kingdom' (27). This fasting meant that they should be itinerants (14), 'passers-by' (42), live a life of poverty and give away what they have (95, 110). The wealthy are excluded from the kingdom. There are no words for, or parallels with, church or community: the ideal is to be solitary (49). The *Gospel of Thomas* clearly represents an ascetic ideal, an impression reinforced by the use of the (originally Greek) term *monachos*, which would enter into Coptic and be used of monks, both hermits and those living in monasteries. The emphasis on salvation through insight, knowledge and asceticism gives *Thomas* a profile that is markedly different from all four canonical gospels, and one which fits well with the emerging monastic movement.

One saying in the *Gospel of Thomas* reflects a culturally traditional and critical attitude towards women. This occurs in the dialogue between Peter and Jesus in saying 114: 'Simon Peter said to them, "Let Mary leave us, for women are not worthy of life." Jesus said, "I myself shall lead her in order to make her male, so that she may become a living spirit resembling you males. For every woman who will make herself male will enter the kingdom of heaven."' Here Peter is identified with a misogynistic position (see, also, the *Gospel of Mary* below), whereas Jesus' solution is in line with a widespread view that male and female identities were found in unequal measures in men and women, and that it was possible for women to 'move up' to 'become male'.

The Gospel of Mary explicitly raises the issue of the role of women in early Christian communities. This text, which probably originated in the second century, belongs to the tradition of dialogues between Jesus and his disciples that are often set after his resurrection and in which he discloses the mysteries of the world. In this example, it is Mary Magdalene who is said to receive his revelation.[11] The role of Mary Magdalene as recipient of the teaching of Jesus develops the scene from John 20:11–17 where she meets Jesus at the tomb after his resurrection. In the *Gospel of Mary* the disciples ask Jesus about the future, the Kingdom of God and salvation. Jesus teaches them that they must liberate themselves from the material world and that they must proclaim this to the world. He then leaves. The disciples are confused and afraid, at which point Mary steps in and explains the words of Jesus for them based on her personal vision of Jesus.

In her vision Mary is praised by the Lord for not 'wavering' at seeing him (7), as her stability indicates conformity with the nature of God: eternal and unchanging. Thus, the writer commends Mary for her spiritual superiority, and that commendation sets the scene

Figure 10. Mary Magdalene and Jesus in *Noli me tangere*. Giotto, after 1305. Fresco in Lower Basilica in Assisi.

83

for a conflict with the apostles Peter and Andrew. From a misogynistic position, Peter questions what she has said: 'Did he really speak with a woman secretly without our knowledge? Shall we all turn around and listen to her? Did he choose her over us?' (17:18–22). But Peter is criticised by Levi for being 'wrathful' or 'hot-tempered', a characterisation which associates Peter with the adversarial powers that oppose the heavenly world in Mary's vision. Levi concludes the dispute: 'But if the Saviour made her worthy, who are you indeed to reject her? Surely, the Saviour knows her very well. That is why he loved her more.' (18:10–15). The *Gospel of Mary* and saying 114 in the *Gospel of Thomas* may reflect tensions between male-dominated culture in second-century Christianity, claiming to represent orthodoxy, and strands of the religion where women were still engaged in leadership and prophecy. We saw some of the same type of conflicts at an earlier stage in the Pastoral letters (see Chapter 1).

Our third example, the *Proto-Gospel of James*, has a different character than the two previous ones.[12] It represents an elaboration of the infancy narratives in Matthew and Luke (see Chapter 2) and is generally ascribed to the last part of the second century. It is, in a sense, a prequel: a story of what happened before the gospel, namely the birth, childhood and marriage of Mary leading up to the birth of Jesus. Its main purpose appears to be to glorify Mary, and the literary style reminds one of the Hellenistic *encomium*: praising a person through a description of his or her family background, formation of character and virtues.

The narrative begins with Mary's miraculous birth, born to an old couple through the power of God. She is brought up in purity in the temple in Jerusalem, but when the time comes to get married she is given to Joseph, a widower, who commits himself to keep her as a virgin in his house. Their arrival in Bethlehem is marked by cosmic wonders, when time stands still. After the birth of Jesus, Mary remains a virgin (*virgo intacta*); this was a miracle to which two midwives in Bethlehem could testify. This gospel has a vivid narrative form that made it popular, but it also served to prove certain dogmatic points, both in terms of Jesus' extraordinary birth and Mary's perpetual virginity. Dogmatically, the *Proto-Gospel of James* was used to support the divinity of Jesus against the position of some Jewish Christians who held that that he was human but adopted by God; it also supported the Eastern Church's elevation of Mary to *theotokos* (literally, God-bearer). The *Proto-Gospel of James* was not as controversial as many of the other apocryphal gospels were. It was obviously an addition to the canonical gospels, not an alternative to them; it was enormously popular in late Antiquity and during the Middle Ages and had great influence on Christian liturgy and art.

THE PROCESS TOWARDS A CANON

The process towards establishing a canon, especially a canon of gospels, started much earlier than Constantine, and was not a unified effort directed by a centralised authority. The geographically disparate and culturally diverse context of early Christianity, lacking as it was in centralised powers, made the process towards canonisation in the first three centuries a local and unstructured affair. The term 'process' is important in any discussion of canon and canonisation.[13] We may distinguish between, on the one hand, evidence for the usage of specific writings and their function as authorities for Christian communities and, on the other hand, the more formal definition of canonisation, for instance through lists of canonical books drawn up by powerful figures, defining which books were included and which were excluded. In the following section I will first focus on evidence for usage of the four, eventually canonical, gospels as sources of authority in the early Church.

An important purpose behind the canonisation process was to decide which texts could be used in worship by Christian groups, and in that way shape the identity of the community. This was a central issue for the bishops, who had authority over the churches to decide on theological and practical matters and were often involved in conflicts with opponents. Some of the most important sources of evidence for the long process of canonisation are letters from bishops to their churches with lists of 'authorised' scriptures. This evidence throws light on considerable regional differences, with some old independent traditions, for instance in Syria.

The four canonical gospels were in use in many churches, especially in the West, from the second century. Towards the end of this century, Ireneus from Lyon, a bishop and very influential writer – not least because of his writings against heresies – was the first to introduce the four gospels as authoritative (*c.* 180). After his criticism of groups that used only one or other of the gospels, he delivered a spirited and multifaceted argument as to why there should be four of them. For instance, he argued that the preference for four gospels cohered with the way that God had created the world with four corners, four directions of the wind, etc. Especially interesting is his use of Revelation 4:6–9, describing the four 'living creatures' around the throne of God: a lion, an ox, a man and an eagle. This symbolism has had a long reception history in art and iconography; indeed, we can still find these symbols in churches today for each of the evangelists: Mark (lion), Matthew (man), Luke (ox), John (eagle).

Irenaeus was very polemical in his defence for the authority of four, and only four, gospels. A less exclusive stance is indicated in the churches in the East, where there are sources that seem to support the authority of the four to-be canonical gospels without excluding other texts from this genre. Clement of Alexandria (*c.* 150–215),

Figure 11. Christ with the symbols of the four Evangelists, Portal, the Cathedral of Saint-Trophime d'Arles.

for instance, quoted non-polemically from the *Gospel of the Egyptians* and the *Gospel of Hebrews*. This did not mean that he held them in the same regard as the Gospels of Matthew, Mark, Luke and John. Indeed, a comparison of how often Clement quoted from these four gospels over *Egyptians* and *Hebrews*, shows 1672 times versus 11.[14] The gospel harmony of Tatian, a disciple of Justin Martyr in the second part of the second century, is another witness to the importance of the four gospels at this time.[15] Tatian titled his harmony *Diatessaron* ('through four'); he drew on material from all four of the gospels and combined them into a single narrative, with John providing the framework. When he returned to Syria, he translated the *Diatessaron* into Syriac and it remained the text used in Syrian churches until the fifth century when it was replaced by the four individual gospels.

When it comes to the scriptural authorities of Jewish Christian groups, from the few fragments we have, supplemented by quotations from their orthodox critics, some such groups appear to have used texts that were adaptations of the Gospel of Matthew (the *Gospel of the Nazareans*) or a harmony of Matthew, Mark and Luke (the *Ebionite Gospel*) in addition to a *Gospel of the Hebrews* and a *Gospel of the Egyptians*. The lack of later manuscript evidence suggests that these Jewish Christian groups and their scriptures disappeared after the second century.

To summarise the situation by the end of the second century: the four gospels appear to have been known as a group and were used in most regions where Christian churches were found; in some places as a privileged and exclusive set and in others read alongside other gospels. From the third century on there are codices where all four gospels are bound together, indicating that they were treated as a unified body of scripture (see Chapter 5). What was the situation with regard to those other seminal texts in the Christian tradition, Paul's letters?[16]

Paul had clearly addressed his writing to specific groups, defined by time and geography, so how could this particularity be combined with universal authority? It seems to have been accepted early on that Paul's advice was also relevant to groups beyond the original recipients. However, Paul's letters were not used and quoted as often as the gospels, especially Matthew. In all probability his letters were collected and distributed at the end of the first century, and most likely this was the responsibility of groups of his disciples and followers. The first to make Paul his theological hero was Marcion, a wealthy merchant from Asia Minor who tried to establish himself in a leadership position in the Church in Rome during the middle of the second century. Marcion found in Paul's writings a gospel that promised freedom from the Jewish law and even the Jewish God. In terms of the Pauline corpus, Marcion was the first to present a list of Paul's letters: ten altogether (the Pastoral Epistles were not included). Several lists appeared, with different ways of ordering the letters according to their length. One was based on the idea that Paul had written to seven churches, so that 1 and 2 Corinthians and 1 and 2 Thessalonians were counted together. Another list followed the length of the individual letters, starting with the longest (Romans), which gives us almost the present sequence in the New Testament.

It appears that by the end of the second century there was a great deal of consensus and common practice, especially in the Christian communities in the West: the four gospels and the Pauline letters belonged to the body of recognised scriptures to be read in church. The Acts of the Apostles, 1 Peter and 1 John also appear to have been in widespread use, but discussions continued in the following centuries about the status of other writings, especially Hebrews and Revelation, with differences again emerging between the Eastern and Western Church. Nevertheless, proto-canons were still very fluid, with a range of Christian literature (eventually excluded from the New Testament canon) still figuring on some lists of scriptures used in some churches, for instance the *Shepherd of Hermas* and the *Epistle of Barnabas*, both from the early second century. There was a variety of reasons for the selection of texts: apostolic authorship; historical links to the apostles; and broad acceptance as containing 'sound' doctrine. This doctrine of course included the divinity of Christ – which may account for the exclusion of the Jewish Christian gospels and their human Jesus – but also a contrary tendency: the dialogue gospels, which presented Jesus as more fully divine than the four gospels, were excluded in most communities.

NO END TO THE CANONISATION PROCESS?

We have now looked at the use of writings which came to be seen as authoritative in early Christian communities, either for their historical or theological merits, but what were the formal processes of establishing a fixed canon? It has been suggested that there were external pressures that started the process, for instance the aforementioned Marcion *c.* AD 150. He was critical of the Jewish heritage of Christianity and presented a list of textual authorities that consisted of Luke's Gospel, which he regarded as the least Jewish, together with the Pauline letters. It is doubtful, however, that Marcion's influence on the process of canonisation was very strong: he and his canon were rejected by the powerful Roman Church before any formal process got underway.

Besides Marcion's list of the writings he would accept, there were many other lists by individual writers,[17] the most famous being the Muratorian fragment. This includes the writings in the present New Testament canon and a few more.[18] The dating of this list has been the cause of much discussion: an early date would be significant for our overall impression of when the New Testament canon came into being. Traditionally, the Muratorian fragment has been dated to late second- or early third-century Rome; however, more recent studies have argued strongly for a date in the fourth century, in the East.[19] The later date would put the list of the Muratorian fragment at about the time of Constantine's reign (306–337), in the first half of the fourth century. So what can we now say about the claim that Constantine was responsible for the creation of canon? Constantine made Christianity a legal religion and took great interest in the Church. Of course he also wanted the Church to serve the Empire, especially to preserve its unity.[20] Thus it is likely that he was interested in the canon in so far as it contributed to Church unity. In his *Church History,* Eusebius, who was close to Constantine, tells the story of how the emperor ordered 50 large bibles for churches in his new capital: Constantinople.

However, Constantine's letter to Eusebius, preserved in his *Church*

History, does not give any instructions about the content of these bibles, neither does Eusebius himself. The best indication we may have is Eusebius' presentation of writings that were in use in the churches of his time.[21] He divides them into three groups:

1) those that were universally acknowledged: 21 or 22, including the four Gospels and the Pauline letters
2) those that were disputed, e.g. the letters of James, Jude, 2 Peter, 2 and 3 John
3) the illegitimate ones, e.g. the *Shepherd of Hermas*, the *Apocalypse of Peter*, etc.

Finally, he gives a list of writings put forward by heretics that are absolutely rejected. Thus, Eusebius presents a canon of 21 or 22 commonly acknowledged writings in the churches of his time. What we do not know for sure, however, is if these were the texts included in the bibles ordered by Constantine, but there can be no doubt that 50 bibles with identical content, placed in the churches of Constantinople, must have influenced the view of what were included in the canon. This makes Constantine indirectly influential in a process of canonisation which started long before his time, and which continued after him.

As noted above, the discussion of the canon continued, but with the attention now on the shorter and 'less important' writings. In his Easter letter of 367, the powerful bishop and theologian Athanasius of Alexandria wrote on the topic of which scriptures should be read in church. Athanasius gave a list of the 27 writings that make up the New Testament as we have it today. This letter does not represent a decision or agreement by all churches. It was more likely an effort to stop churches and monasteries from reading apocryphal writings in their liturgies. Nevertheless, it is interesting to note that, with this letter, Athanasius laid out a preferred canon which the rest of Christendom ultimately came to follow.

But in the end, there never was a universal declaration on the New Testament canon. And it may be for this reason that, in the sixteenth century, Martin Luther felt able to question the authority of the canon when he argued that because the Letter of James did not proclaim Christ it scarcely warranted its place in the New Testament.

CANON AS A COMMON PROJECT

These quarrels over the formation and boundaries of the New Testament canon, accusations of heresy, etc. may seem strange and antiquated to modern readers. Maybe we will understand them better if we realise that similar discussions are still carried on today in a variety of literary and cultural contexts. One example is a collection of essays, *The Canonical Debate Today*, which discusses the importance of a modern literary and cultural canon.[22] The authors are a group of literary scholars who face the challenge of identifying the 'common denominators capable of (re)shaping the identity of European culture as a whole'. One of the editors points out that 'canon building is orientated not only towards the past, but also towards the future. Very often canons are rooted in a societal "ideal", in a collective project, much the same way that "imagined communities" are born'.

A canon based on the idea of an 'imagined community', with the goal of shaping the identity of a group, is a common dominator in the discussion among Christians in Antiquity and the cultural debate today. In the previous chapters I have suggested that letter writing of the kind in which Paul engaged contributed to community formation, while the gospels, as memories of the life of Jesus, served to shape the identities of those who encounter them. The discussions in literary studies, of the kind just mentioned, suggests that the formation of literary and cultural canons constitutes a similar project: a common human enterprise of imaginative community making and remaking. Such modern parallels may make it easier to understand what was at stake in the discussions about the formation of the New Testament canon in early Christianity.

Part 2

SHAPING HISTORY

THE RECEPTION OF
THE NEW TESTAMENT

The writings that make up the New Testament were mostly written in the latter part of the first century. That means that when we read them today, it is almost 2,000 years since they were written. For a long time, interpretation was aimed at becoming a contemporary of the author in order to find the original meaning that the author wanted to convey. This is now in the process of changing; many readers have become interested in the period in between; in how the New Testament writings were read, understood and used in all those years. As a result the history of the interpretation, reception and impact of the New Testament has become a quickly growing field of study. Some universities have established centres on reception history,[1] and there are also commentaries on biblical books that focus especially on the history of their interpretation and reception.[2]

Reception history represents a philosophical and cultural perspective that goes back to the German philosopher Hans-Georg Gadamer who, in 1960, coined the term *Wirkungsgeschichte* which has been translated into English in various ways. The term 'reception history' comes from another German academic, Hans Robert Jauss. He was inspired by Gadamer to develop a theory on reception history (*Rezeptionsästhetik*) that focused on the role of the reader as necessary to create the meaning of the text (reader-response criticism). Various readers would read a text in different ways, depending on their presuppositions: their 'horizons of expectations'. We may say that reception history looks at the ways in which a text or tradition has interacted with the culture of its readers.

The following chapters will deal with different aspects of the reception history of the New Testament. With his commentary on the Gospel of Matthew (1985), Ulrich Luz was the first to integrate the history of interpretation in a commentary on a New Testament text.[3] Luz's focus was on the theological interpretation of texts in scholarly works, but both Luz and Christopher Rowland in Oxford, another initiator of reception history, also wanted to include voices at the margins, those who had not been part of the 'dominant interpretative communities'.[4] From this point of view the history of reception may represent a criticism of established theological positions. Luz speaks of a 'history of influence' [5], while Heikki Räisänen has challenged biblical scholarship to study the 'effective history' of the Bible,[6] in terms of its influence on, and inspiration of, various art forms, as well as on attitudes and ethics. Räisänen urges that not only the positive effects, but also the negative effects be studied.

In this section I will include an aspect of the New Testament texts that so far has not received much interest in reception history; the material production and distribution of the text. We are mostly interested in the content and meaning of the texts, but here we will discuss them as material objects. Therefore, I shall start Chapter 5 with the history of the New Testament as a physical book, the history of the text and the technology of the book. This history closely follows the history of the expansion of Christianity; in fact, in many cases, the translation and production of the New Testament presents early sources of the history of expansion.

Reception history is associated with reader-response criticism, that is, meaning is established in the encounter between the text and the reader or listener. In Chapter 6 I shall look at how meaning was created through the way the narratives of the passion and death of Jesus in Jerusalem were received and re-presented through various media: through sacred meals, through 'following Jesus' in pilgrimage and through 'seeing' the story in images. Chapter 7 is a test case with a study of the reception history of Galatians 3:28 ('There is no longer Jew or Greek, [...] slave or free, [...] male and female'), with different interpretations in three periods: Antiquity, the Reformation period and modernity.

5

'CHRISTIANITY GOES TO PRESS': THE COMMUNICATION HISTORY OF THE NEW TESTAMENT

The headline 'Christianity goes to Press' sounds anachronistic, but it raises an important question, and one rarely considered until recently: How were early Christian writings spread? This headline was also the title of a book, published last century, by an American expert on early Christian literature, E. J. Goodspeed.[1] In his work, Goodspeed pointed out how the development and application of new technologies for producing books contributed to the spread of Christianity. We may think that the spread of Christianity was primarily a matter of faith and theological ideas, but Goodspeed's intervention into this debate points to the importance of the material aspect of ideas and their transmission. So, before we speak of the reception history of the New Testament in terms of ideas, interpretations and ideologies, we will look at the physical and material aspect of the reception of the New Testament: How was it produced and copied? How was it spread and made available? And who exactly used to read it?

To follow the copying, translation, production and use of the New Testament (and the whole Bible, for that matter) penetrates the history of Christianity in a distinctive way. New Testament manuscripts in Greek, or in translation, are often the earliest sources we have to testify to the presence of Christianity in a given geographical area. They introduce us to cultural, social and even political histories of societies, from Ethiopia in the South to Russia in the North; from Georgia in the East to Ireland in the West. This history of textual production also takes us through a history of technological advances: from copying by hand to Gutenberg's printing press and finally the digitalised texts made electronically available on an ever-increasing variety of devices. This story is also part of the history of scientific progress in the study of ancient manuscripts, of establishing methods of textual criticism and systematic analysis.

This history is not only one of technological advances; technology reflects changes in social and economic history. When Constantine ordered 50 large codices of 'the sacred Scriptures' for the churches he built in Constantinople, the cost of such codices meant that they were out of reach except for the absolute elite. More than 1,000 years later, the printing presses created a democratisation of scripture: they made the New Testament, now also in vernacular translations, available for the growing urban middle class that was the bedrock of the Protestant Reformation. Five centuries later, the new electronic world has opened up an enormous variety of New Testament texts to those who have access to it. Translations of the New Testament continue to be at the forefront of democratisation and equality: they are still often the instruments to create written languages, and thereby a literature, for many small groups of people, often in isolated and poor areas of the world.

Finally, a caveat: it was not until the fourth century that the New Testament was established as a collection in its present form, so when I use the form 'the New Testament' for earlier periods, I mean scriptures that eventually formed the New Testament.

MANUSCRIPT PRODUCTION

The production of books in Antiquity was a very different and very taxing enterprise compared with the modern methods we enjoy; not least the fact that each copy had to be made by hand. Writing required skilled people and materials for them to operate with,[2] and we have both paintings and texts which illustrate how writings were produced in the first century of Christian literary creation. The instruments needed were a pen, ink and a sponge for corrections. The texts were written on papyri or parchment, sometimes also clay tablets, pot shards or wooden tablets. The actual writing was often done by scribes, who might be professionals. That seems to be the preferred method of Paul, as he sometimes calls attention to the fact that he is writing a particular section with 'his own hand', such as when he adds his own greeting (1 Cor 16:21, Gal 6:11). It was common to use wooden tablets or small notebooks of parchment to put down ideas and thoughts to be included in the finished text. There may be a reference to such notebooks in (the post-Pauline) 2 Timothy 4:13, when the author makes the following request to Timothy, 'When you come, bring the cloak that I left with Carpus at Troas, also the books, and above all the parchments'.

When a letter was written, the next step was to send it to the addressees. Travel around the Mediterranean was easy in Antiquity, so Christian groups were probably able to have letters delivered relatively quickly. Paul's letters tell us that he usually had co-workers as letter carriers. Within an oral culture, the reading aloud of letters or other texts in the gatherings of Christians represented the 'publication' of the work. The next step was copying the text to produce more copies. Since there were no 'copyrights', there were no formal legal difficulties involved. It was just a matter of finding a copyist. It is possible that many Christian manuscripts were copied not by professional scribes, who were expensive, but by literate members of the community.

DIFFERENT FORMS OF NEW TESTAMENT MANUSCRIPTS

We do not possess any originals of the texts that make up the New Testament. There is nothing unusual about this: that is the normal situation with texts from Antiquity. For instance, with the words of Plato and Aristotle the earliest copies we have of their works date from many centuries after they were written. In comparison, there is a very short time span between the writing of Paul's letters or the gospels – from the middle to the end of the first century – and the earliest copies. The oldest papyri fragment of John's Gospel that has been found, from the second century, may have been produced only 50 years after the Gospel was originally written.

The various types of manuscripts are commonly divided into four groups, in the order of importance and the age when they were produced. The classifications use different criteria: papyri refers to the material of the manuscript; majuscules and minuscules refer to the type of script (capital or small letters); lectionaries are defined by their function – they are liturgical books that have selections of biblical texts used in the liturgy; and papyri make up the oldest and smallest group (125; 2.-8.c.), often existing only in fragments of texts. Most of them were found in Egypt at the turn of the twentieth century, and they are regarded as very important for the reconstruction of early forms of the Greek texts. Before the papyri were found, the majuscules were considered the most important manuscripts (306; 3.-10.c.). Many of them contain most of the writings of the New Testament and sometimes other early Christian writings. The minuscules are numerous (2,800 known today) and they are from a later date; most were in use during the Middle Ages. The lectionaries are also numerous and from later times (2,281; 8.-19.c). Other sources are, for instance, quotations in early Christian literature. There are also a few examples of texts on ostraka (pot shards) and on amulets made out of papyri.

NEW TESTAMENT WRITINGS IN A SOCIAL CONTEXT

These various forms of manuscripts point towards the various uses of the New Testament among Christians in Antiquity. This was basically an oral culture and, with a literacy rate at 10–20 per cent, it is obvious that only a very few Christians could read the manuscripts themselves. But reading aloud to groups was common and the lectionaries, with the texts used for the liturgy, attest to this practice.

Another aspect of the social and religious history opens up if we investigate the cause of variations in the manuscripts. Many differences may be caused by scribal errors, misreadings, etc., but it has been suggested that, in some instances, a copyist may have made intentional changes. This suggestion is based on the idea that a copy of a manuscript reflects a process that takes place within a particular context. One of the experts in this field of study, David C. Parker, suggests that the texts that have been transmitted in the various forms of manuscripts are parts of how the gospels, apostolic letters and the Apocalypse 'have been read, heard, transmitted, and scrutinised. The written texts have no independent function, but are one part of a never-ending sequence of conversations, arguments, and interpretations.'[3]

One of these conversations and arguments in early Christianity was the controversy over Christology: the discussion concerning the relationship between divine and human in the person of Christ. Bart D. Ehrman has studied manuscripts from this period with a view to textual changes in sections that deal with Jesus.[4] In two instances in the infancy narrative of Luke's Gospel, the text speaks of Joseph as Jesus' father – first, in 2:33, Jesus' 'father and mother were amazed', and in 2:48 Mary says, 'your father and I have been searching for you in great anxiety'. In some Greek manuscripts these passages have been changed to avoid such a threat to the virgin birth and Jesus' divine origin – in the first instance to 'Joseph and his mother began to marvel', and in the second, 'Your relatives and I have been grieved'.[5] Ehrman argues that these are intentional changes, from what he calls a "proto-orthodox" position. Of course this cannot be proven, but these changes are strong indications that the manuscripts may also be studied for the insight they give into discussions in early Christianity.

ENTER A NEW TECHNOLOGY: THE CODEX

It is a puzzling situation that most manuscripts of writings that would later become part of the New Testament have the form of a codex, or a book. The common form for publication in Greco-Roman Antiquity, also used by Jews, was the papyrus scroll. The roll was made by attaching sheets of writing material at the end of the previous one, and the length depended on the size of the text. The codex, on the other hand, was similar to modern (well-made) books. It consisted of sheets of papyrus that were folded, so that each sheet made four pages, and attached to one another with binding threads. A large number of sheets could be bound together, and then a cover was attached to protect the book. To produce a codex was, therefore, a labour-intensive process.

Thanks to large databases of ancient manuscripts, it is now possible to make reliable inventories of the number of Christian manuscripts and their forms – scrolls or codices – compared to other

Figure 12. A Psalms Scroll from Qumran (Photograph: the Israel Antiquities Authority 1993)

manuscripts from Antiquity.[6] Over several centuries there was a gradual but slow transition from scroll to codex in all manuscripts from Antiquity, but the process went much more quickly with Christian manuscripts. Although Christian manuscripts from the second and third centuries are a very small part of the overall number, of these there is a much higher percentage of codices, so we may say that the codex became a Christian publishing medium.

Many different theories have been put forward to find explanations for this unique position of the codex among Christians. Some of them are practical (for example that the codex made it easier to search for specific parts of the text) while others are based on suggestions about history (for example that Christian missionaries gave an example by using codices). So far, it seems that there are no hypotheses that have been generally accepted as to why the codex became a Christian 'identity factor'. However, drawing on the databank of information about Christian codices, Larry Hurtado finds interesting information about their use.[7] It turns out that, whereas other early Christian texts were copied on scrolls, texts from Scripture (Old Testament) and the gospels and Paul's letters, that later would become part of the New Testament, were almost exclusively written on codices. Moreover, there are examples of two, even all four, gospels being put into one large codex. There are examples, too, of collections of Paul's letters in the same format. These examples of codices from the second and third centuries provide material evidence of the development towards establishing the New Testament as a fixed collection of writings: a canon. Eventually, the large codices from the fourth century included all of the Christian sacred scriptures in one book: this conveyed their importance for the religion that had only recently become accepted in the Roman Empire.

THE GEOGRAPHY OF THE NEW TESTAMENT: FROM GREECE TO GEORGIA

The early translations of the New Testament writing – and of the Bible generally, especially the Psalms – give a fascinating insight in the spread of Christianity.[8] The need to translate the Greek writings arose when Christianity spread from the Greek-speaking areas of the Hellenistic world. The Acts of the Apostles tell the story of Paul's mission to Asia Minor and Greece, and his subsequent journey to Rome. This trajectory has shaped popular perceptions of the spread of Christianity, not least the idea that it quickly became a Western

Figure 13.
Codex Sinaiticus
(fourth century),
Matt 3:7-4:19, in
The British Library

103

European religion. The record of early translations of Christian scripture tells a different story. The centre for the early Latin translations towards the end of the second century appeared to be the Roman province of Africa (present day Libya, Tunisia, Algeria and Morocco) which, early on, had a strong Christian presence. Translations also appeared in Italy, Spain and Gaul, and a Latin translation (Vulgate) became the biblical text used in the Western part of Christianity.

Various Syriac translations were also very early, reflecting the vitality of the Christian communities towards the Eastern part of the Roman Empire and beyond (in present day Syria, Iraq and eastern Turkey). A significant innovation in Syrian Christianity was Tatian's *Diatessaron* (*c.* 170, see Chapter 4). It is uncertain if the original was composed in Greek or Syriac. The early mission towards the east is also reflected in translations into Armenian, first based on Syriac texts of the New Testament, and into Georgian in the fifth century. Translations from Syriac into Persian and Sogdian (the *lingua franca* along the Silk Road in Central Asia) are signs of the spread of Christianity still further East, even towards China.

Christianity came early to Egypt, perhaps as early as towards the end of the first century, first to Jews and Greek-speaking groups. Translations into various dialects of Coptic in the third and fourth centuries indicate how Christianity moved into the indigenous Egyptian population. From the seventh century onward, translations into Arabic reflect the arrival of Muslim groups into Egypt. Gradually Arabic became the main language for Coptic Christians, but in church liturgies the Bohairic dialect of Coptic remained in use. Even further South, Christianity spread to Ethiopia, probably in the fourth century, with Bible translations following shortly after.

Towards the North, the translation into the first Germanic language, Gothic, came in the fourth century. Further missions among German tribes and the Slavs in the Middle Ages resulted in German and Old Slavonic translations. A common feature of most of these translations was that they were produced around the beginning of the written languages into which they were rendered: in several instances, the translators even created the alphabet for this very purpose, for instance in Armenian and Slavonic (the Cyrillic alphabet). Thus, Christianity and the Bible translations had an enormous influence in starting and making possible a national literature.

MANUSCRIPTS AND MONASTERIES IN THE MIDDLE AGES

While the Western Church in the Middle Ages used the Latin translation – the Vulgate – as their sacred text, the Church in the East continued to use the Greek. As a result, the large majority of later Greek manuscripts come from the East, with Constantinople at the centre, based on the same tradition of copying. The Eastern Church retained close ties to the Empire of Byzantium. In the West the situation changed when the Roman Empire and its institutions collapsed after the Visigoths' sacking of Rome (AD 410). The churches had to fill the political and cultural gap after the fall of the Western Empire, which included the preservation of classical literature and the spreading of Christian literature. It was, for the most part, the monasteries that took up this task by establishing workshops for copying books: the *scriptoria*. New monasteries were spread through several missionary currents, one of the most important was from Ireland to Britain, Gaul and Germany. We can follow this current to some of the oldest and most famous monasteries in Europe, and beautiful manuscripts tell the story of their *scriptoria*, for example the Kells and the Lindisfarne Gospels.

There are few historical sources about the work in these *scriptoria*, but in his famous novel, *The Name of the Rose*, set in a medieval monastery, Umberto Eco gives a fascinating (and fanciful) picture of a monastery with a *scriptorium* and large library. The book also reflects how the times were turning away from the great monasteries situated in the countryside to new religious groups, such as Franciscan and Dominican friars, who were living in the growing towns. The town became the place for the new institution; the university, developed from the schools attached to the cathedrals. In these universities the Bible was at the centre of their teaching and, for a long time, the study of theology was actually the study of the biblical texts. Such was 'the Bible of the learned', that is, of the small groups that made up the elite in European societies.

'The Bible of the unlettered' was the Bible for the majority of the people, delivered in different media from the written Bible. The visual image was an important medium: people encountered them in the stained-glass windows in cathedrals, with typical scenes from the Old Testament parallelling those from the life of Jesus (see Chapter 6). Homilies provided ideals for a moral life by drawing on biblical examples. The *Biblia Pauperum* stood in the same tradition. They were collections of wood prints with a moral message, where the images were more important than the texts, almost like a comic strip. Towards the end of the Middle Ages the growth of towns, with more affluent people, created a market for books and education and encouraged more independence *vis-à-vis* church authorities. This development prepared the way for the next step for the Bible in Europe.

THE PRINTING PRESS: A NEW TECHNOLOGY FOR THE RENAISSANCE AND REFORMATION

The next big technological jump in the history of the New Testament was a result of Gutenberg's invention of the printing press in the middle of the fifteenth century. But this invention, which made mass production of the New Testament possible, was dependent upon three other factors, as technology can only work together with human initiatives and social and cultural factors. The cultural factor was the Renaissance, with its interest in classical languages and in the original Greek text of the New Testament. The Reformation was both a religious and a political factor, beginning with Luther going back to the Bible in his criticism of the Church and its authority. The third factor was the social one: the growth of the middle classes and of literacy, with large groups of the population who could read. Luther and the other reformers therefore put great emphasis on translations of the New Testament as a way to remove authority from the Church elites, who had almost exclusive access to Latin, and to increase the religious self-confidence of 'ordinary' people.

It was the famous Renaissance scholar Erasmus of Rotterdam who edited the first printed Greek New Testament text in 1516. He had only a few manuscripts to work with, and not very good ones, so the quality of the edition was rather poor. However, being first gave Erasmus an advantage and his edition, with later modifications and improvements, remained the dominant text of the New Testament for almost 400 years. His text was the basis for Luther's translation of the New Testament into German, as well as for the English King James Version. These Bible translations were not just part of religious history. They played a large part in the development of the language and literature of the German- and English-speaking worlds.

The influence from the Renaissance is visible in Luther's interest in the original Greek text of the New Testament combined with a hermeneutical emphasis on the relevance of the Bible for his own time. Luther's translation of the New Testament was a *tour de force*, completed in only 11 weeks in 1522. Three thousand copies of the first edition were printed, and new editions quickly followed. The project reached 100 editions before the full Bible

Figure 14. Image of a printing press, *c.* 1520.

Figure 15. Frontispiece to Martin Luther's German Bible, 1541, woodcut by Lucas Cranach the Younger (1515-1586)

was completed in 1534. This had far-reaching consequences for the spread of the Reformation, made possible by the printing press and the mass circulation of books. Ironically, the German humanist Johann Cochlaeus, a critic of Luther, wrote that Luther's New Testament was spread so much 'that even tailors and shoemakers, yea, even women and ignorant people who had accepted the new Lutheran gospel, and could read a little German, studied it with the greatest avidity.'[9] The churches of the Reformation emphasised the importance of reading the Bible for all Christians, not just priests. Protestantism became a 'religion of the book', quite different from the focus on liturgy and tradition in the Roman Catholic Church.

NEW TESTAMENT TRANSLATIONS AND THEIR READERS IN THE ENGLISH REFORMATION

In the English-speaking world, most of the focus has been on the King James Version of the Bible of 1611. However, there is an earlier history to the printing and dissemination of the New Testament and the whole Bible in the Reformation period in England: a history of changing royal politics, market strategies and an unprecedented evolution of popular readership.[10] That said, the possibility of publishing in vernacular translation, and the right to read an English New Testament, shifted many times with the policy of different monarchs over a time span of just 30 years. The English reformer William Tyndale, who was executed in 1536, was the first to translate the New Testament into English and to print it. But it had to be done in exile in Germany, and in a small (octavo) format that was both affordable and easy to hide. Henry VIII authorised the publication of the Great Bible in 1539, printed in a large (folio) format meant for use in churches; however, reading the Bible was still forbidden for lower-class men and women, and was even punishable by death. Under the minority rule of Edward VI (1547–53), subjects of the crown were authorised to read and interpret the Bible, but under the Catholic Queen Mary (1553–8), the publications of New Testament and Bibles were forbidden, only to be resumed under Queen Elizabeth I.

In periods when Bible reading and printing was allowed there were many editions of the New Testament in small formats, intended for private readers. There were even Bibles printed in six parts to make them affordable to poor people. This move made the New Testament and whole Bibles part of the marketplace, with many different editions and revisions of earlier translations competing for customers. The first edition of the King James Version (KJV) in 1611 was in a large folio format for church pulpits, but a third edition was in a very small format, continuing the trend of publishing large volumes for churches and smaller, affordable New Testaments for private readers. It was the seventeenth century before KJV became firmly established, but it went on to gain an exceptional position, both in its influence upon English language and in becoming a symbol for the British nation. It also became the Bible for Protestant America and. for a long time, it had almost complete hegemony among bibles in the English-speaking world.

BIBLE TRANSLATIONS IN THE AGE OF EMPIRE AND (POST-) COLONIALISM

The post-colonial Bible scholar R.S. Sugirtharajah has said that KJV owed its success to the British Empire.[11] The eighteenth- and nineteenth-century expansion in colonisation and empire-building was accompanied by Christian missions and the British and Foreign Bible Society that spread the KJV. The Bible Society was established in 1804 as a result of the evangelical and mission revival in the late eighteenth century.[12] In order not to be involved in conflicts and controversies over biblical interpretation and questions about canon, it was to publish Bibles without comments or notes, and without the apocryphal books. However, this history of good works and good intentions, with the spreading of Bibles and interpretations into new languages, was played out within the context of empire and colonisation. The mission and the Bible were among those factors that created the idea of Britain as a nation with a civilising mission. The role of the English Bible in the consciousness of the British was expressed in a statement that was later used of the British Empire itself; that the English Bible 'is the only version in existence on which the Sun never sets'.[13]

Where the English Bible (KJV) was used, for instance in India, it conveyed a supremacy *vis-à-vis* local culture. It was part of the civilising process, a means to moral improvement of the natives. Since many cultures were so different from the Christian West and lacked not only institutions but also concepts, attitudes and values that were central to the vocabulary of the Christian faith, one of the goals of translations could be to create a vocabulary that expressed the message of the Bible. Additionally, the very text of the Bible was important; the written text was superior to the natives' oral culture.

Understandably, these attitudes were often met with resistance, and eventually translations and interpretations that came from the local culture. Until the mid- or late-twentieth century, most translations

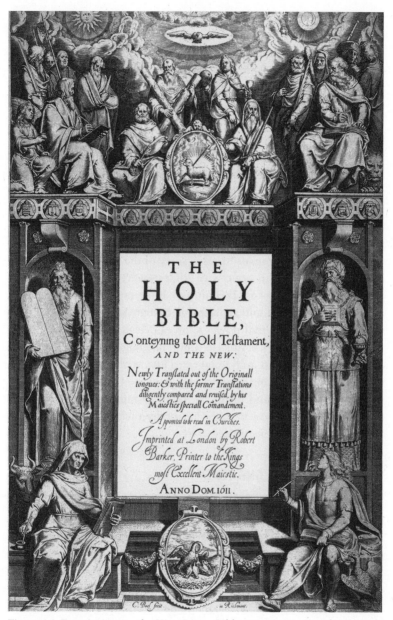

Figure 16. Frontispiece to the King James Bible, 1611, engraving by Cornelis Boel (1576-1621)

were done by missionaries, often with local assistance. At that time, translations became more professionalised, building on expertise for instance in linguistics and anthropology. The other major change was that translations were more and more often done by people translating into their own language. There has also been an explosion of the number of languages that have translations of the Bible or parts of it. To illustrate the growth, consider the following: in all of the nineteenth century, approximately 450 languages were added; in the twentieth century, around 150 new languages were added in each decade.

While the traditional medium to make translations available was the printed book, that has also changed with new technologies. We have now reached the third stage of communication (after the codex and the printing press), that is, the digital stage. An exciting example of this is the MegaVoice audio Bible, based on the initiative of a few dedicated individuals to reach some of the millions of non-readers in the world.[14] It is done with solar-powered digital audio players that can hold up to 320 hours of Bible content. It comes with a built-in solar panel and replaceable battery so that it can be used in areas without external power sources. MegaVoice has a scripture audio library with 8,400 titles in 4,600 languages and dialects which can be downloaded to audio players. Thus, with the help of modern technology, it is possible to jump back over the Gutenberg revolution with printed books and bring the Bible to millions of non-readers through a human voice: in this way, modern technology brings back ancient oral communication.

THE STRUGGLE FOR ONE TEXT[15]

Erasmus' publication of the first printed New Testament in Greek stimulated others to improve his work and to collect more manuscripts and compare them. This was the beginning of textual criticism, which has been central to attempts to establish the best possible Greek text. In 1624, the Dutch publishing firm Elzevir published an improvement of Erasmus' text, marketed with the claim that 'this was the text received by all', which gave it the name Textus Receptus and, for a long time, undisputed authority. In the following centuries, most editions stayed with the Textus Receptus, although there were many studies of textual criticism and improvements of methodology.

German scholars were at the forefront of this first major phase of textual criticism. Thus, J.A. Bengel (1687–1752) was the first to group manuscripts in 'families', based on the similarities between them. J.S. Semler (1725–91) divided the manuscripts into three main groups based on geographical areas: Alexandrian (Syria, Egypt and Ethiopia); Eastern (Antioch and Constantinople); and Western (especially Latin versions). In 1752, J. Wettstein published the Textus Receptus in two large volumes – the space was needed to provide comparison with other manuscripts and quotations from Greek, Latin and Rabbinic literature. Thus, his edition paved the way for the next step of establishing a more satisfactory text.

K. Lachmann (1793–1851) was the first to publish a modern text that was not based on the Textus Receptus, but on four important majuscule manuscripts that he found to be the earliest attainable texts. This break with tradition caused much controversy, but the idea of establishing the oldest text soon captured the imagination of scholars. In this search for the oldest text the fourth-century Codex Sinaiticus, comprising most of the Bible in Greek, played an important role, but its history also shows how biblical scholarship was involved in the nineteenth-century colonial politics of European empires. The German scholar and adventurer Constantine Tischendorf happened to come across the large codex in the ancient Orthodox monastery of St. Catharine in Sinai in 1859 and, at a later visit, used pressure and deceit to get hold of it under the pretence that it should be a gift to the Russian Emperor as the defender of the Christian Orthodox faith. In 1933 the codex was sold by the Soviet government to the British Museum.[16] Tischendorf published several editions of the New Testament, and in the last ones the Codex Sinaiticus played a prominent part.

Two Cambridge professors, B.F. Westcott and F.J.A. Hort, set themselves the goal of replacing the Textus Receptus and published what they called *The New Testament in the Original Greek* in 1881. Their most original contribution was the attempt to identify the oldest possible texts among the different 'families'. They argued that two of the most important texts from the Constantine era, Vaticanus and Sinaiticus, were 'neutral' and free from the corruptions that had coloured other groups of text. This break with the Textus Receptus caused protests, since many regarded it as 'the word of God' (it is still being used by some scholars), but the efforts by Hort and Westcott opened the way for other editions.

THE DIGITALISED ELECTRONIC NEW TESTAMENT FOR A NEW AGE

Instead of editions by individual scholars, typical of the nineteenth century, critical editions of the New Testament in the twentieth century have been undertaken in collaborations between institutions and organisations. From the beginning of the twentieth century, new finds of Greek papyri texts were integrated into existing editions. Towards the end of the century came the third technological innovation, alluded to already: the electronic age which has made New Testament texts and manuscripts more widely available than at any other time in history.

In Germany, this new period began with E. Nestle in 1898, when he published an edition of the New Testament based on Westcott and Hort and two other versions. Nestle's edition was based on the majority decision of the three versions, but later editions, under the editorship of Kurt Aland (and later Barbara Aland), became transparently critical with extensive notes to the text which provided alternative readings from a large number of manuscripts, from which the editors chose what they believed to be the best text.[17] This version, called Nestle-Aland, is now in its twenty-eighth edition. There is a longstanding collaboration between this project, (established at the Institute for New Testament Textual Research in Münster, Germany) and that of the United Bible Societies (UBS). The UBS publish the same text, but present only a few alternative readings, intended for what Bible translators need to consider in their translations.

In addition to the study handbooks of the Greek New Testament, there are various larger projects underway at the Münster Institute and the International Greek New Testament Project,[18] to take into consideration the enormous amount of material afforded by the growing number of manuscripts. These two projects have collaborated to develop a joint system for electronic transcriptions of manuscripts and for analysing manuscript groups. This opens up new and exciting possibilities that earlier generations, working with handwritten catalogue cards, could never have dreamed of.

But these electronic possibilities are not only available for experts as they attempt to create *the* optimal critical text of the New Testament. Electronic culture opens up possibilities for everybody to enter into the world of the New Testament text, in ways that threaten the hegemonic authority of the experts.[19] The webpage The New Testament Gateway (http://NTGateway.com), by New Testament scholar Mark Goodacre at Duke University, illustrates the new possibilities that are available. It has established itself as a very helpful resource, providing access to translations of the New Testament in many languages and information on research and literature in almost all areas of New Testament studies. It also gives access to databases of the Greek text of the New Testament or, rather, the Greek *texts* of the New Testament. It provides texts and searches for translations of words and phrases, not only from the latest edition of the Nestle-Aland and Bible Societies' text, but also from Hort Westcott and various older editions.

Perhaps the most valuable aspect of this whole development is the radical democratisation of knowledge, in that almost everybody may have access to this wealth of material given relatively basic information technology facilities. However, the enormous amount of New Testament texts and translations that is made available also opens up the idea that 'everything is at my disposal, I can choose what I want'. As a result, the idea of a fixed canon of the New Testament text disappears. The attempts to establish an authoritative critical text, accepted by the scholarly community, were based on shared evaluations of the available knowledge. It was a sign of unity in the 1960s when the Roman Catholic Church in the United States also recognised the Revised Standard Version of the Bible, a translation that was initiated by Protestant scholars. Now this notion of an authoritative text may be dethroned in favour of a selection by preference of the reading communities. This possibility may result in a decomposition of the New Testament as a common text, so that groups will select their favourite texts and translations as part of their identity and as a way to distance themselves from other groups. Thus, instead of the New Testament being a sign of unity between Christians, multiple different versions of the New Testament may signal splits and disunity.

6

'. . . THEIR EYES WERE OPENED AND THEY RECOGNISED HIM': GLIMPSES OF RECEPTIONS OF THE JESUS STORY

How were the scriptures of the New Testament received? Since much of this book is concerned with the texts themselves, and their interpretation by expert readers, in this chapter I will focus on how these texts gave rise to other interpretations: interpretations formed as they were encountered through the senses of the common readers, touching both their intellects and their emotions. I will, therefore, attempt to trace cases of reception among 'ordinary people', examining how they encountered the New Testament, its stories and figures and, above all, the figure of Jesus. I will look for evidence of such experiences in communal settings, just as I have emphasised the community-building effect of the letters and gospels within the New Testament. I will follow three different trajectories of experiences.

The first trajectory is the communal experience whereby gospel stories are re-enacted in the life of a Christian community. My example here will be the narrative of Jesus' last supper with his disciples, re-enacted in the holy meals of Christian groups eating together. The second trajectory concerns the bodies of Christians. In the gospels, Jesus called on the disciples by challenging them to follow him: 'following Jesus' becomes a central metaphor for discipleship, and 'the way' a metaphor for the Christian life. One of the ways this 'following' became re-enacted was through pilgrimages to the places associated with Jesus' life; this made it possible for common people to identify with the New Testament stories. The third trajectory creates identification through 'seeing'. Unlike the

116

other Abrahamic traditions of Judaism and Islam, Christianity allowed images of the divine. This made for a very different tradition of worship and symbolism. Here we may speak of 'the power of images',[1] a power forged when the images (or their creators) transmit messages to their spectators, but the spectators themselves also participate in interpreting and giving meaning to the images.

Eating, walking and seeing provided possibilities for everybody to be part of the reception of the New Testament. These activities started in Christian communities and churches but, over time, they continued outside the traditional groups of Christians and became part of the cultural heritage of societies and nations.

MEALS AS RECOGNITION

The reception of New Testament texts by ordinary people has left behind few traces. But we can point to some places where the texts or stories themselves appear to have been influenced by the reception of stories about Jesus which shaped community practice. The title of this chapter, 'their eyes were opened and they recognised him', is taken from the well-known Easter story in Luke 24:13–36, and concerns the two men who met Jesus (without recognising him) on their way to Emmaus. They talked with the 'stranger' about this Jesus in whom they had had great hopes, but who had been executed before those hopes could be realised. It was only at the meal, when Jesus broke the bread that 'their eyes were opened and they recognised him' (24:31). The narrative contains elements that are similar to the story of the last supper, in Luke 22: 14–31, so this story must have served as a mirror of the early Christians' celebration meals, in which 'breaking the bread' was the central act. The participants recognised that this was the same act that Jesus had done together with his disciples, and they could identify with the disciples at table with Jesus.

This tradition became a popular motif in Christian art. It was preserved in churches and monasteries through paintings of Jesus' last supper with his disciples. The best known is of course *The Last Supper* by Leonardo da Vinci (1495–8),[2] with its enormous dimensions (180 x 350 inches; 4.6 x 8.8 metres) and its masterly presentation of the dramatic moment when Jesus reveals that one of his disciples at the table will betray him. The painting fills the end wall of the refectory (dining hall) in the monastery of Santa Maria delle Grazie in Florence. Similar paintings or frescos by well-known artists, from approximately the same period, covered the end wall of the refectories in many monasteries in Florence in the period 1300–1500.[3] These paintings are not just decorative, however. They are situated at the end wall of the refectory, with the table painted as an extension of the refectory, facing the monks, thereby creating an impression of the monks actually sitting at table with Jesus and the disciples: the Lord present among them.

These paintings re-enacted the story and included the communities of monks and sisters within the last supper. The story of the two men who recognised Jesus at the meal in Emmaus also served as invitation to ordinary people to identify with these disciples. This is illustrated in the works by the Italian painter Caravaggio from around 1600. He was a controversial figure, often involved in fighting, but he revitalised religious painting with his focus on dramatic moments and use of light and shadows.[4] He set the Emmaus scene in a tavern from his own time, with local figures everybody could identify with, catching them in the moment when they recognised Jesus. He painted two versions: the first (1603), with dramatic gestures of surprise; and the other (1606), a quieter painting, with Jesus

Figure 17. *The Last Supper* (1495-98), Leonardo da Vinci, in the Convent Santa. Maria delle Grazie, Milan

in reflective mood, an inward drama that is played out in the countenance of the risen Lord. Some will explain the differences between the two versions with reference to experiences in Caravaggio's own life. If so, he has been able to transform these experiences in such a way that the people in the painting became recognisable and plausible in their reactions to Jesus, so the viewer might be prompted to ask him or herself, 'How would I react?'

In John's Gospel, the story of the last supper (John 13) does not have the institution of the Eucharist, but the narrative of Jesus washing the feet of his disciples as an example of servitude and humility. This story has become part of Easter celebrations on Holy Thursday in many churches throughout the world, and the Pope's performance of this ritual feet-washing receives global media attention. Traditionally, bishops and the Pope have washed the feet of 12 priests but, in his first Easter celebration as Bishop of Rome in 2013, Pope Francis broke with tradition and performed the ritual in a prison for young offenders, kissing and washing the feet of 12 youths, including women and two Muslims.

Figure 18. *Supper at Emmaus* (1603), Michelangelo da Caravaggio, British Museum, London

Figure 19. *Supper at Emmaus* (1606), Michelangelo da Caravaggio, Pinacoteca di Brera, Italy.

WALKING IN THE FOOTSTEPS OF JESUS

In the gospels the disciples were called to 'follow' Jesus, and in Mark's Gospel we often hear that Jesus and his disciples are 'on the way' (Mark 8:27; 10:32). This emphasis on place, journey and arrival take on a symbolic function in the gospels; they show what it means to follow Jesus on his way to suffering and death. And in Acts 9:2, 'the way' becomes a metaphor for being a Christian. However, in earliest Christian communities 'the way' was not associated with the physical places where Jesus had lived and died – not even Jerusalem mattered; it was worship 'in spirit and truth' that was necessary (John 4:24).

It was with Constantine, and his building of large churches over the most important places associated with the life of Jesus, that the recognition of 'holy places' started.[5] The royal visit by his mother Helena and the miraculous finding of the cross of Jesus established the Church of the Holy Sepulchre – over the cave where Jesus was thought to have been buried – as a centre of devotion and pilgrimage. There are several reports by early pilgrims, the most well-known of which is by Egeria, a rich and aristocratic Spanish woman and the leader of a convent from the end of the fourth century.[6] She describes in detail the church liturgies in Jerusalem for the Easter feast days, which quickly became the central celebration of the Church: Christ's death and resurrection. She also described other holy places that she and her company visited. At each place they read from the Bible the story that was set in that place. So here, the biblical stories and the places were woven together. And, by the end of Antiquity, the places associated not only with Jesus but also with the figures and narratives from the Old Testament became holy places for Christians, and the area covering all these places was known as the Holy Land.

In the early centuries of the Church it was, of course, mostly people with resources who could make the pilgrimage to Jerusalem, but there were other ways in which the veneration of Christ and the Sepulchre were made available nearer the homes of worshippers: in

Figure 20. The Round Church, Cambridge. Photo by Sailko.

artistic representations, for instance.[7] There are plausible points of contact and influence between the liturgy in Jerusalem and liturgies in the West, with symbolic representations of the cross and Sepulchre, although this history is complex. Nevertheless, it seems clear that the very shape of the Church of the Holy Sepulchre (the tomb in the centre of a rotunda with columns in a circle around it) was repeated in churches in the West as burial churches for saints, but also explicitly as models of the Church of the Holy Sepulchre itself. The Church of Stefano de Rotundo in Bologna is one of the oldest examples, with a tradition that goes back to the sixth century.[8] After the first Crusades in the twelfth century, some of the wealthy participants who returned built round churches that were meant to be representations of the Church of the Holy Sepulchre.[9] Sometimes the connection is made explicit; at Cambridge in England, around 1130, an abbot gave a fraternity of 'the Holy Sepulchre' the permission to build a church 'in honour of God and the Holy Sepulchre'. This is the Round Church in Cambridge that still stands, and the parish maintains the relationship with the Holy Sepulchre Church in Jerusalem through an annual pilgrimage. There are many such churches all over Western Europe, where Christians could visit the Sepulchre of Jesus without having to make the long journey to Jerusalem.

From the twelfth century we have accounts which stress the spiritual importance invested in pilgrimages to Jerusalem.[10] The ceremonies during Holy Week brought the pilgrims into direct contact with the different places associated with the life, death and resurrection of Christ Jesus. This is also the period when the images of Jesus changed in the artistic imaginations of Christian writers and artists. The image of Christ as the suffering Saviour was substituted for Christ enthroned as a king, a change which influenced the ideal of what it meant to follow Jesus. Some of the accounts from this period emphasise the importance of spiritual journey over physical pilgrimage and, in many cases, there are direct criticisms of pilgrimages as being little more than an indulgence of curiosity and the desire for sightseeing! The better way was to take responsibility for one's wife and children, or for the poor in one's own town. Thomas à Kempis, in *The Imitation of Christ* (c. 1418–27), produced one of the most influential spiritual manuals of all times, urging the reader to eschew pilgrimage in favour of an encounter with Christ through the sacraments in one's own church.

In the Reformation period, both Protestant and Roman Catholic reformers were critical of pilgrimages to holy places, considered as part of the worldly structures of the Church. Against that background it may come as a surprise that the Puritan classic, and one of the most beloved and read English books, is titled *The Pilgrim's Progress* (1678).[11] But John Bunyan was unafraid that his book would be misunderstood as providing support for geographical pilgrimages rather than spiritual ones: the subtitle spells out the destination of the pilgrim, 'from this world to that which is to come'. Bunyan used the pilgrim as figurative treatment of the Christian, but this is a pilgrimage set in a symbolic and spiritual landscape. He takes as his model the description of the heroes of faith from the Old Testament in the Letter to the Hebrews (11:13–16): they acknowledged that they were strangers and exiles on the earth and desired a better country, a heavenly one. The book builds heavily upon the Bible, and the story starts with the Christian's determination to follow the words of Jesus, leaving wife and children behind. It is a dramatic and uncompromising scene which marks the beginning of a journey where the Christian will meet many dangers and temptations, illustrated by figures such as 'the Lord Carnal Delight, the Lord Luxerious, the Lord desire of Vain-Glory'.[12] It is no coincidence that in this Puritan spiritual pilgrimage, the ungodly belong to the gentry and nobility while the pilgrims are among the poor of the world.

Despite hostility since the Reformation, pilgrimage to the Holy Land did not stop; indeed, it had something of a new beginning in the nineteenth century after Napoleon's brief expedition and rule over Egypt and Palestine (1798–1801). That event opened up the Orient to political competition among the European powers, explorations by scholars, pilgrimages and general tourism, all made possible by steam boats and travel companies (most famously, Thomas Cook).[13] Geographers and Bible scholars wrote books that were popular among many 'armchair travellers'; churches supported expeditions to make geographical surveys and maps; and the Holy Land became a 'homeland' to many Europeans and North Americans. Many of them were Protestants, and sceptical of the holy places

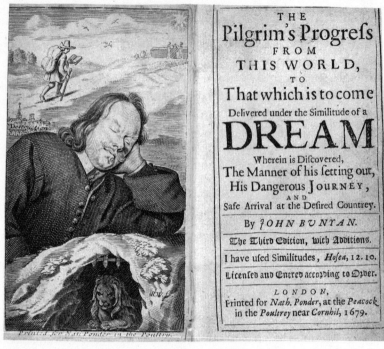

Figure 21. Frontispiece and title page of the third edition of *The Pilgrim's Progress*, by John Bunyan, London, 1679.

that were under the control of Eastern, Orthodox or Catholic clergy and dominated by their liturgies; instead they focused on the land where Jesus had lived and walked, especially Galilee. To them, the landscape was shaped by the close relationship between the geography of Palestine and the biblical texts. Although a Roman Catholic, this experience was best expressed by the French philologist and scholar of religion Ernest Renan in *The Life of Jesus* (1863), the most popular book about the historical Jesus to appear in the nineteenth century. For Renan, Jesus appeared a shadowy figure in the pages of the New Testament, but he came alive for Renan when he saw the land, especially Galilee; indeed, in the book, Renan described this land as 'a fifth gospel': as equally an important source for the life of Jesus as the four gospels in the New Testament.[14]

Since the nineteenth century there has been a steady stream of pilgrims and tourists to the Holy Land. Protestants no longer seem to have any objections to those holy places; indeed, after the establishment of the State of Israel in 1948, evangelical Christians from the USA and elsewhere have come in large numbers. These groups have combined visits to the holy Christian places with strong support for Israel as a Jewish state. This raises the issue of the political context in which pilgrimage takes place. It seems to me that it is impossible to be a pilgrim, 'walking in the footsteps of Jesus', and not to recognise the political problems: that the Holy Land is divided and many of its Palestinian inhabitants live under occupation.

SEEING THE GOSPEL

No examples of Christian art or architecture have survived from the first two centuries, probably because there was very little of it and because there were no separate buildings for Christian worship. Starting in the third century, most of the earliest Christian images are found in funeral chambers in Roman catacombs and on reliefs on sarcophagi.[15] It is difficult to identify early images as specifically Christian as some of them use classical pagan imagery; for example the image of the good shepherd or decorative fruits and flowers. It is only images that are based on narratives from the Bible that can be identified as Christian with any certainty. Old Testament figures and themes, for example Noah, Jonah or Abraham offering Isaac as a sacrifice, were all very popular. From the New Testament the scenes were mostly taken from stories about the life of Jesus: his baptism; healing of the paralysed; the miraculous multiplication of the loaves and fishes; and the raising of Lazarus. Often, themes from the Old and the New Testament were combined, for example in a funeral chamber or on a sarcophagus.[16]

From the fourth century, the time of Constantine and the acceptance of Christianity within the Roman Empire, there are significant changes both in the forms of images, the various media that are used and in the thematic representations.[17] We saw how Constantine built monumental churches, and this new period also initiated Christian art in mosaics, and later in metal works, wood carvings, ivory works and illuminated manuscript. This is, in short, when a distinctively

Christian material culture begins to take shape. The Christians came out of underground catacombs to take full part in their social and cultural context, making use of all of the available media to present Christian images. There is also a change in the themes and motives that are presented. The earliest images presented the works of Jesus' earthly ministry, his healings and other wonder workings. But, from the fourth century, the images shifted to events of dogmatic importance: the nativity; Jesus' transfiguration, passion and ascension; and the final judgement. Towards the end of this period, in the fifth century, the image of a heavenly Jesus seated on a throne (like the emperor) became a popular form of representation, frequently in the apse of churches.

So what was the purpose of these images? It has often been suggested that images were for the common people: those who could not read. In fact, a statement from Gregory the Great in the seventh century may suggest that this was how the ancients saw it: 'what writings present to readers, a picture presents to the unlearned who view it, since in the image even the ignorant see what they ought to follow; in the picture the illiterate read.'[18] But according to one notable expert in early Christian art and literature, Robin Margaret Jensen, this may be too simple.[19] Jensen finds that Christian images are more than just an illustration of written texts. Narrative images (for example of stories in the life of Jesus) have an independent function. They are scripture presented in pictures rather than in words; the images therefore have an edifying function: they present key aspects of Christian belief, particularly the combination of pictures of narratives in the Old Testament with pictures of events in the life of Jesus, representing an interpretation of these events. This typological method became perfected in the Middle Ages, as we shall see in the next section. Christian images were not simple; they had a didactic purpose, and partook in interpretation in a way similar to homilies and expositions in writing. However, they activated senses other than just hearing and reading: they were a visual representation.

A BIBLE IN GLASS: JESUS IN THE STAINED GLASS WINDOWS OF CANTERBURY CATHEDRAL

To move from the frescos and carvings in late Antiquity to the stained-glass windows in medieval cathedrals is to move into another world, created by the unique qualities of that artistic medium: the glass lets the light come through and, by responding to the sun, the oxides in the stained glass absorb the light waves of one colour to create another. Stained glass has been called the first modern medium of communication and compared to cinematography in the way it transmits images by way of light. I have chosen to focus on the stained-glass windows of Canterbury Cathedral, since they are among the cultural treasures of Europe and the cathedral is a world heritage site.[20] The oldest windows go back to the end of the twelfth century and the rebuilding of the cathedral after the murder of Thomas Becket, after which the cathedral became a shrine for the martyr and one of the principal pilgrimage centres in Europe. Many windows are dedicated to the miracles of Becket but our interest is primarily in the series of windows that represent Christ, especially the typological windows that depict the redemption of the world in Christ.

The windows are known as 'typological' because they are based on the theory that events or people in the Old Testament are types that prefigure events or people, especially Christ, as their antitypes in the New Testament. This method of interpretation goes back to biblical times; for instance in the saying of Jesus that, 'For just as Jonah was three days and three nights in the belly of the seamonster, so for three days and three nights the Son of Man will be in the heart of the earth' (Matt 12:40). Here Jonah is the Old Testament type that prefigures the Son of Man (Jesus) as the anti-type. In the Middle Ages this type of interpretation was taken to great lengths,[21] something reflected in the iconographic programme of the Canterbury windows, which combine great art with a complex theology. This theology was, however, also expounded in sermons and teachings – we can imagine priests and monks explaining the deeper meaning of the windows to the pilgrims.

Two examples from these windows will illustrate how the pictorial

Figure 22.

Top Left: Herod meets the Magi, The second typological window n XV, Canterbury Cathedral, (Photo by permission, Painton Cowen). **Top right:** Moses leading the Jews out of Egypt, The second typological window n XV, Canterb Cathedral, (Photo by permission, Painton Cowen). **Left:** Christ leading Gentiles away from a pagan god, The second typological window n XV , Canterbury Cathedral, (Photo by permission, Painton Cowen)

programme was built up. The main motive in the second typological window is the story of the Magi from the East who come to worship the newborn King of the Jews (Matt 2:1–12). The window is high, with seven registers (rows) of images, and the story moves from top to bottom. The Magi are depicted in the centre column with parallel, typological motives in the other columns.[22] The second register shows the Magi together with Herod, who asks them to return and tell where they have found the king (so that he can kill the child). The picture to the left shows Moses leading the Jews out of Egypt, to escape from the killings of Pharaoh (who is a type with Herod as the anti-type). The picture to the right is not from the Old Testament, but develops the image of the Magi as Gentiles who have come to seek Christ. It shows Christ leading gentiles away from the worship of a naked pagan god towards an altar with a cross and baptismal font. Thus the two side pictures develop different aspects of the central image. The idea of Christ leading gentiles away from pagan gods was certainly a popular topic for artistic representation, as references to the conversion of the gentiles appear in several of the registers. In some instances the Gentiles are pictured favourably in contrast to the Jews, reflecting a growing anti-Jewish mentality in England. This was partly caused by resentment that the Jews did not accept salvation in Jesus, and partly because they were looked upon as a suspicious foreign element.[23]

The second example is from the so-called 'Redemption window', which has a very complex composition.[24] The central images are of the crucifixion, the resurrection and Pentecost, each depicted in a square surrounded by four semi-circles that present the Old Testament types for the New Testament story. The top semi-circle above the central scene of the crucifixion shows Abraham's sacrifice of

Figure 23. The Redemption window, Canterbury Cathedral (photo by permission, Gordon Plumb).

Isaac. This is a well-known type of the crucifixion, although the point is made abundantly clear by the way the wooden sticks are placed in a cross at the altar. The bottom semi-circle tells the story of the spies that Moses sent to Canaan, and who came back carrying grapes (to show how fruitful the land was, Num 13:1–29). In the picture the grapes and the stick they are carried on form a Tau-shaped cross (additionally, the grapes are a reference to the blood of Christ in the Eucharist). The right semi-circle shows the killing of the lamb at Israel's Passover in Egypt, when the striking of the blood on the door post would protect them against God's anger with the Egyptians. Finally, the left semi-circle shows how Moses struck the rock with his rod so that water came forth to save the Israelites from thirst. Here the link to the crucifixion was to the water (and blood) that came forth when a soldier pierced Jesus' side with his spear (John 19:34). Once more we see a creative gathering of Old Testament types. They represented different aspects of interpretation; moreover, they provided references to the Eucharist and the homilies in the home churches of the pilgrims. For the observers, then, there were signals in the images that referred to and reflected contemporary concerns.

It is easy to be overwhelmed by the exquisite stained-glass windows in Canterbury and in other large cathedrals in Europe, and to think that they were unique places to experience these images of Jesus and other narratives from the Bible; surprisingly, this was not the case. In the Historical Museum in Oslo I have often admired a painted ceiling from a fourteenth-century stave church from a distant valley in inland Norway. This ceiling is proof that such pictorial interpretations were found even in small peasant communities on the outskirts of Europe.[25] The centre of the ceiling has roundels illustrating the creation story, based on an interpretation in which Christ was present at the creation (John 1:1–4). On both sides there are scenes from the nativity of Jesus: annunciation, visitation, birth, adoration of the Magi, Herod and the massacre of the infants and the flight to Egypt. At either end there are large paintings of the Last Supper and the Crucifixion. The colours and the drapes of the clothing shows the influence of English style, while Adam and Eve are portrayed digging and spinning, illustrating the old English Rhyme from the peasant uprising in 1381,

Figure 24. Roger Wagner. *Walking on Water III*, 2005; used by permission.

Figure 25. Roger Wagner, *The Road to Emmaus*, 2008; used by permission.

'When Adam delved and Eve span, where was then the gentleman?' Thus, we may imagine that not only the narratives about Jesus, but also their interpretations were transmitted to this little parish church. In Norway such interpretations were collected in a book of Latin homilies translated into Old Norse in the late twelfth century and used by priests to preach to their flock.[26]

These medieval images of the Jesus story place the figures in a contemporary context with regard to dress, landscapes and customs, so that the story interacts with the viewers and their context.

In contrast, many paintings from the nineteenth and twentieth centuries do not attempt to relate the images to a modern situation but place them in a romantic version of Palestine. Such images do not present any challenges to the viewer. They remain in a kitsch Disneyland version of first-century Palestine. Not surprisingly, some modern artists have moved away from this and in the direction of non-figurative representations, working with colour and light.

The English artist Roger Wagner works figuratively, but his religious works definitely interact with the modern world.[27] His images from the Jesus story are placed in recognisable contemporary settings, thereby creating an almost surreal atmosphere. *Walking on Water III* (2005) is a good illustration: Jesus and Peter are tiny figures on water that is not the Sea of Galilee, but the Thames, with the Battersea Power Station towering on the other bank. The existential moment that Peter experiences – and which Wagner explores in a poem written to the painting – is almost hidden as a secret in the large industrialised world. We find a similar perspective in *The Road to Emmaus* (2008). Here Wagner shows a modern road along the side of a wadi, with trees and white-plastered houses with flat roofs. If we look carefully, we see some tiny figures under the pergola on one of the roofs. That is all! This is not the dramatic recognition scene in Caravaggio's picture (see page 119), nor the splendid celebration of the Eucharist in a cathedral. The point seems to be that faith in Jesus lives hidden in the modern world: it is barely visible from the outside. Wagner's paintings are more than illustrations of biblical scenes, they are a 'visual literary imagination',[28] a hermeneutical *tour de force* that moves the viewer into the picture and puts them into a situation of existential challenge.

7

RACE, CLASS AND GENDER 'IN CHRIST'?: THE AMBIGUOUS RECEPTION HISTORY OF GALATIANS 3:28

> There is no longer Jew or Greek, there is no longer slave or free, there is no longer male and female; for all of you are one in Christ Jesus.
>
> Galatians 3:28.

Galatians 3:28 is a text that has inspired visions of a new humanity and exercised power over people's lives. In modern times this statement has been called the 'Magna Carta of the new humanity', as a central expression of how faith in Jesus Christ affects basic human relations.[1] Race, class and gender are key factors constituting human life, helping to organise societies and determine power structures. Galatians 3:28 is, therefore, a text that illustrates what is at stake in a reception history of the New Testament. A text is not a stable thing: it is established and given meaning in the interaction with readers or listeners within changing contexts. This is especially true with a text such as Galatians 3:28 which addresses basic human relations, and through which people will construct their own meaning, understanding it through the lens of their own worldview and experiences. The more readers who encounter such a text, the more meanings will emerge.

To try to grasp this interaction between readings of a text and a reader's own worldview, I will use the Canadian philosopher Charles Taylor's concept of 'social imaginaries'.[2] By social imaginaries, Taylor means more than the philosophical systems discussed by intellectuals: it refers to broader understandings of how people understand themselves in their social reality. A social imaginary 'incorporates a sense of the normal expectations that we have of each other; the kind of common understanding which enables us to carry out the collective practices which make up our social life.' But it goes wider than that. It includes what philosophers speak of as 'background' – meaning the understanding of our whole personal, social and cultural situation. An important part of this wider background is 'a sense of moral order', 'the deeper normative notions and images which underlie these expectations.' This sense of moral order is not always determined by status quo; it can also be orientated towards change. Taylor shows the processes whereby 'the modern theory of moral order gradually infiltrates and transforms our social imaginary', but also how in other instances practices may change first, and only later modify the theory of moral order.

I think the notion of social imaginary will be helpful to explore the reception of Galatians 3:28. I will take up this challenge in three periods where very different social imaginaries were in operation. The first is the beginning of reception within early Christianity with its focus on 'oneness in Christ'. The second is the Reformation where faith, without regard for social distinctions, was the basis for salvation, but where preserving these distinctions between people was part of the social order. The last period is modernity, right up to the present, where Galatians 3:28 is used to support equality and equal rights both in the Church and in wider society. One limitation of my study is that I draw on literary material which is, for the most part, written by an intellectual elite consisting of free white men. There are relatively few slaves and women whose voices can be heard within that literature, and so it is difficult to evaluate the effects of Paul's words on the majority of foreigners, slaves and women who have ever been touched by them. That would have required a much broader study that integrated social and intellectual history to a greater extent than is possible here. These elite voices are, nevertheless, an influential part of the history of New Testament reception, and it is to them that we now turn.

GALATIANS 3:28 AS PART OF RECEPTION HISTORY

Before we start on the reception history of Galatians 3:28, we must clarify the place of this text within the context of Paul's letter to the Galatians. Addressing a group of Gentile Christ followers (see Chapter 1), Paul defends his mission to the Gentiles without demanding that they should become Jewish proselytes. In Chapter 3 Paul argues that it is through their faith in Christ, without the (Jewish) Law, that they can be included among the descendants of Abraham, ancestor of the Jews:

> for in Christ Jesus you are all children of God through faith. As many of you as were baptised into Christ have clothed yourselves with Christ. **There is no longer Jew or Greek, there is no longer slave or free, there is no longer male and female; for all of you are one in Christ Jesus.** And if you belong to Christ, then you are Abraham's offspring, heirs according to the promise.

In this saying, Paul has combined three elements: baptism 'into Christ', the unification of opposite groups of humanity and inclusion into the heritage of Abraham. Many scholars think that the central statement in 3:28 goes back to an earlier formula used at baptisms, and that Paul adapts it for his own purpose in Galatians 3:26–8.[3] If this is the case, Paul's text is itself an early example of reception history, where Paul has combined or recast received tradition with his own theological agenda. One indication that Paul is interacting with a traditional formula here – the three parallel contrasting elements – is that in the letter itself he only actually develops one of them. Paul's main point in Galatians 3–4 is to break down the divisions between Jews and Greeks. The two other contrasts, between slave and free, male and female, play no part in his argument in the letter, and scholars have debated whether Paul ever followed through on these sayings with regard to either slaves (1 Cor 7:20–24) or women (1 Cor 11:2–16).

These three pairs are brought together in a new approach in

modern interpretation, known as intersectionality:[4] the three pairs are understood to constitute a totality, combining to envisage what must be incorporated to form a new, whole society. In the history of reception, however, we shall see that Gal 3:28 has sometimes been discussed as a unit consisting of the three pairs, and sometimes with focus on just one pair (for example slaves/free).

GALATIANS IN CHRISTIAN ANTIQUITY: UNITY NOT EQUALITY

We who have become the disciples of God have received the only true wisdom [...] And *the one whole Christ is not divided*: there is neither barbarian, nor Jew, nor Greek, neither male nor female, but a new man transformed by God's holy spirit.
Clement of Alexandria (150–215), *Protreptikos* 11.112.2–3.

The first complete commentaries on Paul's letter to the Galatians were not written until the fourth and fifth centuries,[5] but references to individual passages from Paul were found much earlier, as in this quotation from Clement of Alexandria from around AD 200. The division between the three pairs in Galatians 3:28 (Jew and Greek, slave and free, male and female) reflects the type of society and powers that existed in Mediterranean Antiquity. Such contrasts were well known from Greek city-states which established structural dividing lines in terms of 'gods/humans, Greek/Barbarians; male/female; human/beast; culture/nature, civilised/uncivilised world'.[6] These structures were part of a political system in Greek cities that made up the boundaries of citizenship by excluding 'the others', and it was part of a common, cross-cultural discourse. A tradition preserved in the Babylonian Talmud presents a similar division from a Jewish perspective in the form of a prayer to be recited by a Jewish man every day: 'Blessed be God who has not made me a gentile, who has not made me a slave, who has not made me a woman' (*B.Men.* 43b–44a). This blessing, which is still found in the Orthodox prayer book, has raised controversy in modern times – so much so that some Jewish movements have removed it or have turned the negative into a positive form.[7]

A situation where these divisions were no longer in effect was a utopian vision: the hope for an idealised future. One dominating aspect of a Greek social imaginary was the fear of diversity and divisions coupled with the desire for unity, the 'One'. The ideological presupposition here was that unity meant peace, wholeness and perfection, whereas division and differences resulted in pain, imperfection and conflicts. The early Christian interpreters of Paul came from this Greek background, and their understanding of life, society and cosmos was shared by the early Christians so that fear of divisions and conflicts was a problem uppermost in their minds. Unity was a major issue for Paul in his letters to his communities, most explicitly in 1 Corinthians, where Paul addresses the disharmony in the community and tries to unite various factions (see Chapter 1). The hope, however, was not that the two different parts should be equal, but that the divisions should be removed to create a union.

Clement of Alexandria refers to Galatians 3:28 in several of his writings, often in the form of adaptations and with additions.[8] The quotation from *Protrepticus* (above), an apologetic work for a pagan audience, is an example of how Clement presents Christianity as a philosophy that promises to unite all humanity. In this quotation Clement combines Gal 3:28 with an adaptation of Gal 6:15: 'For neither circumcision nor uncircumcision is anything; but a new creation is everything.' Clement has substituted 'creation' with 'man', and added 'transformed by God's Holy Spirit'. In another instance, where he gives an exact quotation, he introduces Gal 3:28 as a saying 'that is clear of all partiality', to defend the idea of equality with regard to the 'equality of salvation'. The equality without strife and differences that Clement speaks of was part of the unity that was the main goal of the social imaginary of Antiquity:

> Likewise also the apostle writes that no one in Christ is bond or free or Greek or Jew. For the creation in Christ Jesus is new, is equality, free of strife, not grasping, just. For envy, and jealousy, and bitterness stand without the divine choir' (*Strom.* 5.30.4–5)

Nothing less than a 'new creation' was the vision of the early Christian commentators on Galatians, but how did this vision actually play out with regard to the various divisions?

NO JEW OR GREEK – THE 'NEW RACE'?

Paul's term 'no longer Jew or Greek' reflects a Jewish perspective from the earliest period when the Christian groups were predominantly a Jewish movement. But over the next 100 years the situation changed almost completely. Christianity had become a predominantly Gentile movement, and in many communities the internal relations between Jews and gentile was not a very pressing issue. What was a problem, however, was the relationship with Jews who had not become Christians.

One of the first to discuss that issue was the Christian philosopher Justin Martyr (c. 100–65) in his *Dialogue with Trypho*, a fictional dialogue with a Jew. Justin argues a similar case to that of Paul in Galatians: Gentiles who have a faith like Abraham, and who believe in Christ, are now the descendants of Abraham; they have received the promises to Abraham and are now the new holy people, a 'new race' (*Dial* 119–20). The idea that the Christians were a new race or a new people used an ethno-racial discourse but opened access to this race or people through belief and practices.[9] This created a new identity for Christians, but at the same time it raised the question of the place of the Jews, who also traced their ancestry to Abraham. Justin's response would become the common Christian position: those Jews who did not believe in Christ did not belong to the people that God had promised Abraham (Gen 12:1–3). The Christians appropriated Abraham and the promises for themselves and excluded those Jews who did not have faith in Christ. Together with the accusation that 'the Jews killed Jesus', these forms of theological interpretation portrayed Jews as 'the Other' with respect to Christians. Such interpretations supported and increased negative attitudes to Jews among many Christians and were one of the major contributors to anti-Judaism in the coming centuries.[10]

Among early Christian theologians, Augustine was the only one to have a more positive evaluation of the Jews.[11] From an earlier negative view, he became critical of the anti-Jewish tradition among his contemporaries. It was indeed remarkable that Augustine recog-

Figure 26. The promise to Abraham that he and Sarah shall have a son (Gen 18:9-15), Woodcut for *Die Bibel in Bildern*, 1860, Schnorr von Carolsfeld

nised that even Jews who did not convert to Christianity were part of God's plans for the world. Instead of condemning the Jewish practices of Sabbath and holiday observance, food laws, sacrifices, etc. as 'fleshly practices', Augustine held that they fulfilled God's commands. And instead of saying that God had rejected Israel, Augustine emphasised that God maintained an abiding relationship with the Jews. The Jews actually confirmed the Christian understanding of the biblical texts that had foretold their stubbornness. To Augustine the Jews represented the figure of Cain, upon whom God had put his mark to protect him: God likewise protected the Jews and their traditional practices.[12]

'NO LONGER SLAVE OR FREE' – IN A SLAVE SOCIETY?

Did the second pair of Galatians 3:28, 'no longer slave or free', have any practical results among early Christian groups? Ancient Greece and Rome were slave societies, and slavery was much more pervasive than most of us can begin to imagine; it was a social institution that was taken for granted among the first Christians.[13] Indeed, the subject rarely surfaces at all in many early Christian writings, and when it does it is liable to be obscured for most readers by the fact that the Greek words for 'slave' are often translated into English as 'servant', which has less problematic connotations: slaves in the early Christian world have become invisible to modern eyes. It is important not to forget that not only men, but women, too, were slaves and, moreover, these women were used to bear children to supply the need for new slaves. The attitudes to slaves in early Christian writings, including those of Paul himself, are ambiguous. But in later texts, especially the 'Household codes' (Ephesians 6:5–9; Colossians 3:22–5; 1 Peter 2:18–21), there is no ambiguity. They put heavy emphasis on the obligation of slaves to obey even unjust and violent masters. These texts indicate that there were many slaves among these early Christians, but we do not have any sources where slaves speak themselves: it is always the masters who speak.

There are many examples of slaves who play an active part in Christian communities in the first centuries. One prominent example is the slave women Felicitas who, together with her mistress, Per-

Figure 27. Funerary relief of former slaves Aurelius Hermia and his wife Aurelia Philmatium, portrayed as Roman citizens. *c.* 80 BC, British Museum

petua, became a martyr in North Africa in the late second century.[14] And several early Christian authors argued for consideration from owners towards slaves, but there was little discussion of actually freeing them. However, in the fourth century, perhaps because many elite men who owned slaves became Christians, there are several examples of discussions of slavery. These discussions often combined specifically Christian ideas with Stoic ideas of the unity of humanity. One example is a text (falsely) attributed to Ignatius of Antioch which used Galatians 3:28 to urge Christian slave masters to 'be gentle towards your slaves, [...]; for there is one nature, and one family of mankind. For "in Christ there is neither bond nor free".'[15] The common attitude of early Christian writers who identified with the slave-owning class was to speak of slaves as part of the one family of mankind, but without arguing for an end to slavery.

The strongest known criticism of slavery as a system came from Gregory of Nyssa (335–95) in Asia Minor. Gregory came from an elite family and his brother and a friend, both prominent bishops, defended slavery, so Gregory must have been an exception in his criticism. He likewise drew his conclusions from the idea of the unity of humankind, based on Gen 1:26–7. This text about God creating man and woman 'in his image' was often used together with Galatians 3:28. In a sermon on Ecclesiastes 2:7 ('I bought male and female slaves'),[16] Gregory argued that if man was created by God to be free and sovereign, another human being could not reduce to slavery somebody who was created in the image of God. Although the text said 'male and female slaves', Gregory subsumes the female slaves under masculine terminology. The practical results of Gregory's radical sermons are, however, uncertain.

This emphasis on Christian slaves being 'brothers', and on masters showing leniency, may have had the effect of stopping Christian slaves from interpreting Galatians 3:28 with their feet and fleeing from slavery altogether. That may have worked for almost 300 years, but in the fourth century there are indications that many Christians did flee from slavery, and that they got support from some free members of the Christian community. Groups of 'heretical' monks in Asia Minor and North Africa argued for a radical interpretation of Galatians 3:28 and put it into practice by welcoming into their communities slaves who had fled from their masters. This practice was met with condemnation from various Church councils but it also made many early Christian writers modify the Church's teaching on slavery and encourage the freeing of slaves.

NO LONGER MALE AND FEMALE BUT THE MASCULINE ASCETIC IDEAL

In the last contrasting pair in Galatians 3:28, Paul does not use the gendered terms for people, 'man and woman' (that would be parallel to the first two pairs), but the adjectival forms 'male and female'. These forms suggest that it was not only the social differences, but also the biological, sexual distinctions that had lost their significance,[17] and it was the rejection of sexual distinctions in the 'new creation' that was in focus for the earliest commentators. The idea of the new creation made several of them look to the story of the first creation in Genesis 1:27, of how God created humankind in his image. This verse (in Greek) has the same terminology as Galatians 3:28: '*male and female* he created them.'

The early commentators described the unity of male and female, not in terms of social roles or equal rights, but as their equal access to spiritual knowledge and virtue. This idea of unity can be explained in the context of the ancient understanding of gender. It was not dualistic, based on two different sexes, but on a 'one-sex model' where men and women were physically the same, but at different levels of completeness.[18] The masculine was, of course, the ideal, closer to completeness, but the female could advance towards greater maleness and, thereby, towards unity. When sexual distinctions between men and women were taken away, there was no longer any sexual desire. For Clement of Alexandria, 'no longer male and female' meant that all 'who have abandoned the desires of the flesh are equal and spiritual before the Lord' (*Paed.* 1.6.30–31) John Chrysostom (347–407) used 'no longer male and female' to argue that they are the same 'before God', in that they now can learn virtue in the same way.[19]

When sexual attraction was removed it was possible to reach the ideal of asceticism. Male theologians imagined that the female would stop being female in the course of her progress to virtue, which was construed in masculine terms: Jerome (347–420) used Gal 3:28 as proof that through celibacy a woman could 'become male'. Often 'no longer male and female' has been interpreted as a return to the image of the *androgyne*, the idea of the human being before it was divided into male and female. But it is more likely that the *androgyne* was understood as masculine. For instance in the *Gospel of Thomas* 114, salvation for women was expressed in terms of 'becoming male'.[20] Thus, in the reception of 'no longer male and female' by the male theologians of the early Church, there was no suggestion of equality between the sexes; instead, the feminine was subsumed into the masculine: they became 'one [that is, one masculine form] in Christ Jesus'.

The reception of Galatians 3:28 in Antiquity focused on unity 'in Christ'. This reflects how the early Christian writers struggled to shape a new social imaginary that corresponded to their experiences of being many small groups spread over the vast Roman Empire. They also struggled to find an identity where they preserved a continuity with Jewish traditions at the same time as they expressed their identity as 'a new race'. And the most dramatic expression of what it was to be a new man was the ideal of ascetic asexuality, where women could 'become male'.

SOCIAL ORDER IN THE REFORMATION – NOTHING AND EVERYTHING

> For in Christ Jesus all social stations, even those that were divinely ordained, are nothing. Male, female, slave, free, Jew, gentile, king, subject – these are, of course, good creatures of God. But in Christ, that is, as a matter of salvation, they amount to nothing, for all their wisdom, righteousness, devotion, and authority.
>
> Martin Luther, *Lectures on Galatians 1535*, p. 354.

The Reformation resulted in great changes in how European societies were organised, and how the individual understood themselves and their world. One question that became important for the individual was the question of the basis for salvation. This question involved the role of institutions, especially the Roman Catholic

Church and its authority over individuals. The Protestant reformers challenged the distinctions between ordinary people and the religious: monks and nuns who were regarded as more perfect models of the faith. If, as the reformers argued, salvation was a result of a person's faith in God's grace, independent of a person's station in life, that was a revolutionary idea.

All these issues come up in Luther's lectures on Paul's letter to the Galatians, a New Testament text which played a significant part in the development of the new systems of thought that resulted in the Reformation. Indeed, Luther's lectures on Galatians became the most important of all his commentaries, with a wide circulation and influence not only in German, but also in English translation. The first English translation was published in 1535, while later editions greatly influenced the likes of the Wesley brothers, John and Charles, who were pivotal in founding the Methodist movement. Luther's lectures, on both Galatians and Romans, shaped the interpretation of Paul among Protestant New Testament scholars for generations. Only recently have there been reactions against that tradition, with the charge that Luther turned the Pauline letters into dogmatic and 'introspective' reflections (see Chapter 9). But this critique does not seem to be an apt characterisation of Luther's lectures on Galatians. Instead, Luther combined a historical exposition of Galatians with a hermeneutical address to his contemporary German readers. Using very direct and simple language he struck up a new 'social imaginary' of what Christian life in Germany should be. Luther started his comments on Galatians 3:28 by giving examples of what Jew or Greek, slave or free, male and female might correspond to in his own time: 'there is neither magistrate nor subject, neither professor nor listener, neither teacher nor pupil, neither (house) lady nor (female) servant'.[21] These were examples that immediately situated the text in a German contemporary situation and in a discussion of salvation and social responsibility.

The issue in Luther's reading of Galatians 3:28 is no longer the distinction between two groups, one superior and one inferior, and how this imbalance is dissolved 'in Christ'. Instead, the issue is the value of the work that each person does as part of their obligations in life. Luther commends the slave who works truthfully and the free man who performs all the required duties, for example 'getting married, administering his household well, obeying the magistrate'.[22] Likewise he commends the housewife who 'lives chastely, obeys her husband, takes good care of the house, and teaches her children well'. Luther speaks of all these deeds as 'truly magnificent and outstanding gifts', ordained by God. However, they do not count for anything towards 'righteousness in the sight of God'; they cannot 'take away sins or deliver from death or save'. It is only through baptism, by putting on Christ, that the 'new man' comes into existence, therefore there is no value in what people have produced in life. In Luther's exposition Paul's arguments, directed against Jewish laws in his own time, were applied to the time of the Reformation and directed against the Roman Church, its teaching and its practices. Additionally, Judaism and the Jews in Luther's own time came in for strong criticism because they would not accept the Christian reading of the Old Testament as a prophecy of Jesus Christ.[23] Luther's main criticism of the Jews was that they claimed to be God's chosen people because they were descendants of Abraham, and he defended Paul's position that only Jesus and his followers were the descendants of Abraham. Thus, Luther had a negative view of Jews for theological reasons, and in addition he was influenced by the virulent and widespread anti-Jewish accusations and slander of the late Middle Ages. He wrote a number of pamphlets, directed at Jews in the German states of the time, which became increasingly negative. Luther's most infamous writing, *On the Jews and Their Lies* (1543), participated in the political discussion of the role of Jews in Christian states and argued that they should be expelled. If they remained in the land, he suggested prohibiting their worship and burning down their synagogues. Luther's attitude towards the Jews is one of the darkest aspects of his heritage, and one which was revived in Germany during the Nazi period.

He also accepted traditional structures with regard to social mores and organisation, arguing that such social structures did not mean anything 'in the sight of God', but that did not mean that they had lost their importance in society. Luther here pursues a strange line of argument: he repeats over and over again that life in these social structures has no value with respect to salvation, in 'the sight of God', but these disclaimers are combined with a belligerent insistence on how these social stations were divinely ordained. Luther is very concerned that equality 'in the sight of God' must not be used to challenge the system of difference and inequality in society. It would upset the order and social stations 'if a woman wanted to be a man, if a son wanted to be a father, if a pupil wanted to be a teacher, if a servant wanted to be a master, if a subject wanted to be a magistrate'.[24]

These traditional positions reflect the fact that Luther remained rooted in medieval social imaginaries.[25] He did not question the social and political structures in society, but focused on the individual and their responsibility within this system: it was the duty of the inferiors to obey their superiors. Even if obedience was not one-sided (masters also had obligations), Luther's position supported the existing power structures: they must not be upset by movements of the radical Reformation or peasant revolts. On this issue, the other main Reformation leader, John Calvin, in his *Commentary on Galatians,* is in full agreement with Luther. Calvin made it clear that Galatians 3:28 should not be understood to authorise the removal of social distinctions:

> Paul does not mean here that there are no differences of status with regard to the society of this world. For as we know, there are servants and masters, rulers and subjects; in the home, the husband is the head, and the wife must be in subjection. We know this economy to be inviolable, and that our Lord Jesus Christ did not come into this world to confuse everything by overturning what God the Father had established.[26]

We may say that there was a liberating potential in speaking of equality in the sight of God in Luther's interpretation of Galatians 3:28, but it was soon lost in the defence of the social order that became a mark of a Protestant social imaginary. It is possible, however, to see it as a social imaginary with conflicting elements. The Reformation's contribution to secularisation – in setting human society apart from the control of the Church – and the emphasis on the independence of the individual, may also be seen to point towards the Enlightenment and, later, the ideas of equality and autonomy.

MODERNITY BETWEEN DIFFERENCE AND EQUALITY

> There can be no doubt that Paul's statements have social and politi-
> cal implications of even a revolutionary dimension.
> Hans Dieter Betz, *Galatians*, 1979, p.190.

The third period of the reception of Galatians 3:28 comprises 'modernity', a long period starting, for our purposes, with the Enlightenment
and leading up to and including our own times. One of the major
changes in social imaginaries in this period was the transition in attitudes, from pre-modern societies, with regard to the position of the
individual. The idea of equality, and equal rights for all individuals
and for all groups, is fundamental in those modern societies that are
influenced by the Enlightenment and its legacy. The Enlightenment's
emphasis on individual rights arose in the same era as the historical-critical method came to dominate biblical scholarship within
German universities. During the late eighteenth century, political events
such as the American and French Revolutions were beginning to realise ideals of equality, albeit ideals only enjoyed by men in the first
instance: 'liberty, equality, brotherhood'. Equality was denied to slaves
and women for considerably longer. The idea was raised and discussed
in the late eighteenth and nineteenth centuries and resulted in the
eventual abolition of slavery, but equality for women was slow and
only brought to (partial) fulfilment in the twentieth century. During
this period the idea of equality has undermined the previous general
acceptance of privileges as part of the natural order of things. And,
from the mid-twentieth century, human rights have become a central
feature of modern social imaginaries as the older biblical points of
reference for such moral and political issues have receded in the public
consciousness. What follows is a discussion of these seismic changes.

'NO LONGER JEW OR GREEK' BUT MANY 'CHILDREN OF ABRAHAM'?

From late Antiquity through the Middle Ages and beyond, it was
in the role of 'the Other' that Jews lived within Europe and were

represented in Christian literature. This 'othering' of the Jews received an academic platform in the historical-critical study of the Bible in the nineteenth century. Within much of the scholarship of this era Jesus was portrayed in opposition to the Judaism of his day, and Paul's polemics against Jews were regarded as historically accurate and representative descriptions of Jewish teaching. These views dominated Christian biblical studies, especially as they were carried out in Protestant German universities with their Lutheran anti-legalistic legacy. These scholarly studies served to legitimise expressions of anti-Judaism, discrimination and, in some extreme cases, the final catastrophe that was the Holocaust. In the aftermath of the Holocaust, many Christian churches have been concerned to look at some of the religious causes of anti-Semitism, especially in interpretations of the New Testament and its presentation of Jews and Judaism (see Chapter 9).

An example of the growing awareness of such responsibilities came in the form of a report from the Pontifical Biblical Commission of the Roman Catholic Church from 2002: *The Jewish People and their Sacred Scriptures in the Christian Bible.*[27] This report represented a dramatic change from a traditional view, one going all the way back to Justin Martyr, a position known as supercessionism.[28] Instead, the Commission recognised that the People of Israel have an eternal covenant with God.[29] On that basis, the Jewish people are given the special status of 'elder brother' and 'a unique place among all other religions' (§ 36). When the Commission claims that the New Testament never says that the Jews have been rejected, it finds its strongest arguments in Paul's own struggle with that very question (Romans 9–11).

The issue most relevant to the discussion of 'Jews or Greek' in Galatians 3:28 is the question, 'Who are the children of Abraham?'. For Paul it was those who belonged to Christ *and* who believed in the promise of God to Abraham. Therefore, the conclusion of the Commission in this section is unclear: 'In this way, Paul confirms and accentuates the universal import of Abraham's blessing and situates the true posterity of the patriarch in the spiritual order.' The 'universal import' appears to open the blessing to all, including Jews, but 'true posterity' and 'in the spiritual order' sounds like a veiled reference to Christians.[30]

Figure 28. Pope Benedict XVI greets Sir Jonathan Sacks, Chief Rabbi of the United Hebrew Congregations of the Commonwealth, (CNS/Reuters)

The importance of the report is that it leaves behind the earlier supercessionist tradition of interpretation, that is, the idea that Christianity has displaced Judaism in God's plan. However, the report does not engage sufficiently in a hermeneutical reflection on the almost 2,000 years that have passed since Paul wrote his letters to establish a really new position. Paul wrote within a first-century social imaginary of distinctions between Jews and Greeks, where his goal was to give Gentiles (Greeks) equal rights with the Jews to be 'the people of God' through Christ. I suspect that his social imaginary is quite distant for many today, Christian as well as Jew. Therefore, the attempts to make the Jews – who today might be seen as the discriminated group – equal with (Gentile) Christians, based on readings of Paul, are not all together convincing. Between Paul's text and today there is a history of Judaism and Christianity existing as separate religions for at least 1,700 years, with a long history of Christian dominance. Therefore, Christians should respect Jewish traditions and use of Scripture without attempting to integrate them in a Christian interpretation of history.

Moreover, the social imaginary today includes a pluralistic, interfaith world where three faiths can trace their roots to Abraham:

Judaism, Christianity and Islam share this common ground.[31] A Christian vision of oneness in Christ must be shared in dialogue – between Jews, Christians and Muslims – on the meaning of being Abraham's children. Furthermore, in a social imaginary that does not take patriarchy for granted, Abraham should not be the only common figure of authority: the 'foremothers' should also be included. The slave woman Hagar, who bore Abraham a son, Ismael, spans all the categories of 'the other': a slave, a woman and mother of the Arabs, but she has nevertheless become a recent focus for dialogues between Jews, Christians and Muslims.[32]

THE ABOLITION OF CHRISTIAN SLAVERY

> God is no respecter of persons (Acts 10:34), but gave his son to die for all, bond or free, black and white, rich or poor.
> Greensbury Washington Offley, former slave, 1808–96.[33]

In the discussions about slavery in the United States in the nineteenth century, interpretations of the Bible and social imaginaries of the time were deeply entangled.[34] Until around the time of the American Revolution slavery was taken for granted – it represented a hegemony that did not need defence or justification. The early protests from abolitionists and from African–American slaves questioned this hegemony where slavery was considered natural, and the situation became one of conflict where each party developed its ideology, either defending or attacking the former hegemonic position.

As the Bible was written in a slave society, the pro-slavery defenders had an easier task than the abolitionists. They could point out that, since slaves figured in many of Jesus' parables, Jesus supported slavery and therefore the hierarchical structure of society. They argued that 'there is no slave nor free' should not be taken in its literal sense. It had a metaphorical, spiritual sense that left the social differences between slaves and free in place, just as 'no male and female' indicated a spiritual equality but preserved the gender differences in place in this world. The pro-slavery advocates defended the 'old' society: they wanted the future to be a continuity of the past, based on hierarchy and patriarchy.

The abolitionists, on the other hand, represented liberalism with democratic ideals of equal rights. In order to make the Bible useful, the abolitionists developed various hermeneutical principles: for instance, the Golden Rule as a key to the ethics of Jesus and Paul. The fact that there are few direct statements by Jesus and Paul that reject slavery was explained with the theory of 'the seed growing secretly', that is, Jesus and Paul had inspired a slow development towards the abolition of slavery. This idea was combined with the common nineteenth-century idea of history as progress. At the same time there was a movement in England to end the slave trade from Africa (1807) and eventually the total abolition of slavery (1833), led by William Wilberforce, Thomas Clarkson and other evangelical Anglicans and Quakers. They held that slavery was contrary to the universal brotherhood of all humanity.[35]

In the USA the discussion was not only carried out between white slave owners and abolitionists: slaves made their own voices heard. In some cases, enslaved Christians had a stronger attachment to the Bible than their white owners, and they developed varied strategies to make the Bible useful to their cause. For instance, they initiated a hermeneutics of suspicion towards slaveholders and their readings of Paul. The first African–American novel, *Clotel* by William Wells Brown, himself an escaped slave, gives an illuminating example of this hermeneutics, which aimed at denaturalising slavery.[36] Here Galatians 3:28 was interpreted as Paul's critique of the mythological structures of slavery, stripping it of its religious justification.

Galatians 3:28 was central to the image of Paul as a champion of liberation, and the verse occurs in memories and biographies of former nineteenth-century slaves and early advocates of African–American civil rights. Women were also active in this advocacy of rights. They found that Galatians 3:28 gave them confidence in their calling to ministry and combined the oppositions listed by Paul with other contrasts that were part of their lives: 'No Jew nor gentile, no Catholic nor Protestant, no black nor white'.[37] Alone or combined with other statements such as Acts 10:34, Galatians 3:28 became a model for unity and equality of humanity, and enabled African–Americans to criticise racism, gender and class differences in American society on biblical terms.

Figure 29. William Wells Brown (1814-1884) former slave, author of the first African-American novel

More than 100 years later many people are still held in slavery, although in forms other than those of the nineteenth century. But there are now few who will defend slavery on a moral basis, and an 'abolitionist' reception of Galatians 3:28 has become generally accepted. An illuminating example is how, in 1995, the Southern Baptist Convention (SBC) repudiated its previous stand on slavery.[38] This denomination was actually founded (in 1845) to defend slavery as part of biblical teaching. In 1995, the Convention presented it as a timeless truth that the Bible was against slavery, based on Gen 1:27 and Gal 3:28. Moreover, in 2012 the SBC elected its first African–American president.

Today, many African–Americans in the USA are descendants of former slaves who identify with their heritage and see parallels between discriminations based on race and class today and those characteristic of ancient slavery. There are also obvious similarities between modern phenomena – for example sex trafficking, child labour and the exploitation of foreign workers – and traditional slavery.[39] Poverty is one of the most enslaving of human conditions and, with growing inequalities in many parts of the world, 'no longer slave nor free' might be translated as 'no longer poor and rich'.

FINALLY, EQUALITY BETWEEN THE SEXES?

The reception of 'there is no longer male and female' in recent biblical studies cannot be understood separate from the social and economic changes for women and their place in society.[40] The road towards equal rights started at the end of the nineteenth century, with women gaining access to universities, academic degrees, professions and democratic voting rights. The road towards equality accelerated with women entering the external workforce in many Western countries, first during the world wars (when many men were conscripted into military service) and on a general basis in the last part of the twentieth century. Together with strong feminist movements in many countries, the results were changes in family structures and relations between men and women with regard to responsibilities for children and the family home. Equality and equal rights between women and men now constitute one of the key ideological dimensions of many modern societies.

Protestant churches, in particular, have moved towards equal rights for women with regard to ordination and leadership positions. As is well known, this is not a universal development. The largest Christian churches, the Roman Catholic and the Orthodox, have not followed suit and, likewise, many conservative evangelical denominations. In general, the move towards gender equality started in the Northern and Western regions of the world, but it has now been taken up by women's movements in churches in the Global South. So it seems fair to say that this is a situation of conflicting social imaginaries, with changes happening at differing speeds, depending on theological and cultural contexts. Galatians 3:28 has been read as a foundational text in support of this trend. It was one of the texts that were used by early feminist readings of the Bible that challenged the all-male biblical scholarship at universities or Church institutions in the nine-teenth century. A prominent example is Elizabeth Cady Stanton in *The Woman's Bible* (1895).[41] By exposing the presuppositions of male interpretations of the Bible, feminists opened up biblical studies to gender criticism. These major developments, hinted at by Stanton, began to be realised from the last part of the twentieth century onwards, with women entering and influencing the field of biblical studies.

The most thorough argument for a liberationist and egalitarian interpretation of Paul is the classic study by Elisabeth Schüssler Fiorenza, *In Memory of Her*.[42] Fiorenza discusses Galatians 3:28 at great length, and sees it as a key text for understanding earliest Christianity. She argues that the pre-Pauline baptismal formula represented an equality between the sexes, and that it was followed up by Paul's social practice in his mis-

Figure 30. Frontispiece of Elizabeth Cady Stanton, *The Woman's Bible* (1895)

sion and in the communities he established. Central to Fiorenza's reconstruction was that she wanted to go beyond a feminist critique of patriarchy: she coined the term 'kyriarchy' (lordship) to indicate domination not just of women, but of all who were in a lower position, such as subordinate men and slaves. Fiorenza held that this first Jesus movement was an egalitarian movement, including all these groups, but that this was only the first phase; in later stages there were backlashes against this egalitarian period.

Fiorenza's main thesis – that Paul's 'no male and female' is a statement about equality between men and women – has also been accepted by many traditionally conservative evangelicals.[43] The discussion has centred on whether this equality applied only 'in Christ' or also in social structures. However, Fiorenza's presentation of the early Jesus movement as egalitarian has been criticised, including by other feminist scholars who find that it misrepresents the androcentric and patriarchal character of the first Jesus groups.[44] Nevertheless, Fiorenza and her feminist critics share a common ground: they find that what Paul said still makes a difference and that it has the power to affect women's situations today, either as an oppressive force or as a potential for liberation. Feminist receptions show that meaning cannot be frozen in time: when a text is moved into a different social context and social imaginary it has a different potential for meaning.

THE FUTURE OF RECEPTION HISTORY: UNITY WITH EQUALITY?

This brief survey shows that Galatians 3:28 has been understood in different ways from Christian Antiquity, through to the Reformation and into modernity. For much of this history I have read the reception of this text as separate histories of the various binary pairs: Jew/Greek, free/slave, male/female. This was a result of the way in which Gal 3:28 has usually been used, focusing on the separate aspects and not seeing how they are interrelated. For instance, male liberation theologians in Latin America, who worked for the liberation of the colonised from the colonisers, have been accused of overlooking the inequality of women in their own societies. In other social contexts, white feminists have been accused of not including other women, for example African–American women, who might be more concerned with communal issues than with their own individual rights. These examples point to the complexity and interrelatedness of differences and discriminations, and to the need to see them together.

Human rights provide such a possibility. They have become a global force that determines the social imaginary of how 'we', that is to say, more and more of us, view the world. Human rights have become one of the major political and social instruments to create equality and oppose discrimination in the world today. They have been extended from the classical liberal rights of free speech to include social and material rights. The United Nations, in particular, has been concerned to see the combination of factors that result in the lack of rights. This development in practical and political work has been combined with a new theoretical approach, known as 'intersectionality'. Intersectionality developed from feminist activism and studies and provides a way to see the interconnectedness of discrimination in many areas. It is a theoretical approach with a focus on marginalised subjectivity and how identity is constructed at the intersections of race, class, gender, sexuality and political power. This approach may lead to questions of where we find the intersections of identities and marginalisation in today's world. In addition to race (white/non-white), gender and class (rich/poor), other factors such as age (old/young/children) and place (peaceful country/war zone) are obviously important where there are boundaries that need to be broken down to create a human society for all. Such an intersectional approach will also raise new questions at Paul's pairing of categories in Gal 3:28.[45] To say that groups were united and equal 'in Christ' becomes more complicated when we realise that the 'Greek' might be free male, free female, or male slave, female slave, and the same is true for the 'Jew'.

Paul's statement in Galatians 3:28 has turned out to be one that can be used to discuss what it is to be human. Many readers of this passage have read it against the statement of how God created humans 'in his image', as male and female (Genesis 1:27); others have read it in the face of a dramatic encounter with Christ Jesus in an act of faith. Creation and re-creation – this is the stuff that great thinkers, artists and writers struggle with to shape their masterpieces. And it is the stuff that all of us, consciously or unconsciously, have to struggle with when we shape our own lives.

Part 3

READING AND MEANING-MAKING

THE HISTORY OF HOW TO READ THE NEW TESTAMENT

There are many different ways of reading the New Testament. Perhaps the most common way to read it, whether alone or in a group, is as Scripture: as a sacred text, important for one's religious faith. Pastors, priests and religious educators may read it to find material for their preaching and teaching, asking themselves, 'What does the New Testament mean for the church and larger community today?'. There are also the performance readings of the New Testament by actors or other vocal artists, often conducted in theatres, read for the literary and dramatic qualities of the texts, and sometimes set to music. In this book, however, I am thinking of scholarly readings of the New Testament: critical, methodological readings based on theories of how to read texts to answer specific questions. But these readings do not stay the same. The following chapters will review some of the key questions which arose during different periods of history, and consider how those questions reflected the cultural and intellectual climate of the societies in which it was read.

Some intellectual readers of the New Testament had always been concerned with questions of history, but today the historical-critical method is shorthand for a number of interconnected reading strategies developed during the early modern period. It began with a few lonely and largely unwelcome voices in the early Enlightenment and grew into full maturity when it became possible to engage in biblical interpretation as a more or less independent academic discipline in the European universities of the eighteenth and nineteenth centuries. Over the next two chapters, we will consider how the questions and issues underpinning the historical-critical method actually developed. These questions and issues laid the groundwork for the present situation in academic biblical studies, which is characterised both by continuities and discontinuities with historical-critical scholarship. Chapter 8 will start with a brief glance at the earliest periods of reading the New Testament, from Antiquity until the Reformation, before it focuses on the seminal Enlightenment and the nineteenth century. My examples will draw on nineteenth-century discussion of the gospels and the historical Jesus and Christian origins, and I will track later developments until the end of the unchallenged hegemony of historical criticism *c.* 1960. Chapter 9 will introduce the reader to changes in methods and perspectives which have taken place in the last generation of scholarship, and I will take most of the examples here from the interpretation of Paul's letters during this period. Some thematic overlap between the different periods is unavoidable, but the value of discussing the history of scholarship on the two main genres of writings in the New Testament – gospels and letters – is to be preferred over a strictly chronological presentation of research methods. I have tried to present New Testament scholarship as part of broader intellectual trends, but I must refer to larger reviews of the field for a more substantial picture (See Further Reading to Chapters 8 and 9).

8

HISTORICAL READINGS: HOW MODERNITY SHAPED NEW TESTAMENT SCHOLARSHIP

PRE-MODERN READINGS OF THE NEW TESTAMENT

As a brief introduction to how the modern academic study of the New Testament was established, we need to first look at the long history of reading New Testament writings, from the earliest commentaries on gospels and letters in the third century to the brink of modernity and the Enlightenment. The examples from the early reception history of Galatians 3:28 in Chapter 7 will hopefully have provided some sense of the interpretative interests of early Christian readers. But the creative interpretation of Scripture started long before that: it began with the authors of Scripture itself and the common practice of 'rewriting' in the Hebrew Bible. In the Hebrew Bible, for instance, there are ostensibly historical writings which rewrite the information given in earlier texts (for example 1–2 Chronicles partly rewriting the material of 1–2 Samuel and 1–2 Kings). Matthew and Luke's Gospels rewrite and thereby interpret the material in the Gospel of Mark. And when one considers how the gospels, especially Matthews', frequently refer back to the Hebrew Scriptures, the gospels themselves might actually be understood as exercises in the interpretation and rewriting of those earlier biblical texts. The notion of the story of Jesus as a rewriting of the Hebrew Scriptures would need qualifying, of course, but there is no doubt that the 'new' message about Jesus Christ was presented against the backdrop of those Jewish texts, which were the only authoritative documents for the first members of the Jesus movement.

Paul's letters are good examples of this interpretative situation. In Romans 4 Paul recalls the story of God's promise to Abraham from Genesis 15, arguing that God counted Abraham as righteous on the basis of his trust (or faith) in God. He then develops that foundational Jewish text to argue that, 'the words "it was reckoned to him" were written not for his sake alone, *but for ours also*'(4:23–4). Paul's use of the Abraham story was characteristic of the attitude to Scripture among the first followers of Jesus. In the first instance this attitude indicated that the followers of Jesus were part of the larger Jewish community, but such was the dependence of the story of Jesus on the longer story of the Israelites that the Jewish writings remained sacred Scripture even after the Jesus movement separated from those Jewish communities centred on the synagogue. That separation happened at different times among different groups, but there are writings from the second century which show that some Christ followers insisted on their right to reject that God's covenant was 'both theirs and ours', and to claim that 'it is ours' (*Letter of Barnabas* 4:6–7).

Thus began a division between Jews and Christians with regard to the Hebrew Scriptures. We often think of them today as common to Jews and Christians, but it may be more accurate to see them as contested ground from the outset. For one thing, the Christians who wrote the New Testament used the Septuagint version of Hebrew Scriptures. This was a Greek translation, but it also contained a number of texts that were excluded from the Tanakh (the final Jewish Hebrew canon). After the Reformation those texts, the so-called 'Old Testament Apocrypha', were also rejected by the Protestant churches who insisted that, in future editions of the Bible, the Old Testament should be brought into line with the Tanakh. But even more important than the textual content, were the differences in reception and interpretation.

The Christians claimed that the Jewish Scriptures (the 'Old Testament') should be read in light of the revelation of Christ: specifically, that the prophecies of Scriptures were fulfilled in the life, death and resurrection of Jesus, and that they continued to be fulfilled in the life of the Church. Therefore, many of the discussions among Christians in the first centuries about how to read Scripture dealt with how to explain this relationship between Scripture and Christ. Christian approaches to this relationship were, of course, unacceptable for the vast majority of Jews, who never joined the Jesus movement and regarded the appropriation of their texts as a foreign imposition on Jewish scripture.

Even if Paul's statement that Scripture was written 'for our sake also' originally applied to Jewish scripture, it became relevant to the writings of the New Testament. Gradually the teaching of Jesus, and the preaching about him, was written down and the fruits of that process gained a similar authority: texts about Jesus became Scripture. Like the Old Testament, the New Testament was read to illuminate the experience of its readers: its meaning transcended the original historical context of its production and extended into the lives of the faithful. This type of reading unites Christians, reading within their faith communities, across the generations.

But this type of reading is very different from the historical-critical readings which have dominated modern scholarship, whereby the scholar attempts to find the intention of the authors of New Testament texts, or at least the probable meaning of texts for their original recipients. This difference in interpretive style cannot be understood apart from the intellectual and academic contexts in which it operates. In Christian Antiquity and the Middle Ages biblical interpretation was carried out by learned Christians, either independently or in churches and monasteries. From the twelfth century the locus of biblical interpretation switched to the universities of Europe, but these universities were usually Church foundations with theology as the main discipline. Moreover, for most of this long period, theology was not divided into different sub-disciplines – such as biblical theology, historical theology, systematic theology or moral theology – and so the interpretation of Scripture was inseparable from all of these theological concerns. In contrast, modern historical-critical readings of the Bible developed in (more or less) secular universities, where its study has developed as an independent discipline – or rather, two disciplines, Old and New Testaments.

Returning to the pre-modern period, the earliest Christian theologians raised different types of questions about New Testament texts and emphasised different levels of meaning.[1] As examples of the different 'schools' of interpretation in the ancient world one could point to the Alexandrians – who argued for the allegorical (symbolic) meaning as the primary sense of Scripture – and those belonging to the Antioch tradition, who argued for the primacy of the literal meaning. In late Antiquity and the early Middle Ages, these theories were refined.[2] The literal sense, which always came first, provided the historical narrative which could then be given several symbolic meanings, corresponding to three theological virtues: faith, hope and love. The allegorical meaning of the text tended to be associated with the Church, its mission and beliefs (faith). The moral sense of Scripture taught the faithful the appropriate habits of action they should cultivate (love), and finally, the anagogical sense pointed towards the future consummation of God's covenant in Christ (hope). These three forms of interpretation were known, collectively, as the 'spiritual sense' of Scripture. Despite the emphasis placed on the spiritual meaning, however, Thomas Aquinas and other Medieval interpreters emphasised the importance of the literal sense as the basis from which the spiritual sense was derived.

RENAISSANCE AND REFORMATION

The priority of the literal sense was emphasised even more by interpreters in the Renaissance and the Reformation. The Renaissance was characterised by a fascination with classical Antiquity. One of the most fundamental changes this brought about with respect to biblical interpretation was the return of scholars to the original languages of the Bible – Hebrew and Greek – as they were no longer satisfied by Latin translations of their sacred texts. Christian humanists, such as Erasmus of Rotterdam, interpreted the Bible with the same methods as they interpreted other texts, looking for the literal sense. Erasmus also made reason a criterion for interpretation. Historically, the leading intellectuals and ecclesiastical figures of the Church, especially the Pope, were the guardians of biblical interpretation. However the Protestant reformers, with Martin Luther and John Calvin the most prominent, rejected the notion that the Bible could only be interpreted with the tradition and authority of the Church.

Figure 31. *Erasmus of Rotterdam* (1466–1536), portrait by Hans Holbein the Younger. 1523, National Gallery, London.

Despite their rejection of the need for authoritative intermediaries between the Christian reader and the Bible, Luther and Calvin were so steeped in the traditions of medieval exegesis that many of the latter's interpretative assumptions remained firmly in place. Both reformers continued to see the Old and the New Testaments as a unity and a consistent witness to Christ and the life of the Church. For instance, Calvin would acknowledge that texts about the 'Suffering Servant' in Isaiah 42–53 spoke of the hope of the Jews in exile, while insisting that they also anticipated God's sending of Christ into the world and its saving potential. Moreover, on Calvin's reading, such passages extended well beyond their prophetic anticipation in Christ and spoke to the situation of the Church in his own time. Thus, Calvin could also use texts polemically against the Catholic Church so that the prophetic voice of Isaiah is turned against the iniquities of Rome, no less than it once was against the iniquities of Judah.

In the case of Luther, the literal sense of Scripture was no less spiritual than the moral, allegorical or analogical: from first to last, the biblical text bore witness to the revelation of Christ.[3] Even at the literal level, then, biblical interpretation was not just a grammatical task, but a theological one; more specifically, it was the catalyst to preaching. The gospel was an oral revelation in the first instance, and the living word of God should continue to be communicated through word of mouth.

The Renaissance and the Reformation brought with them tremendous political, social and intellectual changes. The Reformation broke down the unity of Church and created new possibilities for Europe's political classes. Kings and princes who rejected the religious authority of Rome were able to forge new alliances and power blocks based, very often, on these worldly interests. The Reformation did not immediately produce individual religious liberty – far from it – but it did help create a culture where authorities, religious and political, could be questioned. In the aftermath of this cultural shift, there emerged a new breed of radical religious and philosophical thinkers who would interpret religious liberty in ways that the early reformers would never have sanctioned and who laid the intellectual foundations for the religious liberties enjoyed in Western societies today.

THE ENLIGHTENMENT AND THE BIRTH OF HISTORICAL CRITICISM

One of the main impacts of the Reformation on biblical interpretation was that the literal sense of Scripture was given a new spiritual priority and, at least in narrative features of Scripture, the literal sense was identified with the historical sense. Thus it has been suggested that the Reformation prepared the ground for historic criticism. However, to fully understand the origin of the historical-critical method, we must take into account the intellectual revolution of the early modern period which fundamentally challenged a view of history largely based on the Bible. Living in the twenty-first century, where the Bible is regarded as a text for the personal or communal use of people with a particular religious sensibility, it may be difficult to imagine a time when the Bible could be invoked with confidence as an authoritative source in almost any sphere of human knowledge, especially history. The intellectual and political convulsions of the seventeenth- and eighteenth-century Enlightenment dethroned the Bible from this position as a repository of secure knowledge about the past. As a result of discoveries in geology, astronomy and anthropology inspired by the great voyages of discovery,

> the Bible had to be incorporated within a newly discovered, vastly expanded reality, thereby taking its place as just one among many literary monuments to the ancient world and its religions, to be examined and evaluated using the same critical methods that were applied to the study on non-Christian antiquity.[4]

Therefore, it is not sufficient to look at the rise of historical criticism merely within the confines of a history of New Testament interpretation. The shift towards a historical-critical approach needs to be understood within the wider socio-cultural transformations of early modernity.

The Earth's cosmic decentring in the minds of Western intellectuals, largely due to astronomy during the early modern period, emerged alongside the decentring of the Bible in the Western story of human existence, knowledge and achievement. Even in matters of religion the Bible was no longer the unassailable touchstone of truth, with an increased confidence in the power of natural reason to evaluate the truth claims of religions. However, when the Bible lost some of its religious authority during the Enlightenment, at least among intellectual elites, as a cultural force it remained *the* canonical text for European civilisation. In this sense, the possibilities for biblical interpretation actually increased, as the Bible was mined for moral and political insights, quite independent of its use by the Church. Thomas Hobbes (1588–1679) was concerned with theology and biblical exegesis as tools for political theorising.[5] After the trauma of the English civil wars, with their sectarian divisions,

Hobbes interpreted the Bible in such a way as to legitimate the subordination of the Church to the State. The combination of a Machiavellian tradition of political philosophy, based on human interests, and a materialist cosmology provided the intellectual framework within which Hobbes read the Bible. Hobbes can be regarded as a trailblazing figure of modern critical exegesis, purging the Bible of immaterial spirituality, banishing angels and demons alike from serious consideration in biblical interpretation. Hobbes's *Leviathan* is one of the foundational texts of modern political philosophy but it was also an opportunity for Hobbes to insist on a new approach to interpreting Scripture which prioritised civil peace as the highest human good. Hobbes judged that religion was too powerful a force to be left to private interest groups and must be managed by the sovereign, who alone had the right to determine the meaning and uses of Scripture.

Baruch Spinoza (1632–77) shared the political interests of his forerunner, Hobbes, and probably had more impact on the history of biblical interpretation,[6] such was his influence on other radical thinkers of the Enlightenment. In his *Tractatus Theologico-Politicus* Spinoza showed a similar disdain to Hobbes for the supernaturalism of the Bible but was much more sophisticated in the scientific methodology he proposed to study the text. He outlined this method in three steps. The first was very much in the tradition of humanistic philology, calling for a good working knowledge of the original biblical languages. The second step was to identify topics or themes within the Bible and understand their internal relationship without importing theological and philosophical ideas which were foreign to the text. The finale step was to explore the historical circumstances of specific biblical books, gathering any information about the author and the occasion of writing, as well as its reception history. This general form of interpretation will be recognised by many students even today as a prototype of modern historical criticism, and Spinoza's conclusions as a radical challenge to Jewish and Christian interpretive practice. His most radical judgements were informed by his rejection of substance dualism in favour of metaphysical monism, where God became identified with 'nature', broadly conceived. This had implications for the interpretation of biblical miracles, which were widely understood by Christians and Jews to be interventions into the natural order by a transcendent God, usually implying the breaking of natural laws. But God, on Spinoza's understanding, was immanent with respect to nature and could no more alter the laws of nature than he could alter his own nature *qua* God.

THE QUEST FOR THE HISTORICAL JESUS

The historical study of Jesus is a striking example of the impact of a historical-critical approach to the New Testament, particularly when practised by intellectuals outside the Church. Historical reimaginings of the life and mission of Jesus and early Christianity were taken up with considerable enthusiasm by critics of orthodox Christianity, conscious of the post-Reformation importance of primitive Christianity. Most of the earliest writers of this kind in the seventeenth and eighteenth centuries operated outside academic institutions, although their claims to independence must be qualified by the patronage they relied upon. English and Irish writers were among the first to publish books either on the historical Jesus, or with direct implications for the historical Jesus: John Toland (1696) Matthew Tindal (1730) and Thomas Chubb (1738) are just three notable examples.[7] Often classified as 'deists', these freethinkers are actually difficult to define in terms of their religious outlook, but a number of overlapping concerns can be identified in their work. They argued for a religion based on reason and understood the historical Jesus primarily as a moral teacher: their interpretive assumption being that the content of Jesus' own teaching in the gospels could be separated from the theological interpretation of him, both by the Church and the gospels writers themselves.

Inspired by some of this English Anglophone criticism, along with the continental rationalism of biblical scholars such as Jean Le Clerc (1657–1736), Herman Samuel Reimarus (1694–1768) made the most celebrated contribution to historical Jesus studies of the eighteenth century. So controversial were Reimarus' theories about Jesus and Christian origins that, as a respected member of the academy, Reimarus only circulated his ideas among friends in manuscript form. They were finally published, anonymously, after his death.[8] In the aforementioned manuscript, Reimarus agreed with his British and Irish predecessors that the religious significance of Jesus does indeed lie with his moral teachings, but he identified a major political motivation in the life of Jesus, suggested by his proclamation of the coming Kingdom of God: on this reading, Jesus' messianic self-understanding was tied to the future of Israel as a political entity, and he saw his own role as the leader of a restored Kingdom. When this political revolution failed to materialise, and Jesus was put to death, the disciples self-consciously and self-interestedly reinterpreted Jesus' messianic role as one concerned with spiritual salvation in a heavenly Kingdom of God. On this reading, the birth of Christianity had its origins in the falsification of history: the conscious misrepresentation of Jesus' teachings aims. These theories were judged to be too subversive for the German academy. It is ironic, then, that this same academy would soon become the centre of historical Jesus studies.

THE UNIVERSITIES AND HISTORICAL CRITICISM

Although the roots of historical-critical readings of the New Testament lay in the work of more or less independent writers in the seventeenth and eighteenth centuries, the institutionalisation of biblical studies represented a significant new beginning. Historical-critical approaches to the Bible became domesticated, constituting a standard methodological approach to both teaching and research at the universities. This potentially dangerous approach to Scripture was now supported by the state authorities, and it was part of the theological education of students who would go on to become leaders within society whether as ministers, teachers or in other forms of public service.[9]

European universities underwent great changes in the period that followed the French revolution and the Napoleonic wars as part of larger transformations in the political, social and intellectual order. Many old universities, in which theology and related disciplines had been narrowly confessional and dogmatic, were closed and new universities were established based on the critical pursuit of knowledge, often with a secular foundation. The ideal was *Wissenschaft* (knowledge, in the broadest sense) directed towards the improvement of human character. In matters of religion, this pursuit of knowledge in the German academy was overwhelmingly undertaken within the context of Protestant theology, albeit one less constrained by the confessional demands of the various Protestant churches. The most influential to appear during this period was the new Berlin University, established in 1810 (now the Humboldt University), whose theology faculty boasted some of the foremost intellectuals of the age, not least G. W. F. Hegel (1770–1831) and Friedrich Schleiermacher (1768–1834).

Schleiermacher's vision for academic theology was at one with his vision of the mission of the university in general: it should be based on the new ethos of science. History was firmly established as a critical discipline of *Wissenschaft*, and it carried an interest which extended across the Academy and into general culture. Historical enquiry was very often concerned with investigating the origins of particular phenomena, which paralleled the concerns of other disciples: biologists went in search of the origin of species (most famously Charles Darwin), and linguists and anthropologists went in search of the origin of language. A sign of the changing times here was the displacement of biblical Hebrew as the favoured candidate for the original language of humanity, succeeded as it was by Sanskrit.[10] In the same manner, the purpose of the study of the New Testament became the original, historical meaning of the texts and the historical causes for the rise of Christianity.

Perhaps the most important legacy of Enlightenment biblical criticism was the recognition that the Bible could be read, and in the university it should be read, as any other book: there was no special method for interpreting the Bible as distinct from other texts of the ancient world. Schlei-

Figure 32. Friedrich D.F. Schleiermacher (1768-1834), woodcut by Leopold Hugo Bürkner (1818-97).

ermacher, a founding figure of modern hermeneutics and Protestant thought, insisted on this latter point when laying out his guiding principles for the scientific reading of texts. When he started his lectures on the historical Jesus, the first question he addressed was what it actually meant to write a biography; what kind of statement it made. For Schleiermacher, to choose the literary form of a biography for Jesus was to interpret his life on the same terms as other human beings examined within that genre. Despite the challenges to orthodoxy in the Enlightenment, this choice of literary genre was still controversial for many within the German academy of the nineteenth century, representing as it did a break with dogmatic Christology. Such a position was not only controversial at the level of theological conviction, it was politically subversive. The belief in the divine Christ, seated 'at the right hand of the father', represented a spiritual cosmology of the world where the king or political equivalent was nothing less than the representative of Christ on Earth. Critical readings of the gospels that presented Jesus as a human being deconstructed this symbolic unity of Christ and king. To undercut the status of Christ was to undercut the status of his representatives on Earth. Schleiermacher's lectures avoided censure, but they were not actually published until 30 years after his death.

By the time they appeared, their capacity to shock had been eclipsed by the Jesus-biographies of David Friedrich Strauss (1835–6) and Ernest Renan (1863), who escaped neither censure nor social stigma. The government of Switzerland withdrew Strauss's appointment to a position in Zürich following the appearance of his two-volume study which insisted on a mythological reading of large parts of the gospels. Strauss never got another academic position for the rest of his life.

In his opening lecture as a professor in Hebrew at the Collège de France in Paris, Renan said that Jesus was 'an incomparable man' whom some 'call God'. Such a description may seem benign today but four days after this lecture the Emperor himself, Napoleon III, personally intervened to relieve Renan of his academic duties (he was later reinstated). The lives of Jesus produced by Schleiermacher,

Strauss and Renan illustrate three important aspects of nine-teenth-century New Testament scholarship; scholarship which still influences the way the New Testament is read today.[11]

THE GOSPELS AS HISTORICAL SOURCES: JOHN OR THE SYNOPTICS?

In his lectures Schleiermacher argued that John's Gospel was the best historical source for a biography of Jesus. This was a common opinion at the beginning of the nineteenth century, but it is of inter-est to see how Schleiermacher arrives at the conclusion. He builds on the contemporary discussion of the nature of history at the very time it was being established as a key discipline in the modern universites. One view, which captured Schleiermacher's imagination, was that what separated modern history from, say, the ancient tra-dition of the chronicle, was that it presented events within a unified perspective. It was the task of the historian to bring order and coherence to the passage of time and accumulation of events. For Schleiermacher, the synoptic gospels were mere chronicles, lacking this unifying and explanatory perspective. John, by contrast, had an organising principle of unity which, for Schleiermacher, was the relationship between Jesus and the (Jewish) nation.

Strauss had a different perspective. Reading the gospels from the perspective of myth, Strauss found that John was more easily absorbed into this category than the synoptic gospels. On this view, John was less, not more, historically reliable. Strauss' teacher, F.C. Baur, reached the same conclusion, albeit by a different route: Baur judged that the narrative and discourses in John's account were shaped by highly developed theological ideas of divine dignity and glory, and that this was a gospel with little interest in the factual details of Jesus' life. The details of the arguments may differ but, from the middle of the nineteenth century, it has been the dominant view of New Testament scholars that the synoptic gospels contain more reliable historical data than the Gospel of John.

But what was the relationship between the historically prioritised Matthew, Mark and Luke? Any comprehensive answer would have to explain both the striking similarities and the significant differences. In *Synopsis of the Gospels of Matthew, Mark & Luke* (1776), Johann Jakob Griesbach (1745–1812) printed the complete text of the first three canonical gospels in columns, so that scholars could compare parallel passages in each text at a glance. *Synopsis* is a Greek term meaning 'seen together,' and has become the standard term of reference for these three texts, and the kind of synopsis employed by Griesbach remains an important tool in the academic study of the gospels.[12] On the basis of this kind of comparison, Griesbach suggested a historical relationship whereby the Gospel of Matthew was written first, followed by Luke who used Matthew as the primary source. Finally, the Gospel of Mark was written using both Matthew and Luke. This hypothesis is called the Griesbach or 'two-gospel hypothesis'. The alternative to this in the nineteenth century, and the theory which has commanded the most widespread support ever since, is the 'two-source hypothesis'. This theory reverses the position of Mark, making this gospel a primary source, but proposes an additional source, consisting largely of *logia* (sayings), to help explain the material common to Matthew and Luke but absent from Mark. In a study of the origin and historical character of the synoptic gospels in 1863, H. J. Holtzmann gave the most comprehensive argument for the two-source theory.[13]

In later scholarship, the *logia* came to be identified with the technical term 'Q' (from the German *Quelle,* meaning 'source'). The late twentieth century witnessed an increased focus on Q but, as there are no remains of this document, the content of the source must be established on the basis of discourse material common to Matthew and Luke. There is also a discussion of whether Q was ever actually a written source, or an oral tradition shared by the authors of Matthew and Luke (see Chapter 2). Since there is little narrative material in this shared content, some have argued that Q represents the view of a group of Christ followers where the teachings of Jesus were more important than his death and resurrection. This idea has become more plausible since the discovery of the *Gospel of Thomas* (see Chapter 4) which fits this very profile even if, lacking proof, Q must remain a hypothetical document.

MYTH AND HISTORY

Perhaps the most influential discussion of the historical Jesus in the nineteenth century was D. F. Strauss' *The Life of Jesus, Critically Examined* (1835–6). Ironically, the book stands as one of the most powerful arguments for the impossibility of writing a biography of Jesus. Strauss started his large project with a section on myths and placed the gospels within that conceptual context before making a detailed analysis of the gospel stories. The main focus of Strauss' critical analysis were the miracles of Jesus. This feature of the gospels had been a matter of immense controversy since the Enlightenment, during which there had been a long discussion between advocates of supernaturalism, which accepted extraordinary divine action in the world, and rationalism, which sought natural explanations of events which may have appeared extraordinary at the time. Strauss wanted to find an alternative to this discussion, both sides of which had insisted that the status of these miracles turned on the question of the correct interpretation of historical facts. Strauss found an alternative in the category of 'myth'.[14] A myth was a narrative that was

David Friedrich Strauß.

Figure 33.
David Friedrich Strauss
(1808-74), drawing
from *The Life of Jesus
Critically Examined*
(1860).

historical in form, but fictitious in content. And although a myth was not historical, Strauss argued that there was an inherent truth in these stories. The historical figure of Jesus inspired these stories by triggering the idea that he was indeed the Jewish Messiah of Jewish prophecy. Once this belief was triggered, however, the story of his life began to be told in mythical terms drawn from the narrative and images of the Hebrew Bible. Jesus as a historical person disappeared behind myths which grew spontaneously out of the historical imagination of early Christian communities. Myths about Jesus revealed truths about humanity and their relationship to God, and for Strauss, at least during the period he wrote these volumes, those truths remained untouched by historical criticism.

Strauss' book drew enormous criticism; it offended the religious, moral and political sensibilities of a generation. Strauss may have expected a backlash from conservative Christian readers, but he probably could not have anticipated the political impact of his work.[15] German nationalist movements, trying to break the power of kings and princes, read his argument that myths about Jesus were shaped by grassroots Christian communities as a support for power arising from the people, not from the kings. In the standard histories of New Testament scholarship, Strauss is remembered for his historical criticism, whereas the political ramifications of his work barely register.

For Albert Schweitzer, Strauss was the most important historical Jesus scholar of the nineteenth century, setting the standard for historical criticism of the gospels. The classic presentation of historical Jesus scholarship up to the beginning of the twentieth century is Schweitzer's *Quest of the Historical Jesus,* with the first German edition appearing in 1906.[16] Schweitzer criticised most of the scholars he reviewed for painting a picture of Jesus that resembled their own religious ideals and aspirations, and so he set up an alternative Jesus – one who belonged to the thought world of Jewish apocalypticism, and who could never be modernised.

The combination of radical criticism of the gospels, rejecting claims to historical truths but maintaining other forms of truth, is a recognisable, though controversial, tradition of modern theology.

Following Strauss and Schweitzer in this tradition, Rudolf Bultmann (1884–1976) was probably the most influential Protestant theologian and New Testament scholar of the twentieth century. His most important contribution to the history of interpretation of the New Testament was the programme of 'demythologisation',[17] that is, translating the mythical categories in the New Testament into forms that were common to life in the modern world. This programme of demythologisation made him one of the most challenging and controversial interpreters of his time. For Bultmann, the modern Christian must recognise that the New Testament world of spirits and miracles makes Christian faith in that form unacceptable in the modern world. That critical point has been accepted in much of the Western world, but the intellectual question of how one translates the underlying truths of the gospels to appropriate modern categories has, not surprisingly, produced no definite answer. Bultmann's own category translations were those of the existentialist philosophy which was so fashionable in the early and middle parts of the twentieth century. Bultmann combined his existential interpretation of the gospels with features of Lutheran theology which, on both counts, would significantly limit the appeal of such a modernising programme. The categories and philosophies of modernity are perhaps no less contested than those which belong to the world of the gospels. But perhaps Bultmann's central point can be maintained. Demythologising need not, and should not, imply the establishment of another set of 'facts' – say, the truth claims of modern existentialist philosophy – rather, it demands that we ask ourselves how the gospels relate to 'the realities that shape my existence' *today*. In that way Bultmann's general programme need not be outdated, even if his 1950s European existentialism almost certainly is.

ORIENTALISM, JUDAISM AND THE RACE OF JESUS

Ernest Renan's *Life of Jesus* (1863) was a major international bestseller, translated into many European languages and reprinted innumerable times. But its picture of Jesus was also controversial, particularly among Catholic theologians and clergy in Renan's native France. It has been characterised as a romantic idealisation, portraying Jesus and his disciples walking around Galilee in endless sunshine. What was not noticed at the time, probably because it supported rather than jarred with common political and cultural assumptions in Europe, was how the picture of Jesus supported ideologies of empire and what we now speak of as 'Orientalism'.[18] Although Orientalism can be used in a non-polemical way to refer to intellectual and cultural curiosity towards non-Western peoples and places, it is a term made famous by Edward Said[19] for the way in which Westerners, mostly Europeans, created an image of the Orient as 'the Other', different from 'us'. Orientalism was (and is) an ideology that supported colonialism and empires, and it is telling that Renan wrote his *Life of Jesus* on an expedition to Syria and Palestine to acquire antiquities for the Louvre museum in Paris, under the protection by the French navy.

Renan was a well-known philologist, and with his studies of Semitic languages he was one of the key figures in nineteenth-century Orientalism, distinguishing as he did between 'dead' Semitic languages and the living languages of the Indo-European tradition. For many Orientalists, it was a short leap from the characterisations of languages to the people who spoke these languages. Europeans considered their linguistic and cultural heritage superior to the Semites, so how did this prejudice manifest itself in Renan's treatment of Jesus? Renan found parallels between the Jewish scribes, discussed in the gospels, and the Arab Muslims he encountered when researching his *Life of Jesus*. And just as Renan considered himself, as a European, superior to the Arabs, Jesus was superior to the representatives of Judaism with whom he clashed in the gospel accounts of his ministry. For Renan, Jesus transcended the confines of Judaism, representing the totality of humanity instead of the particularity of Judaism. Renan discusses the gospel stories about Jesus' conflicts with the Jerusalem scribes, and draws the general conclusion: 'He proclaimed the rights of man, not the rights of the Jew; the religion of man, not the religion of the Jew; the deliverance of man, not the deliverance of the Jew.'[20]

This is a typical example of how the Orientalist paradigm worked in the reading of the gospels, and Renan represents some of the roots of modern readings of Jesus, placing him in opposition to his Jewish context. Little historical Jesus scholarship shows awareness of how Orientalism influenced nineteenth-century interpretation, and scholars have therefore not considered the ideological context of their readings.[21] This paradigm of opposition between Jesus and

Figure 34.
Ernest Renan (1823-92).

Judaism was popular with historical Jesus scholars, and it seemed
to be given a firm evidential grounding when the synoptic gospels
were recognised as the best historical sources for a life of Jesus. In
these gospels it is easy to find contrasts between the positive image
of Jesus during his work in Galilee and the negative view of him
among the Scribes in Jerusalem. But how was this supposed historical contrast interpreted and used to legitimise other contrasts of
identity that involved the distinction between 'we' and 'the Other'?

In nineteenth-century Europe, race had emerged as a popular
mode of classification for peoples past and present. In a historical
study of Jesus, therefore, the issue of Jesus' *race* inevitably surfaced.
The question here was whether Jesus was a Jew not only in terms
of his religious outlook, but according to genealogy and descent.
Much of the discussion of this question centred on Jesus' Galilean
context. It was commonly held by biblical scholars that, at the time
of Jesus, Galilee had a mixed population of Jews and Gentiles. If
this was true, there existed the possibility that Jesus himself may
have come from the non-Jewish part of that historical community.
It was on the basis of such speculation that the now infamous concept of *The Aryan Jesus* was born. In the book which carries that

very title, Susannah Heschel shows how some New Testament scholars seized on this idea, promoted it in influential circles and supported its political consequences: discrimination against Jews, support of anti-Semitism and, finally, the programme to exterminate European Jews during the Third Reich.[22]

It is easy to say that these are extreme consequences of some perverted academic readings of New Testament texts, readings that few scholars accepted at the time, and which are categorically repudiated by scholars today. But Heschel documents a real and troubling phenomenon which serves as an example of how speculative academic interpretations can be marshalled for ideological purposes. In *Racializing Jesus*, Shawn Kelley[23] has studied this paradigm of interpretation and the influence of racial thinking on later periods of scholarship. He is not suggesting that prominent scholars he discusses, such as Bultmann, R. Funk and J. D. Crossan, are racist in outlook; on the contrary, they reject such pernicious values. But by tracing the influence of German philosophers and scholars who structure their analysis in terms of binary contrasts – with a positive 'we' versus a negative 'other' – we can see how this way of thinking permeates the approach of later scholars to the gospels and the figure of Jesus.

It took a long time for Christian New Testament scholars to break with the oppositional analysis of Jesus over the Judaism of his day. Contrary to what one might think, it did not happen as an immediate result of World War II and the Holocaust. In the so-called 'New quest for the historical Jesus', the ethnic Jewishness of Jesus was affirmed, but his teachings were still portrayed against the negative background of Jewish religion.[24] It was in texts such as E.P. Sanders' *Jesus and Judaism*[25] that Jesus was first seen as a prophet within Judaism, and where it was accepted that the negative picture of Jewish religion was generated by an uncritical reading of the internal polemics against Jews in the gospels and Paul's letters. Jewish scholars, who had protested against the picture of Judaism in their scholarship since the time of Strauss and Renan, finally got a hearing, and their expertise began to penetrate mainstream New Testament scholarship. Jewish scholars have continued to make significant contributions to New Testament and historical Jesus studies: Geza Vermes, Amy-Jill Levine and Paula F Fredriksen to name but a few.[26]

Since the end of the twentieth century, studies of the historical Jesus and of the New Testament in general have been an ecumenical enterprise including Christian, Jewish and non-religious scholars. This is particularly true in North America, with proportionally more Jews in New Testament and religious studies than in Europe. The common denominator for historical Jesus studies in the last period (often described as 'the third quest') is that Jesus was a Jew, not only in ethnicity but in religious orientation. This does not end the discussion, however. There is still the question of what kind of Jew Jesus was: from the documents discovered at Qumran to the ancient witnesses to Hellenistic Judaism in Palestine and the Diaspora, it is clear that Judaism manifested itself in many different ways. The diversity of approaches, seeing Jesus within different cultural contexts with a wider or narrower focus, is signalled by titles such as John Dominic Crossan's *The Historical Jesus. The Life of a Mediterranean Jewish Peasant*[27] and Sean Freyn's *Jesus, a Jewish Galilean: A New Reading of the Jesus Story.*[28] In addition, there is still a discussion to be had about whether the Judean milieu provided an exhaustive context for the historical Jesus and the movement he initially inspired, or whether Jesus' message and his early gathering of disciples can be seen as the beginning of a Jesus movement that eventually split the Jewish community.

READING THE GOSPEL TEXTS

So far we have followed the studies of the historical Jesus in the nineteenth century, and considered how they set the pattern for twentieth-century scholarship. But there were new developments in the beginning of the twentieth century which are very important to note. Possibly exhausted by the so-called 'quest for the historical Jesus' and its reconstruction of the gospels, a new generation of scholars focused on the oral transmission of his words and the stories about him in the first communities, prior to the written form of the gospels. This approach was known as 'form criticism' and, once again, it was German scholars who led the way: figures such as Karl Ludwig Schmidt, Martin Dibelius and Rudolf Bultmann.[29]

Partly inspired by modern folkloristic studies, these scholars

181

attempted to identify small units that existed as oral forms before they were gathered into larger collections: for example paradigms (short stories that preserve a word by Jesus) and Jesus' sayings, parables, miracle stories and legends (for example the birth stories of Jesus).[30] From Old Testament studies, especially the Psalms, came the interest in identifying 'the place in life' (*Sitz im Leben*) for various forms of sayings. This 'place in life' was, above all, identified as the context of worship, the cultic gatherings of early Christian communities.

From the perspective of a contemporary New Testament scholar, early Christian worship looks like a rather narrow understanding of the place for oral traditions about Jesus, and its focus on worship seemed to offer little to those concerned with the use of the gospels in the modern world. New Testament scholarship taking place in the United States at the same time showed a different approach, especially the Chicago School during the era of the socio-historical method in the first part of the twentieth century. Here the combination of gospel studies with sociology constituted a methodological innovation in New Testament studies, but it had an even greater impact on the application of the gospels to contemporary social and political issues. In publications such as *The Social Teaching of Jesus: An Essay in Christian Sociology* and *Jesus on Social Institutions*,[31] Shailer Mathews insisted that Jesus proclaimed a social gospel with the potential to transform modern society as well as his own. With its use of sociology the 'Chicago School' was something of an exception at the time, but their study methods, along with the socio-political focus, laid the groundwork for the 'social-scientific interpretations' towards the end of the century (see Chapter 9).

Form criticism had focused on small units and likely oral forms of the gospels, and for many students the result could be a fragmentary appreciation of the gospels. However, in the 1950s the pendulum swung back to an interest in the individual gospels and the theological intentions of their authors or, increasingly, their editors. Once again, the technical terminology for a new approach in New Testament studies was provided by German scholars: *Redaktionsgeschichte*, literally translated as 'redaction criticism' and focusing on the process of editing the gospels.[32] Building on form criticism and its identification of small units, scholars noticed that in some cases these had been combined in different ways to form larger units and sometimes given a different context or treated to some kind of explanatory commentary in the various gospels. Thus, by studying these combinations, alternative wordings and alternative framings, it was possible to make suggestions about the theological views of each evangelist as they adapted the material at their disposal.

An early, famous example of redaction criticism is a study of how Matthew transformed the simple story of Jesus stilling a storm with his disciples on the Sea of Galilee (Mark 6:45–52).[33] Matthew's version of the story in 14:22–33 adds some elements – for example the address 'Lord, save me' – and, instead of a confusion among the disciples when rescued, a confession: 'Truly you are the Son of God'. In this way the evangelist turns the story into an allegory for the community of believers at Matthew's time (and constitutes the beginning of a tradition that depicts the Church as a ship). The idea that the evangelist is a theologian who speaks to a community in a particular situation has been very popular; however, definitive results have been blocked by the failure to reach agreement about the historical situation behind the various gospels.

Redaction criticism started out with the idea of the evangelist as an editor, working with traditional material. Under the influence of more recent trends in literary criticism, however, the focus shifted towards the evangelist as an *author*, not just an editor, and each gospel as a narrative in its own right. While the historical critic is interested in the story behind the text, or the sources of the story, narrative criticism focuses on the world of the text itself. The text is a communication between a sender and a receiver and, in an oral culture, the receiver is more likely to be a listener than a reader. But, according to one literary theory, both the sender and the receiver exist within the text, as an implied author addressing an implied audience. This is a structure that encourages the actual audience (we as readers) to identify with the implied audience. Narrative criticism looks for certain elements to get at the meaning of a text, especially characters, settings, plot and rhetoric. We get to know the characters by what they say or do in relation to Jesus or one another. Settings describe times or places that signify meaning (for example 'the third day', 'the wilderness'). Plot is the sequence of events within a story and what drives these events to happen: conflicts between individuals or groups, for instance. And finally, rhetoric is the way the story is told, or how the narrative addresses the audience in a compelling way. The presentation of John's Gospel in Chapter 2 illustrates some of these elements.[34]

With its focus on the text of the gospels as self-contained literary universes, rather than on their relations to the historical Jesus or the early community of Christ believers, narrative criticism has left the area of historical studies. Literary questions are central to its interpretation, rather than historical concerns. So, even if narrative criticism does not represent an end to historical readings of the New Testament, it signals the end of the absolute hegemony of historical criticis. We now enter a new phase with a much larger theoretical and methodological pluralism in the readings of the New Testament, which will be the topic for the next chapter.

9

'READING FROM THIS PLACE': PAUL IN RECENT INTERPRETATIONS

In the 1960s, when I started theological studies at university, the book that was used to teach New Testament methods had a very simple and telling subtitle: *The Historical Critical Method.*[1] The title took for granted that there was just one recognised method. It included various features, for example the history of oral traditions before the written stage, and the history of the individual literary forms that make up the New Testament writings. But there was no doubt what the point of enquiry was: to find the historical – that is, the original – meaning of the individual writings of the New Testament. And the ideal interpreter was the objective scholar, who evaluated the material on the basis of historical criteria.

These once-established norms of the *original* meaning and the *objective* reader have been subjected to serious challenge since the 1960s. I have chosen as the title of this chapter an alternative method which emerged from this period of disciplinary self-criticism – 'Reading from this place' – which was originally the title of two collections of essays that came out of a conference on the impact of different social locations on the fruits of biblical interpretation, with a particular emphasis on the effects of globalisation.[2] Scholars from different parts of the world, women and men, presented interpretations of biblical texts from their particular social, racial, geographic and gender location. Writing from the perspective of postcolonial biblical criticism, R.S. Sugirtharajah puts his finger on what was at stake in this methodological shift, and what breaking the hegemony of historical-critical reading has meant: 'Postcolonial criticism enabled us for the first time to frame our own questions rather than battling with somebody else's'.[3]

Raising new and different questions of the New Testament is the most important result of the new approach of 'reading from this place'. Today, books on method in New Testament studies present a plurality of methods and perspectives, with the historical-critical method listed as one among many. What has happened since the 1960s to have changed the picture so much? First, I think that our understanding of the *world*, politically and socially has changed. Second, the groups of *readers* and interpreters of the New Testament have expanded beyond the old boundaries. And finally, I think that our understanding of *what a text is* has changed. These changes are not just a matter of intellectual trends, they are directly linked to cultural, social and political changes that have had a great impact on the world at large.

At least four major events in the twentieth century have directly influenced new ways of reading the New Testament: 1) the impact of the Holocaust and the questions it raised about the relations between Jews and Christians; 2) the Vietnam War, which indicated the end of direct colonisation by Europe and the USA; 3) the Civil Rights movement of African–Americans in the USA, which carried a symbolic importance for human rights in all nations; and 4) the feminist movement, focusing on women's rights and gender equality, starting in Western countries but spreading to other parts of the world. A characteristic of all of these 'events' is that they have changed the world by de-centring the influence of previously dominant social forces: religious, imperial, ethnic and male hegemonies. Together these events have changed our perspectives of history, with a new interest in the stories of small local communities and various minorities. The formative global events identified here demanded that the world be understood in a new way, one that was open for new understandings, including new and more inclusive ways of arranging the pieces of our various histories.

At the same time, intellectual movements and initiatives at the universities (with 1968 being a symbolic year) brought new questions, theories and methods to the table, with Marxist criticism and names such as Derrida, Foucault and Said at the forefront of critical discourse. Moreover, the experience of independence for previously colonised peoples, and the achievements of the civil rights and

Figure 35. Student protesters at the University of Wisconsin-Madison during the Vietnam War era (Photo: uwdigitalconnections).

feminist movements, brought new people into the recognised guilds of qualified readers and writers. All of this affected the study of the New Testament. Paul's words 'no longer Jew or Greek, [...] no longer slave or free, [...] no longer male and female' were partially realised in the field of New Testament scholarship: Jews, former colonised people, African–Americans and women entered the field of New Testament studies in increasing numbers. These changes posed challenges to those who previously had the balance of power in biblical interpretation: primarily white, male, middle-class European and North American academics, and required scholars to recognise and reflect on their own place in power structures, in terms of political, intellectual, religious, ethnic and gender hegemonies.

Political protest movements, often associated with the student protests of 1968, also influenced our understanding of texts. These movements accused texts of coming from the powerful, from the political regimes; they did not reflect real life as people actually experienced it, but presented a picture which reflected how a dominant regime wanted the world to be seen. The notion of texts as ideological constructions, and the relationship between texts and power, became a key part of discourse analysis. This is often referred to as the 'linguistic turn', one that de-constructs texts as a reference to 'real' history, and instead sees texts as a shaped by certain interests. This linguistic turn also influenced interpretations of New Testament texts as well as the constructions of the history of the New Testament period.

PAUL FROM CANON TO CONTEXT

The development of studies of Paul over the last 40 years exemplifies some of the changes I have described. Modern scholars of earlier generations had adopted a *diachronic* perspective on Paul: Paul and his theology were regarded as the beginning of Christianity and, in a sense, the benchmark for 'true' Christianity. In important periods in the history of the Church, and in intellectual history more generally, Paul has been 'rediscovered' and has exerted a massive influence on the intellectual climate of opinion. This was true of Augustine's formative contribution to Christian theology in the fourth and fifth centuries; it was true of Martin Luther's 'Reformation Discovery' in the sixteenth century; and the pattern was repeated in the twentieth century, when Rudolph Bultmann made Paul the pre-eminent theologian of the then-dominant philosophical movement of continental Europe, existentialism.

Less eye-catching, but no less influential, was the influence of Pauline scholarship on the concept of religion as it tended to function in the nineteenth century: it was understood as personal faith in contrast to works and empty rituals. Although it was obviously a concept with a Protestant origin, it also became dominant in religious studies where 'faith' became the criterion for 'true' versus 'false' or 'higher' versus 'lower' religions.[4] It was used to characterise Protestantism versus Roman Catholicism and to distinguish Christianity from Judaism. Since early modernity, religions come to be defined as entities that made up a distinct sector of society, centred on some set of beliefs and practices. In New Testament interpretation of the eighteenth and nineteenth centuries, this modern construction of religion was transported to the first century and conditioned scholars' understandings of Christian origins and its wider religious context. So, for instance, with his teaching of 'justification by faith' Paul became the authority for the distinction between 'faith' and 'works', which was now objectified as a category in the history of religion. In that sense we can say that Paul was regarded as 'canon', that is, as an authority for 'true' religion, which for most scholars still meant Christianity.

The twentieth-century interest in histories of small communities and localities was a major influence on the way scholars interpreted the New Testament generally and Paul in particular. Instead of the diachronic perspective, it created an interest in a synchronic perspective: that is, reading Paul within the context of his own time and place. Within a synchronic perspective a crucial question emerged – How to place Paul within the three overlapping contexts of his life? These contexts included his Jewish home, the Hellenistic cities of the Eastern Mediterranean and the politically dominant Roman Empire. From this perspective, it wasn't just the theological issues that were relevant for understanding Paul. It was important to understand Paul within the socio-political and religious systems of his time. This emphasis on the local combined with the rise of feminist analysis of text to make Paul's treatment of women in his letters a major focus of discussion in such synchronic interpretation. This new interpretative stance also meant that it was no longer just Paul as a singular authority who was of interest, but also the larger communities in which he was, to different degrees, embedded. Finally, when reading Paul from a synchronic perspective, contemporary with his own time, the question of *when* we can say that Christianity emerged as a religion separate from Judaism became much more complex than had once been assumed.

These new questions resulted in new methods, models and approaches which have come to characterise New Testament studies today. Some refer to specific methods or models brought in from other areas; for example from the social sciences, or from literary studies such as narrative, rhetorical and structural criticism. Some are more perspectives or approaches, applying a combination of methods: feminist, post-colonial, African–American and Asian perspectives have all impacted on New Testament scholarship. These perspectives have also influenced historical criticism, for instance by discussing Paul's letters in a broader context than before, including their Jewish, Hellenistic and Roman contexts (see Chapter 1). In the following, we shall focus on the contextual approach to the study of Paul as a figure of history.

THE NEW JEWISH PAUL

Paul's relationship to his Jewish roots has become one of the biggest issues in the historical interpretation of the apostle over the last 40 years, and it plays a role in the relations between many Jews and Christians today. We may say that it was a belated effect of the Holocaust during World War II: it took a long time before the Holocaust actually entered the general public consciousness and, likewise, it took time to become an issue that actually made New Testament scholars stop to question representations of Jews in biblical scholarship. German New Testament scholarship is a case in point. Although many scholars were personally opposed to the Nazi regime, the war on European Jewry did not immediately impact on their interpretation of Paul. Paul's teaching of justification by faith was the key to scholarly descriptions of his negative relationship with his Jewish context. This was true of the most influential New Testament scholar in the first part of the twentieth century, Rudolf Bultmann, and his existential reading of Paul, inspired by Luther's classic interpretation. He described Paul's conflict between faith and law as paradigmatic of conflicts within human nature. Before the arrival of Christ, 'man' was determined by his sin, understood to be his self-righteousness: the desire to be autonomous and free from God. Thus Paul's criticism was not specifically directed against the Jews, but against human nature in general. The problem with this view, however, was that the Jews remained historical models for a sinful humanity. Bultmann's reading of Paul was highly influential, especially within Protestant theology, and cohered with the existentialism which came to dominate continental philosophy and associated social attitudes in the period after World War II.

With hindsight, it is possible to see a small essay from 1963, by Harvard Professor Krister Stendahl, 'The Apostle Paul and the introspective conscience of the West' as an early and eventually highly influential criticism of this whole image of Paul.[5] Stendahl argued that when Paul advocated righteousness by faith and not by the law, at issue was not human (and Paul's own) existence as a theological problem, but the historical question of whether Gentiles could be

Christians without first becoming Jews. The dramatic encounter with the risen Christ outside Damascus that changed Paul's life should not be understood as a conversion and a turning away from Judaism. Rather, it was God's calling Paul to become an apostle to non-Jews. Stendahl also suggested reading Romans specifically from a collective perspective, with Romans 9–11 as the centre of Paul's theology. These chapters deal with the relations between Jews and non-Jews, with Paul proclaiming the ultimate salvation of all Jews.

The most influential break with the traditional Protestant image of Paul, however, came with *Paul and Palestinian Judaism: A Comparison of Patterns of Religion* by E.P. Sanders.[6] Sanders criticised the dominant picture of Judaism among Christian New Testament critics and history of religion scholars: namely, that they accepted Paul's polemics against the Jewish teaching of 'righteousness through the Law' as indicative of historical truth about ancient Judaism. Based on his readings of Jewish sources at the time of Paul, Sanders suggested 'covenantal nomism' as a positive term to describe what was actually characteristic of Judaism as religion at that time:

> [it] is the view that one's place in God's plan is established on the basis of the covenant and that the covenant requires as the proper response of man his obedience to its commandments, while providing means of atonement for transgression.[7]

In his view, for Paul there was nothing wrong with the law or those who followed it, but now God had shown that salvation came through Jesus, and in no other way. The insistence of Sanders that Paul's rhetoric against the law was an ideological stance and not objective truth was an important observation, and one that is applicable to many New Testament texts. But Sanders continued to describe Judaism and Christianity as two different religious systems, something which had been abandoned by most advocates of what came to be called the 'new perspective on Paul', originally inspired by the work of Sanders. Some writers in this tradition would say that during Paul's own time there was no clear division between Judaism and Christianity.

The trailblazing studies by Sanders were followed up by important contributions to the understanding of Paul by James D.G. Dunn, who first coined the phrase the 'New Perspective on Paul' in an article with that very title.[8] Major European scholars of Paul, such as Heikki Räisänen and N.T. Wright, joined Dunn in this new critical paradigm. They maintained Sanders' criticism of traditional Protestant interpretations of Paul, built around the contrast between faith and law, but kept some of the older features of Pauline interpretation, for instance the view that Paul was not only concerned with a local mission to non-Jews, but also with the more general reconciliation of sinners with God. They emphasised the Jewishness of Paul, while suggesting that Paul had nevertheless abandoned many of the essential aspects of the Torah. Thus, we might say that Dunn and Wright represent a middle position in their recognition of Paul's continued Jewishness. A more radical new position on Paul, would see him as remaining within Judaism even after his calling outside Damascus.[9] This reorientation in the interpretation of Paul, and of the New Testament more generally, is not explicitly confessional, not only with regard to Christian confessions, but also to Judaism and Christianity. Several Jewish scholars of the New Testament have been very active in this radical perspective on Paul. The title of a book by Pamela Eisenbaum, *Paul Was Not a Christian*,[10] illustrates this very well.

How is Paul's criticism of the Law to be understood if he did not break with the Judaism of his day? One solution to that problem, associated with the new perspective, is the suggestion that Paul's discussion of the Law primarily concerned the issue of gentiles and how they could be included within the chosen people of God. Thus, his criticism of the Law was directed not at Jews, but at non-Jews: that they need not, and should not, become followers of the Torah. According to a more radical version of this view, however, Paul not only accepted that Jews should continue to live according to the Law, but that he himself continued to follow the Torah. This radical position has been taken up by scholars who have been concerned that Christian theology should not influence the historical interpretation of Paul. Perhaps the most controversial position within this new trends of interpreting Paul is the suggestion by the aforementioned Eisenbaum that Paul did not hold that his fellow Jews needed the saving power of Jesus' death: Jesus only saved Gentiles – because they did not have the benefit of the Torah and therefore were not in relationship with God. Not surprisingly, these new readings have caused strong reactions and criticism by scholars who, while accepting Sanders' general reorientation in our understanding of first-century Judaism, are committed to a traditional 'Protestant' view of Paul.[11] The new approaches have sought to distance him from contemporary Christian concerns and have claimed to be less theological and more historical. But the decision to read Paul within a Jewish context, to the point of rejecting any links to future Christianity, also implies ideological and normative interests.

Francis Watson takes up this very debate in his book *Paul, Judaism and the Gentiles*. The subtitle of Watson's book, *Beyond the New Perspective* indicates that he is critical of some aspects of this 'new' tradition of Pauline scholarship. This is interesting, not least because Watson was one of the earliest critics of the 'Lutheran Paul'[12] and still stands by the view that Paul was not just a theologian, but also a missionary working to unite Jews and Gentiles in communities orientated towards Christ. It is here, however, that the difference emerges with proponents of the 'new perspective on Paul'. Watson reads Paul's polemics as part of an argument to create a new fellowship, separate from the synagogue, and finds that Paul's letters reflect a transitional moment in the early communities of Christ followers. With the help of sociological analysis, Watson suggests that this is the transition from a reform movement into a sect. Using this model, Watson explains the contrast between Paul's opponents, who want the Gentile Christians to keep the Law (that is, remain a Jewish reform movement), and Paul himself, who rejects this acceptance of the Law so that the group becomes a sect, clearly differentiated from the Jewish community. Furthermore, Watson views Paul's polemics as criticisms directed against Jews (both Christ believers and non-believers) facilitated by a radical reinterpretation of Jewish traditions about identity in which Abraham is now claimed as a rightful ancestor for all Christ believers (non-Jewish and Jewish). In the end, I side with Watson on this, since I consider him to have presented the most satisfactory (synchronic) approach to Paul in his own context: taking Paul's polemics against Jewish positions on the law seriously, while offering a plausible sociological paradigm of group development.

PAUL IN THE HELLENISTIC CITY

What was most important for Paul, his Jewish or Hellenistic milieu? This question, and answers to it, has gone through several phases in the last 100 years. Within the so-called 'history of religion' school at the beginning of the twentieth century, Hellenism was regarded as the dominant influence upon Paul: he was responsible for (or guilty of) transforming the Palestinian Jewish Jesus movement so that it could plausibly be integrated into the Hellenistic world. But by the middle of that century, studies such *Paul and Rabbinic Judaism* by W.D. Davies[13] were showing the extent to which Paul remained integrated within Rabbinic thought structures and styles of argumentation. The Jewish context was the primary focus of E.P. Sanders in *Paul and Palestinian Judaism*, but there was a growing sense by then that it was not possible to put up a strong division between Jewish and Hellenistic cultural forms. Jewish faith and practice, including within Palestine, was already part of Hellenism and shaped by its place within it.[14] More recently, there has been renewed interest in the Hellenistic influence upon Paul. This has partly been expressed in detailed studies of how Paul adapted Hellenistic letter forms in his own writings,[15] and his use of Hellenistic rhetorics.[16] Often this kind of analysis features within broader studies of the influence of Hellenistic philosophy on Paul's intellectual and literary formation. Troels Engberg-Pedersen in particular has argued for Stoicism as a formative influence upon Paul (see Further Reading).

Perhaps the most innovative approach in Pauline and New Testament studies in general has been a new interest in the location and place of the groups that Paul and other missionaries established. The title of the now classic book by the Yale professor Wayne A. Meeks, *The First Urban Christians: The Social World of the Apostle Paul*,[17] signalled a shift away from a history of ideas approach to early Christianity to a focus on the geographic setting and social structures of these groups. Instead of giving a presentation of Paul's theology, Meeks read his letters with the following question in mind: 'What was it like to be an ordinary Christian in the Pauline congregations?' Thus the very understanding of religion underwent a transformation:

Figure 36. *St Paul Preaching in Athens* (1515), Raphael, Royal Collection of the United Kingdom.

it was not only an intellectual and theological enterprise; it included social praxis and rituals, not least baptism and Eucharist.

The German scholar Gerd Theissen helped to initiate sociological studies of early Christianity, showing many (initially sceptical) colleagues that studies of the social context, utilising sociological methods, could help solve traditional problems of interpretation (see Further Reading). One example was the conflict over the celebration of the Eucharist in the community in Corinth (1 Corinthians 11: 17–34). Theissen suggested that this conflict was not caused by differences in theological perspectives on the Eucharist. Based on his study of social stratification in the Corinthian community, which had both well-to-do people and slaves as members, he suggested that this composition caused social tensions. These tensions came to the fore in the eucharistic meal, where the rich brought their own food but the poor had nothing to eat.[18]

As the early Christian groups gathered in the houses of wealthy members, they were already integrated within existing household structures. A new fruitful area of research, therefore, has been studies of household and families in Hellenistic and Roman times (see Further Reading). They are examples of how it is possible to combine social history, concerned with family structures and roles in early Christian groups, and ideological criticism, concerned with the ideals of families and gender roles which were used to establish authoritative structures. The issue of slavery illustrates the need to combine the history of social praxis with analyses of ideology.

In his social reconstruction of the community in 1 Corinthians 11, Theissen succeeded in making the slaves visible. As I pointed out in Chapter 6, slavery has been a topic on the fringes of New Testament studies: in the texts themselves it is mostly mentioned in passing, something that was just taken for granted. Since the Hellenistic and Roman worlds were slave-owning societies, slavery was an essential component of social structures and so, not surprisingly, it features in many parables and metaphors. Because slavery in its traditional form is alien to most modern societies, this is one illustration of just how 'foreign' the New Testament is, in its cultural and social systems, to modern readers.

This focus on foreignness made social anthropological studies of foreign or traditional societies relevant for New Testament interpretation, with the biblical critic adopting a role similar to that of the anthropologist.[19] Studies by social anthropologists Mary Douglas, Claude Lévi-Strauss and Clifford Geertz were among the first resources used by biblical scholars. Mary Douglas introduced specific models (purity and boundaries; the body as a symbol) for analysis,[20] and Geertz inspired many biblical scholars with his understanding of religion as a cultural system and of cultural anthropology as a form of interpretation, not a hard science.[21] New Testament students cannot undertake interviews – which usually provide explicit material on customs, perceptions and mentalities – with the authors or subjects of their literary sources. Therefore, context has been provided through material derived from more general studies of Mediterranean societies in Antiquity, and in traditional communities today. Characteristic elements were the social institutions of kinship and marriage, values such as honour and shame, and a group orientation. These elements have been used to illuminate the historical context and to describe the 'social imaginary' of New Testament writings.

Social science approaches to New Testament studies were initiated by a group of scholars who established a collaboration in the Context Group.[22] Their introduction of theories and models from the social sciences was viewed with some suspicion in a field that traditionally collaborated with disciplines within the humanities such as philology, history and literary studies. However, social science readings have gradually become widely accepted and applied by many scholars, although often without the strong theoretical interest of the members of the Context Group. At first, New Testament students employed theories and models from sociology and social anthropology; increasingly, however, other fields of study have been drawn into the process, especially social psychology, studies of memory transmission and, most recently, social cognition.[23]

FEMINIST CRITICISM

Feminist studies have developed from questions of social history (making women visible) to ideological criticism following the

Figure 37. *A sinful woman anoints Christ's feet.* Etching by Jan Luyken (1649-1712) in the Phillip Medhurst Collection of Bible illustrations, Belgrave Hall, Leicester, England.

so-called 'linguistic turn' (statements about women by male writers are not treated as history, but as the attempt to define 'women's place'). The last step has been a rewriting of the theology and history of early Christianity from a feminist perspective. Starting with historic reconstruction, the most prominent example is the now-classic book *In Memory of Her: A Feminist Theological Reconstruction of Christian Origins* by Elisabeth Schüssler Fiorenza (1983). Here she outlines a history of early Christianity based on a theory of the *possibility* of equal participation of women in leadership and authority roles. This has been followed up by many other studies, in which a common element is a shift of focus from Paul as the unique religious authority to the wider communities he formed, for instance by foregrounding texts that make visible local leaders and collaborators, among them women (for example, 1 Cor 14–15; Rom 16). By reading 'behind Paul' to find the ongoing discourses in the communities he founded, it may be possible to locate the place of women, for example as prophets and participants in cults in Corinth.[24]

Central to feminist criticism is the insight that all texts reflect the dominant ideologies in a society, and in Hellenistic texts such as Paul's letters and the gospels, that means patriarchy and hierarchy, or the neologism 'kyriarchy', that Schüssler Fiorenza created to indicate a pattern of domination over all who were in inferior positions, not just women. Therefore feminist criticism does not apply only to texts about women: all texts are 'gendered' in the sense indicated above. This has resulted in collaborative works of commentaries or studies of New Testament books, such as the series 'Feminist companion to the New Testament and early Christian writings' (see Further Reading).

Feminist criticism illustrates in an exemplary way the significance of 'speaking from this place', entering as it did into a field of study that was dominated by an all-male group of scholars who claimed objectivity as the main ideal of scholarship. Feminist scholars had their work cut out on several fronts, both in terms of questioning the traditional ways of writing the history of early Christianity, and in exploring the ideological underpinnings of texts and their interpretation.[25] They have shown that historical work is also always ideological work, which is to say that the search for historical representation is also a search for a meaningful history shaped by a symbiotic relationship between ideas and interests of the past, and those of the present. This openness about ideological perspectives has, however, resulted in criticism, especially of the theory of equality between men and women in the early Jesus movement – the criticism being that it brings in a modern perspective that was alien to societies in Antiquity.

Feminist criticism is only one of the ways in which women scholars have contributed with new perspectives in New Testament studies. This chapter and Chapter 8 both indicate that women are active in all areas of New Testament studies, for instance on the New Paul (Eisenbaum), the historical Jesus (Fredriksen, Heschel), household and families (Osiek, MacDonald), slavery (Glancy), post-colonialism (Dube, Kahl) and new methods such as intersectionalism (Kartzow).

ROME – FROM BACKGROUND TO FOREGROUND: POLITICAL READINGS OF THE NEW TESTAMENT

Rome and the Roman Empire have always been in the background of the study of the New Testament. Sometimes it comes to the fore, as in discussions of the meaning of Caesar's coin (Mark 12:13–17), or Paul's exhortation to obey the emperor (Romans 13:1–7), but most of the time it was only the given political context for the interpretation of the New Testament. So how did the Roman Empire enter into the foreground in New Testament studies? Once again, it may be an effect of the political changes in the twentieth century, with the end of colonisation and (at least some) global empires. Many biblical scholars in the West were critical of US imperial politics in the Vietnam War, and new groups of readers from Africa, Asia and Latin America used their political insights in the study of New Testament texts. New Testament criticism was also inspired by studies of literature and history from a post-colonial perspective, by writers from both former colonies and previous colonial powers.[26] The aforementioned Edward Said and Michel Foucault helped to inspire such critical perspectives, raising provocative and enduring questions. Typical of this body of literature, which acquired the name 'post-colonial', was the foregrounding of tensions with imperial powers, and the distancing of itself from the assumptions of the imperial centres of Western regimes.

Post-colonial approaches challenge the traditional hegemony of interpretation that was founded on the intellectual traditions which developed from the Enlightenment and which was undertaken by people in privileged positions in former or present colonial powers. Not surprisingly, then, post-colonial approaches in New Testament studies have often been initiated by scholars who themselves write from a disadvantaged place in terms of political, racial, and gender power structures, writers such as Fernando F. Segovia, R.S. Sugirtha-rajah and Musa Dube.[27] They began to ask new questions of the New Testament texts: What was it like to live under the Roman Empire, which determined the political order, the economic system and the dominant ideological universe? And how were these experiences reflected in New Testament writings? When one started raising such questions, the clear distinctions between religion and politics started to blur. Studies of the language of Paul's letters showed that what had been considered theological terminology turned out to have strong political overtones. For instance, the Greek word *dikaiosyne*, was often translated as 'righteousness', referring to an individual, but it might better be translated as 'justice', referring to how God would put an end to an unjust social order. And the word *euangelion*, when translated as the familiar 'gospel' or 'good news', loses its links to common Roman usage, for example to proclaim Emperor Augustus and acknowledge his accession to power.[28]

There are similarities but also differences between empire studies and postcolonial studies in New Testament scholarship. Empire studies often takes as a starting point the comparison between the Roman Empire and modern empires, especially USA and (previously) Great Britain. Studies of how New Testament texts interact with and nego-tiate the Roman Empire often result in interpretations that present Paul and other biblical writers as critical of Empire,[29] suggesting analogies with criticism of modern-day empires. Post-colonial approaches are often more self-critical, reflecting on the impression that the contrast between opposition to empire and adaptation to empire are not always clear-cut. This may be the most challenging task: to expose biblical texts to political criticism and to analyse their message not only in terms of their explicit message, but also in terms of implicit and hidden messages. For instance, when Paul protests against the Roman Empire, he also borrows its logic when he speaks of God, so that God's victory becomes a political counterpoint to Rome's system of domination.[30] Perhaps the most obvious example of this in the New Testament, however, is the Book of Revelation, where violence and warfare are found on the sides of both evil and good (see Chapter 3). The post-colonial approach changed the paradigm of reading Paul's letters as non-political, Christian-theological tracts to a reading that integrates the politics within the theological meaning. For instance, Neil Elliott suggests that it is 'anachronistic to read Romans as an early specimen of Christian theology. The letter is rather one expression of the range of Judean responses to the Roman Empire.'[31] But how is it possible to turn around a traditional reading of Paul, especially in Romans and Galatians, as addressing a Christian/ Jewish conflict, and instead read the letters as responses to the Roman Empire? Part of the problem is that Paul's letters give so little information about their context within the Empire that it is very difficult to establish the position to which he is responding.

Brigitte Kahl and Davina Lopez have found a very creative approach to establishing this context by using Roman art as expressions of Roman imperial ideology. They are inspired by Paul Zanker's *The Power of Images in the Age of Augustus*,[32] which shows how Augustus used iconography – for instance, idealised statues of himself – to spread the ideology of the empire. The power of the Roman Empire was also expressed by urban structures, streets and major buildings such as temples and stoae. This was part of an environment that impressed itself on the people and made them all aware of the power structures under which they lived. Kahl uses the Pergamon Altar, and the well-known statue of the dying Gaul, to illustrate the oppressive Roman power structures.[33] This was the 'law' that Paul addresses in Galatians. His argument was directed, not against Judaism, but against Roman imperial monotheism. Kahl argues that Paul advocated the inclusion of all nations in a movement of peace and justice, as part of Jewish messianic monotheism. Lopez's main example is from the friezes from Sebastaeion in Aphrodisias in Asia Minor.[34] Many of them present Roman emperors together with the peoples they had conquered, often represented by a female figure in an enslaved position. Lopez uses the ideology of these images to explain the meaning of the Greek

Figure 38. Bust of Roman Emperor Nero. Antiques Museum in the Royal Palace, Stockholm. (Photo Wolfgang Sauber)

term *ethne*, 'nations, Gentile' in Paul's rhetorical flourishes in Galatians (1:16; 2:8, etc.). Lopez argues that '*ethne*' must not be read as indicating the opposite to Israel or Jews as a religious category (designating non-Jews); instead, it should be seen within the ideological and political context of the Roman Empire and as a broader social category. Lopez's thesis is that Paul, with his mission to the Gentiles, identifies with the oppressed peoples and that his gospel represents a counter-image to Roman imperial ideology.

PAUL AND THE PHILOSOPHERS

The readings of Paul we have looked at so far may be described as readings 'from this place', where meaning is derived through an interaction between the questions raised by the location of the reader and the historical texts under investigation. Many of these locations are found within religious contexts, typically Christian or Jewish, where Paul has traditionally been placed. That there is now a strong interest in Paul outside of these religious contexts is significant, not least of which is the sustained recent interest by Western philosophers.[35] Central to this new trend are a number of left-leaning and Marxist thinkers, for instance Jacob Taubes, Alain Badiou and Slavoj Zizek (see Further Reading). While Taubes reads Paul from a Jewish and political perspective, it is characteristic of the others that they read Paul from their interest in universalism; consider the title of Badiou's book, *St. Paul: the Foundation of Universalism*.[36] A central text in this book is the well-known Galatians 3:28: 'There is no longer Jew or Greek, there is no longer slave or free, there is no longer male and female'. For Badiou, political change can be initiated by a decisive event, and it is this category he applies to Paul when he sees his presentation of the resurrection of Christ as an event that is important for contemporary politics. For Badiou 'life and death' in Paul are allegories of the human condition, where death is represented by world capitalism and, maybe surprisingly, identity politics (for example women's rights, gay rights, etc.), which only claim rights for themselves without any concern for truth. There is therefore a need for something which is truly universal. In contrast to the Greek figure of the philosopher (who speaks of wisdom) or the Jewish prophet (who speaks of law), Paul introduces a new figure, the apostle, who speaks of truth and life. The Christ event has abolished Greek and Jew, which are symbols of identity differences, and established an absolute and true universal.

It must be said that these philosophers pay little attention to recent New Testament scholarship on Paul. Most of their references are to older literature which still worked with stereotypes of Judaism as 'particular' and Christianity as 'universal'. Not surprisingly, therefore, their readings of Paul have met with criticism from biblical scholars, especially from those associated with the new perspective on Paul, whether in its moderate or radical incarnation: a universalism that is founded on the destruction of the Jewish identity is deemed unacceptable.[37] However, this criticism should not detract from the fact that the philosophers have brought back Paul as a central figure in discussions of what it is to be human and how to create a truly universal society and, in doing so, have recaptured something of the revolutionary potential of his writings, which was in danger of being lost in the understandable attempt to modify his perceived conflict with his own Jewish tradition.

CONCLUSION

The changes that we have seen in the reading of Paul's letters illustrate many of the changes in New Testament studies in general. The hegemony of the historical-critical method carried with it the ideal of the objective scholar who, by following this method, could establish the historical meaning of New Testament writings, as well as the intention of the author. The understanding that we all read 'from this place' has fundamentally changed the landscape of New Testament interpretation. It has changed the relationship between centre and periphery in many ways, most fundamentally in the way that we cannot any longer distinguish between a universal, authoritative interpretation at a political and academic centre and a contextual – that is, less universal – interpretation in peripheries consisting of 'the others'. In addition, scholars at 'the centre' must realise that we all perform contextual interpretation, shaped by the places that influence our readings.

The advantage of accepting our own 'placedness', is that we become more aware that the New Testament writings are also placed in a specific time and context. For instance, post-colonial and empire-critical readings, to a large extent, reflect experiences of readers who have lived under empires or postcolonial conditions and who are critical of the way New Testament writings have been used to support positions of authority and power. But a more serious problem is that not only the interpreters, but the New Testament texts themselves may present positions that are deemed unacceptable. The criticism of the images of Jews in many New Testament texts is a well-known and accepted case; more controversial cases have been the ideology regarding women or the rejection of same sex acts. It is possible to understand these views in their original, historical context but, if interpretation shall include hermeneutics – that is, bring the texts into a contemporary context – they must be exposed to moral criticism.

On the other hand, by being placed in a different context, ancient texts may receive new relevance. This is characteristic of the new interest in Paul among philosophers, who read Paul not primarily within a religious context, but for his contributions to political philosophy. They find in Paul a resource for their work to create a universal society. This usage suggests that Paul's letters – as well as other New Testament writings – are not confined only to a religious world. They belong to world literature and, perhaps to the surprise of professional biblical scholars, many readers outside religious groups find them relevant in discussions about the future of humanity.

Conclusion

WHERE IS THE FUTURE OF THE NEW TESTAMENT?

This book began with the claim that the New Testament was a small book that had changed the world. I don't know if you as a reader have been convinced by my attempts to substantiate that claim but, at the very least, we may say that the New Testament has participated in many of the changes that have happened in the world. And it has become obvious, I hope, that we can only speak of the New Testament as it has been read, interpreted and used by people in specific contexts and times. The history of the readings of the New Testament shows how they have been integrated into their contemporary cultural, political and religious contexts.

This history of the New Testament is obviously written from the perspectives and experiences of the West, and that represents a limitation within a global world. In *The New faces of Christianity: Believing the Bible in the Global South*,[1] Philip Jenkins has reminded us that the demographic centre of Christianity is shifting towards the South, to Latin America, Africa and South-East Asia. Particularly in the latter two regions, the absolute authority of Scripture shapes the way in which biblical texts are used. Christians in the global South often have an immediate rapport with the Bible since many of them live in oral cultures and experience the Bible as coming from a similar culture. The similarities cover a broad range of areas, in world views, social mores and gender roles, as well as in the challenges of life in terms of poverty, illness and demon possessions. This also affects the study of the New Testament, with a closer contact between human experiences and academic interpretations, less influenced by Enlightenment and secularisation. And, from the demographic predominance of Christians in the South, in the future the greatest readership and impact of the New Testament will be found there.

I find it sobering to reflect upon the scenario that Jenkins opened up; it is salutary that Western scholars and readers recognise that we will lose the hegemony of New Testament interpretation, just as Britain gradually lost its Empire. What we should learn from the South is to read the New Testament not as a private text, for the religious individual only, but as writings that address communities living in and interacting with a larger society.

In a time and context where Christianity can no longer be taken for granted as a system of belief, the stories and parables, the sayings of Jesus and letters of Paul have a unique possibility to create images with which people can identify and enter into dialogue. One example is the 'new' philosophers, who find in Paul's letters a radical advocacy of a politics of universalism in today's world. Another is the way in which stories about Jesus may be used as models with which to identify for those individuals and groups who experience discrimination. These are examples of how readers may engage with the New Testament not just as a historic artifact, but as a text dealing with 'real life'.

One of the purposes of this book has been to enable readers to become active dialogue partners with the New Testament. One of the new approaches to study of the New Testament, reader-response criticism, with its emphasis on the role and responsibility of the reader, illustrates this goal. A text is not an object that has its meaning in itself, and a reader is not a passive recipient of meanings that an author has placed in the text. Rather, a reader has an active role, and meaning is created in the interaction between the text and the reader. If this book has helped to establish such a dialogue between readers and the text, it has fulfilled its task.

Further reading

INTRODUCTION

Bart D. Ehrman, *The New Testament: A Historical Introduction to the Early Christian Writings*, 5th ed. (New York, NY: Oxford University Press, 2012). This is the all-time bestseller; large, comprehensive, well written.

Dale B. Martin, *New Testament History & Literature* (New Haven, CT: Yale University Press, 2012): an explicitly historical introduction to the New Testament writings.

Luke Timothy Johnson, *The Writings of the New Testament: An Interpretation*, 3rd ed. (Minneapolis, MN: Fortress, 2010): a literary and theological introduction.

FROM JESUS TO THE GOSPELS

E. P. Sanders, *The Historical Figure of Jesus* (London: Allen Lane, 1993), a classic study of the historical Jesus. Among the many studies of Jesus in his Galilean context, see Jonathan L. Reed, *Archaeology and the Galilean Jesus: a re-examination of the evidence* (Harrisburg, PA: Trinity Press International, 2000).

1: BECOMING CHRISTIANS – LETTER WRITING AS COMMUNITY FORMATION.

On letter writing

William G. Doty, *Letters in primitive Christianity* (Philadelphia, PA: Fortress, 1973), a brief introduction to Hellenistic letter writing.

Stanley Stowers, *Letter Writing in Greco-Roman Antiquity* (Philadelphia, PA: Westminster, 1986). Stowers places Early Christian letters in their wider contexts and presents the different types of letters in Greco-Roman letter writing.

E. Randolph Richards, *Paul and First-Century Letter Writing: Secretaries, Composition and Collection* (Downers Grove, IL: InterVarsity Press, 2004), is good on the practical aspects of letter writing.

Hans-Josef Klauck, *Ancient Letters and the New Testament: A Guide to Context and Exegesis* (Waco, TX: Baylor University Press, 2006). This is a well-documented book with large bibliographies for the advanced student.

On Paul's letters

See suggestions under Chapter 9 for books on methods and theories for studies on Paul's letters.

Halvor Moxnes

Wayne A. Meeks and John T. Fitzgerald (eds), *The Writings of St Paul: Annotated Texts, Reception and Criticism*, Norton Critical Editions 2nd ed. (New York, NY: W.W. Norton, 2007). In addition to the Pauline letters the book includes the history of interpretation, as well as modern approaches by well-known scholars.

Wayne A. Meeks, *The First Urban Christians: The Social World of the Apostle Paul* (New Haven, CT: Yale University Press, 1983). A classic early study of Paul's letters in their social Hellenistic context.

David Horrell, *An introduction to the study of Paul* (Edinburgh: T&T Clark, 2006).

J. Paul Sampley (ed.), *Paul in the Greco-Roman World: A Handbook* (Harrisburg, PA: Trinity: 2003).

Stephen Westerholm (ed.), *The Blackwell Companion to Paul* (Oxford: Blackwell, 2011).

Amy-Jill Levine (ed.) with Marianne Blickenstaff, *A Feminist Companion to Paul* (Sheffield: Sheffield Academic Press, 2004).

Amy-Jill Levine (ed.) with Marianne Blickenstaff, *A Feminist companion to the Deutero-Pauline Epistles* (Sheffield: Sheffield Academic Press, 2004).

Discussion of individual letters

Karl P. Donfried (ed.), *The Romans debate*, rev and exp. ed. (Peabody, MA: Hendrickson, 2001).

Mark D. Nanos (ed.), *The Galatians debate: Contemporary issues in rhetorical and historical interpretation* (Peabody, MA: Hendrickson, 2002).

2: MEMORY AND IDENTITY: THE GOSPELS AS JESUS-BIOGRAPHIES

Orality

Werner H. Kelber, *The Oral and the Written Gospel: The Hermeneutics of Speaking and Writing in the Synoptic Tradition, Mark, Paul, and Q* (Philadelphia, PA: Fortress, 1983). This book initiated oral studies of the gospels. For an evaluation of contemporary studies, see Tom Thatcher (ed.), *Jesus, the Voice and the Text: Beyond the Oral and the Written Gospel* (Waco, TX: Baylor University Press, 2008). For studies of orality in contemporary societies, see Jonathan A. Draper (ed.), *Orality, Literacy, and Colonialism in Southern Africa* (Atlanta, GA: Society of Biblical Literature, 2003).

Genre and content

Richard A. Burridge, *What are the Gospels? A Comparison with Graeco-Roman Biography*, 2nd ed. (Grand Rapids, MI: Eerdmans, 2004). An influential study of the gospels as biographies.

For an introduction to all the gospels, as well as the historical Jesus, see the excellent presentation by Graham Stanton, *The Gospels and Jesus* 2nd ed. (Oxford: Oxford University Press, 2002).

Individual gospels

David Rhoads, J. Dewey and D. Michie, *Mark as Story: An Introduction to the Narrative of a Gospel* (Minneapolis, MN: Fortress 1999/ 2012).

Mary Ann Tolbert, *Sowing the Gospel: Mark's World in Literary–Historical Perspective* (Minneapolis, MN: Fortress, 1996).

John S. Kloppenborg, *Q, the Earliest Gospel: An Introduction to the Earliest Stories and Sayings of Jesus* (Louisville, KY: Westminster John Knox, 2008).

Graham Stanton, *A Gospel for a New People: Studies in Matthew* (Edinburgh: T&T Clark, 1992).

Halvor Moxnes, *The Economy of the Kingdom: Social Conflicts and Economic Relations in Luke's Gospel* (Philadelphia, PA: Fortress, 1988).

Turid Karlsen Seim, *The Double Message: Patterns of Gender in Luke-Acts* (Edinburgh: T & T Clark, 1994).

R. Alan Culpepper, *Anatomy of the Fourth Gospel. A Study in Literary Design* (Philadelphia, PA: Fortress, 1983).

3: ACTS AND APOCALYPSE – AMBIVALENT LIVING UNDER THE ROMAN EMPIRE

Acts

Peter Oakes (ed.), *Rome in the Bible and the Early Church* (Grand Rapids, MI: Baker, 2002); highlights attitudes to Rome in the early Church, especially in Luke and Paul.

Loveday Alexander (ed.), 'Images of Empire' *Journal for the Study of the Old Testament*, Supplement series 122 (Sheffield: Sheffield Academic Press, 1991); introductions to how the Roman Empire was viewed by Jewish and Early Christian writers, reading Acts as partly copying Roman imperial ideology.

David Rhoads, David Esterline and Jae Won Lee (eds), *Luke-Acts and Empire: Essays in honor of Robert L. Brawley* (Eugene, OR: Wipf and Stock, 2011); these essays read Luke-Acts as critical of the Roman Empire.

The Apocalypse

Stephen D. Moore, *Empire and Apocalypse: Postcolonialism and the New Testament* (Sheffield: Sheffield Phoenix Press, 2006); argues that resistance to Roman imperial ideology actually mimicked the Empire in important respects.

Steven J. Friesen, *Imperial Cults and the Apocalypse of John: Reading Revelation in the Ruins* (Oxford: Oxford University Press, 2001), reads the Apocalypse in light of the history and archaeology of imperial cults.

4: INCLUDED OR EXCLUDED: WHEN WAS THE NEW TESTAMENT CREATED?

Apocryphal gospels

Bart D. Ehrman, *Lost Scriptures: Books that did not make it into the New Testament* (New York, NY: Oxford University Press, 2003).

Helmut Koester, *Ancient Christian Gospels: Their History and Development* (London: SCM, 1990).

Stephen J. Patterson and James M. Robinson, *The Fifth Gospel: The Gospel of Thomas Comes of Age* (Harrisburg, PA: Trinity, 1989).

Collections of texts

J. K. Elliott (ed.), *The Apocryphal New Testament* (Oxford: Clarendon Press, 1993).

Robert J. Miller (ed.), *The Complete Gospels: Annotated Scholars Version* (Sonoma, CA: Polebridge, 1992).

James M. Robinson (ed.), *The Nag Hammadi Library in English*, 3rd rev. ed. (Leiden: Brill, 1988).

On the diversity of Early Christianity

Walter Bauer (trans. R.A. Kraft and G. Krodel), *Orthodoxy and Heresy in Earliest Christianity*, (Philadelphia, PA: Fortress, 1971[1934]).

Bart D. Ehrman, *Lost Christianities: The Battles for Scripture and the Faiths we Never Knew* (Oxford/New York, NY: Oxford University Press, 2003).

Karen L. King, *What is Gnosticism?* (Cambridge, MA / London: Harvard University Press, 2003).

The canonisation process of the New Testament

Bruce M. Metzger, *The Canon of the New Testament: Its Origin, Development, and Significance* (Oxford: Clarendon Press, 1987); a classic account.

Lee Martin MacDonald and James A. Sanders (eds), *The Canon Debate* (Peabody, MA: Hendrickson, 2000); the most comprehensive discussion of the canonisation process.

Joseph Verheyden, 'The New Testament canon' in James Carleton Paget and Joachim Schaper (eds), *The New Cambridge History of the Bible vol. I: From the Beginnings to 600* (Cambridge: Cambridge University Press, 2012), pp. 389–411; the most recent general overview.

In support of the 'conspiracy theory': Bart D. Ehrman, *Lost Christianities*, and Lee Martin McDonald, *The Formation of the Christian Biblical Canon* (Nashville, TN: Abingdon, 1988).

See a lively criticism of this theory: C. E. Hill, *Who Chose the Gospels? Probing the Great Gospel Conspiracy* (Oxford: Oxford University Press, 2010).

5: 'CHRISTIANITY GOES TO PRESS'. THE COMMUNICATION HISTORY OF THE NEW TESTAMENT

On the early history of the production, textual history, translations and spread of the New Testament, see James Carleton Paget and Joachim Schaper (eds), *The New Cambridge History of the Bible vol. I: From the Beginnings to 600* (Cambridge: Cambridge University Press, 2013).

Robert F. Hull Jr., *The Story of the New Testament Text: Movers, Materialism, Motives, Methods, and Models* (Atlanta, GA: Society of Biblical Literature, 2010).

Larry W. Hurtado, *The Earliest Christian Artifacts: Manuscripts and Christian Origins* (Grand Rapids, MI: Eerdmans, 2006).

Bart D. Ehrman, *The Orthodox Corruption of Scripture: The Effect of Early Christological Controversies on the Text of the New Testament* (New York / Oxford: Oxford University Press, 1993).

Bruce M. Metzger and Bart D. Ehrman, *The Text of the New Testament: Its Transmission, Corruption, and Restoration* (New York, NY: Oxford University Press, 2005).

David C. Parker, *Textual Scholarship and the Making of the New Testament* (Oxford: Oxford University Press, 2012).

For the history of modern translations and their cultural and political role, see R.S. Sugirtharajah, *The Bible and the Third World: Precolonial, Colonial and Postcolonial Encounters* (Cambridge: Cambridge University Press, 2001).

Hannibal Hamlin and Norman W. Jones (eds), *The King James Bible after 400 Years: Literary, Linguistic, and Cultural Influences* (Cambridge: Cambridge University Press, 2010).

6: '. . . THEIR EYES WERE OPENED AND THEY RECOGNISED HIM'. GLIMPSING RECEPTIONS OF THE JESUS STORY

The focus in this chapter has been on how 'ordinary people' might receive the New Testament stories, through their participation in liturgies, in churches and in pilgrimages. See the footnotes to this chapter for literature I have found useful. I have not followed the more common approach of presenting individual artists, writers, musicians etc. who have interpreted New Testament narratives and figures, and how these re-presentations have moved outside a church context and become integrated parts in cultural and secular contexts. Therefore I list a few books that introduce these various fields.

John Drury, *Painting the Word: Christian Pictures and their Meanings* (New Haven, CT: Yale University Press, 1999), beautifully contextualises paintings from the Medieval to Early Modern periods within their Christian world views, and teaches modern spectators to see their meanings. The catalogue for the exhibition *Seeing Salvation* at the National Gallery in London, *The Image of Christ*, by Gabriele Finaldi *et al.* (London: National Gallery, 2000), addresses the challenges faced by artists, from earliest times to the late-twentieth century, when representing Jesus as God who became man. Vocal and instrumental music has travelled along the same route, starting in churches and monastic liturgies, to become an integral part of the repertoire of choirs and orchestras, and spanning many different musical forms. Tim Dowley, *Christian Music: A Global History* (Oxford: Lion, 2011), gives a fascinating overview of Christian music from the earliest times to today, and covers all continents. New Testament (Bible) and literature is a theme which it is impossible to cover satisfactorily, but the interested reader should begin with the seminal book by Northrop Frye, *The Great Code: The Bible and Literature* (London: Routledge and Kegan Paul, 1982), which presents a study of the Bible from the point of view of a literary critic. David Jasper and Stephen Prickett (eds), *The Bible and Literature: A Reader* (Oxford: Blackwell, 1999), presents comments or reflections upon some of the best known New Testament passages by (mostly) English authors.

Since the beginning of film-making more than 100 years ago, films about Jesus have been very popular. For an overview of studies of these films, see W. Barnes Tatum, *Jesus at the Movies: A Guide to the First Hundred Years*, 2nd ed. (Santa Rosa, CA: Polebridge Press, 2000). Adele Reinhartz, *Jesus of Hollywood* (Oxford: Oxford University Press, 2007), views the representations of Jesus and other figures in the gospels in films from the perspective of a New Testament scholar. Lloyd Bauch, *Imagining the Divine: Jesus and Christ-Figures in Film* (Franklin, WI: Sheed and Ward, 2000), gives a theological and aesthetic evaluation not only of Jesus films, but also of films that picture (often hidden) images of Christ.

7: RACE, CLASS AND GENDER 'IN CHRIST'? THE AMBIGUOUS RECEPTION HISTORY OF GALATIANS 3:28

John Riches, *Galatians Through the Centuries* (Oxford: Blackwell, 2008), in the Blackwell series on reception history, focuses on major commentaries and theologians from Antiquity to the twentieth century.

For collections of sources from ancient commentaries on Galatians, see Mark J. Edwards (ed.) *Galatians, Ephesians, Philippians*, Ancient Christian Commentary on Scripture: NT VIII (Downers Grove, IL: InterVarsity, 1999). Martin Luther's famous commentaries, in English translation, are printed in *Lectures on Galatians 1535, Chapter1–4*, and *Chapters 5–6 (1535)* and *Chapters 1–6 (1519)*, in J. Pelikan (ed.), *Luther's Works* vols. 26–27 (St. Louis, MO : Concordia, 1963).

There is an enormous amount of literature on the three main areas of identities referred to in Galatians 3:28: ethnicity and race, slavery, and gender, so it is possible to list only a few:

On the formation of early Christianity among Jews, Greeks and Romans, see Judith Lieu, *Neither Jew nor Greek?: Constructing early Christianity* (London: T&T Clark, 2002); Denise Kimber Buell, *Why this New Race: Ethnic Reasoning in Early Christianity* (New York, NY: Columbia University Press 2005).

For the history of the relations between Christians and Jews through history, see Charlotte Klein, *Anti-Judaism in Christian Theology* (Philadelphia, PA: Fortress, 1978). For individual theologians, see Paula Fredriksen, *Augustine and the Jews: A Christian Defense of Jews and Judaism* (New York, NY: Doubleday, 2008); B. Schramm and K.I. Stjerna (eds), *Martin Luther, the Bible, and the Jewish People: A Reader* (Minneapolis, MN: Fortress, 2012).

For recent books on slavery in Early Christianity, see Jennifer A. Glancy, *Slavery in Early Christianity* (Oxford: Oxford University Press, 2002) and J. Albert Harrill, *Slaves in the New Testament: Literary, Social and Moral Dimensions* (Minneapolis, MN: Fortress, 2006). Harrill also discusses slavery in nineteenth-century USA.

For a discussion of slavery from an African–American position, see R.C. Bailey (ed.), *Yet with a Steady Beat: Contemporary U.S. Afrocentric Biblical Interpretation*, Semeia Studies 42, (Atlanta, GA: Society of Biblical Literature, 2003). For religion and modern forms of slavery, see Bernadette J. Brooten (ed.), with assistance of J. L. Hazelton, *Beyond Slavery: Overcoming its Religious and Sexual Legacies* (New York, NY: Palgrave McMillan, 2010).

For discussion of models for understanding gender, see Thomas Laqueur, *Making Sex: Body and Gender from the Greeks to Freud* (Cambridge, MA: Harvard University Press, 1990); for the Judeo-Christian tradition, see Kari E. Børresen (ed.), *The Image of God: Gender Models in Judaeo-Christian Tradition,* (Minneapolis, MN: Fortress, 1995). For the history of gender in Galatians 3:28, For the history of gender in Gal 3:28, see Pauline Nigh Hogan, *"No longer Male and Female": Interpreting Galatians 3.28 in Early Christianity'*, Library of New Testament Studies 380 (London, New York: T & T Clark, 2008), and for the modern discussion, Dale B. Martin, *Sex and the Single Savior: Gender and Sexuality in Biblical Interpretation* (Louisville, KY: Westminster John Knox, 2006).

For modern interpretations of Gal 3:28 see Hans Dieter Betz, *Galatians: A Commentary on Paul's Letter to the Churches in Galatia,* Hermeneia (Philadelphia, PA: Fortress, 1979). Richard N. Longenecker, *New Testament Social Ethics for Today* (Grand Rapids, MI: Eerdmans, 1984), makes Galatians 3:28 the centre for a presentation of a New Testament social ethics. The classic feminist perspective on Gal 3:28 is Elisabeth

Schüssler Fiorenza, *In Memory of Her: A feminist theological reconstruction of Christian origins* (London: SCM,1983).

8: HISTORICAL READINGS: HOW MODERNITY SHAPED NEW TESTAMENT SCHOLARSHIP

Reviews of historical critical scholarship from its beginning:

Robert M. Grant with David Tracy, *A Short History of the Interpretation of the Bible*. 2nd rev. ed. (London: SCM, 198). A popular book that covers the history from the beginning until 1980.

William Baird, *History of New Testament Research, Vol 1: From Deism to Tübingen, Vol 2: From Jonathan Edwards to Rudolf Bultmann*, (Minneapolis, MN: Fortress, 1992);

W.G. Kümmel, *The New Testament: The History of the Investigation of Its Problems*, 2nd ed. (Nashville: Abingdon, 1972).

John Riches, *A Century of New Testament Study* (Cambridge: Lutterworth, 1993), covers the last 100 years.

Editions of the Synoptic Gospels in English tranlations

Kurt Aland (ed.), *Synopsis of the four Gospels: Greek–English edition of the Synopsis Quattuor Evangeliorum* (Stuttgart: German Bible Society, 2001).

R. W. Funk (ed.), *New Gospel Parallels* (Sonoma, CA: Polebridge Press, 1990), English, includes also apocryphal gospels.

Zeba A. Crook (trans.), *Parallel Gospels: A Synopsis of Early Christian Writing* (New York / Oxford: Oxford University Press, 2011).

Historical Jesus Scholarship

Translations of classic works from the nineteenth century:

Ernest Renan, *Life of Jesus* (Amherst, NY: Prometheus Books, 1991 [1863]).

Friedrich Schleiermacher, *The Life of Jesus* (with an introduction by Jack C. Verheyden) (Philadelphia, PA: Fortress, 1975 [1864]).

David Friedrich Strauss, *The Life of Jesus, Critically Examined*, 2 vols. (Cambridge: Cambridge University Press, 2010 [1835–6]).

Albert Schweitzer, *The Quest of the Historical Jesus*, trans. of 2nd German ed., Edited by John Bowden, (Minneapolis: Fortress, 2001 (1913), the classic study of Jesus scholarship, primarily German, in the nineteenth century, and one of the most influential theological books in the twentieth century.

Gregory W. Dawes, *The Historical Jesus Question: The Challenge of History to Religious Authority* (Louisville, KY: Westminster John Knox, 2001), in depth presentations of important scholars from Spinoza to Bultmann. A companion volume to the collection of sources in:

Gregory W. Dawes (ed.), *The Historical Jesus Quest: Landmarks in the Search for the Jesus of History* (Louisville, KY: Westminster John Knox, 2000).

Wayne A. Meeks, *Christ is the Question* (Louisville, KY: Westminster John Knox, 2006), a brief introduction to the history of the quest for the historical Jesus.

H. Moxnes, *Jesus and the Rise of Nationalism: A New Quest for the Nineteenth Century Historical Jesus* (London: I.B.Tauris, 2012); nineteenth century Jesus scholarship in light of the ideologies of nationalism in Europe.

For Jewish Jesus scholarship in the nineteenth century, see

Susannah Heschel, *Abraham Geiger and the Jewish Jesus* (Chicago, IL: Chicago University Press, 1998).

For modern Jesus studies, see especially Geza Vermes, *Jesus the Jew: A historian's Reading of the Gospels* (London: SCM Press, 1983)

———*The Religion of Jesus the Jew* (London: SCM Press, 1993).

Paula Fredriksen, *From Jesus to Christ: The Origins of the New Testament Images of Jesus*, 2nd ed. (New Haven, CT: Yale University Press, 2000).

Introduction to historical and literary readings

The series *Guides to Biblical Scholarship* that Fortress Press started in the 1970s has a number of short introductions that are still worth reading; see Edgar Krentz, *The Historical–Critical Method* (1975); Edgar V. McKnight, *What is form criticism?* (1969); Norman Perrin, *What is redaction criticism?* (1969); Mark Allan Powell, *What is Narrative Criticism?* (1990). See also the general introductions to methods in the next chapter.

9: 'READING FROM THIS PLACE'. PAUL IN RECENT INTERPRETATIONS

The diversity of methods and perspectives used in the interpretation of the New Testament comes to the fore in James G. Crossley, *Reading the New Testament: Contemporary Approaches* (London: Routledge, 2010), and Paula Gooder, *Searching for Meaning: An Introduction to Interpreting the New Testament* (London: SPCK, 2008). There are helpful introductions to methods for individual writings, for example Janice Capel Anderson and Stephen D. Moore, *Mark and Method: New Approaches in Biblical Studies*, 2nd ed. (Minneapolis, MN: Fortress. 2008).

Magnus Zetterholm focuses on readings of the 'New' Jewish Paul in his *Approaches to Paul: A Student's Guide to Recent Scholarship* (Minneapolis, MN: Fortress, 2009); a broader range of approaches is presented in Joseph A. Marchal (ed.), *Studying Paul's Letters: Contemporary Perspectives and Methods* (Minneapolis, MN: Fortress, 2012).

Classic books on the 'New Paul' are Krister Stendahl, *Paul among Jews and Gentiles and Other Essays* (Philadelphia, PA: Fortress, 1976) and E.P. Sanders, *Paul and Palestinian Judaism: A Comparison of Patterns of Religion* (London: SCM, 1977). Daniel Boyarin engages with the issues of ethnicity and gender from a post-modern Jewish perspective in *A*

Radical Jew: Paul and the Politics of Identity (Berkeley, CA: University of California Press, 1994).

Contrast the 'ultra-new' perspective in Pamela Eisenbaum, *Paul Was Not a Christian: The Original Message of a Misunderstood Apostle* (San Fransisco, CA: HarperOne, 2009) with the sociological and theological interpretation in Francis Watson, *Paul, Judaism and the Gentiles: Beyond the New Perspective* (Grand Rapids, MI: Eerdmans, 2007).

For studies of Paul within a Hellenistic context, with sociological approaches, see Gerd Theissen, *The Social Setting of Pauline Christianity: Essays on Corinth* (Philadelphia, PA: Fortress, 1982), and Wayne A. Meeks, *The First Urban Christians: The Social World of the Apostle Paul* (New Haven, CT: Yale University Press, 1983). On social-scientific methods in general, see John H. Elliott, *What is Social-Scientific Criticism?* (Minneapolis, MN: Augsburg Fortress, 1993). For the growing field of studies on early Christian families, see Carolyn Osiek and D.L. Balch, *Families in the New Testament World* (Louisville, KY: Westminster John Knox, 1997); and Carolyn Osiek, Margaret Y. MacDonald with Janet H. Tulloch, *A Woman's Place: House Churches in Earliest Christianity* (Minneapolis, MN: Fortress, 2006).

For the philosophical context of Paul, especially Stoicism, see the studies by Troels Engberg-Pedersen (ed.), *Paul and his Hellenistic Context* (Minneapolis, MN: Fortress, 1995), and the sole-authored, *Paul and the Stoics* (Edinburgh: T&T Clark, 2000), and *Cosmology and Self in the Apostle Paul: the Material Spirit* (Oxford: Oxford University Press, 2010).

The classic feminist study is Elisabeth Schüssler Fiorenza, *In Memory of Her: A feminist theological reconstruction of Christian origins* (London: SCM,1983). Fiorenza is also editor of a large collaborative feminist project, *Searching the Scriptures, vol. 1: A Feminist Introduction*, and *vol. 2, A Feminist Commentary* (London: SCM, 1994–5). T & T Clark (now Bloomsbury) has a series called *The Feminist Companion to the New Testament and Early Christian Writings*, edited by Amy-Jill Levine with Marianne Blickenstaff, with volumes on Luke (2002), John (2003), Paul (2004), and Acts of the Apostles (2004).

For introductions to the empire-critical approaches see Warren Carter, *The Roman Empire and the New Testament: An Essential Guide* (Nashville, TN: Abingdon, 2006); Richard A. Horsley (ed.), *In the Shadow of Empire: Reclaiming the Bible as a History of Faithful Resistance*, (Louisville, KY / London: Westminster John Knox, 2008).

For post-colonial readings of the Bible, see Musa W. Dube, *Postcolonial Feminist Interpretation of the Bible* (St. Louis, MO: Chalice Press, 2000), and R.S. Sugirtharajah, *Exploring Postcolonial Biblical Criticism: History, Method, Practice* (Oxford: Wiley-Blackwell, 2012); specifically on Paul, see Brigitte Kahl, *Galatians Re-Imagined: Reading with the Eyes of the*

Vanquished (Minneapolis, MN: Fortress, 2010), and Christopher D. Stanley (ed.), *The Colonised Apostle: Paul Through Postcolonial Eyes* (Minneapolis, MN: Fortress, 2011).

For an introduction to recent readings of Paul by modern philosophers, see John D. Caputo and Linda Martin Alcoff (eds.), *St. Paul Among the Philosophers* (Bloomington, IND: Indiana University Press, 2009), and Ward Blanton and Hent de Vries (eds), *Paul and the Philosophers* (New York, NY: Fordham University Press, 2013). For important studies by individual philosophers, see A. Badiou, *Saint Paul: The Foundation of Universalism* (Stanford, CA: Stanford University Press, 2003); J. Taubes, *The Political Theology of St. Paul* (Stanford, CA: Stanford University Press, 2004); and Slavoj Žižek, *The Fragile Absolute: Or, Why is the Christian Legacy Worth Fighting For?* (London / New York, NY: Verso, 2000).

Notes

CHAPTER 1

1 This perspective is inspired by Wayne A. Meeks, *The First Urban Christians: The Social World of the Apostle Paul* (New Haven, CT : Yale University Press, 1983)

2 It is uncertain whether Paul wrote the letter from prison in Ephesus or in Rome. This accounts for the differing hypotheses of dating, either *c.* 56 or *c.* 62.

3 Richards, E. Randolph, *Paul and First-Century Letter Writing: Secretaries, Composition and Collection* (Downers Grove, IL: InterVarsity Press, 2004).

4 Meeks, *First Urban Christians.*

5 For justfication as the centre of Paul's theology, a common Protestant focus, see Rudolf Bultmann, *Theology of the New Testament* (London: SCM, 1974), Ernst Käsemann, *Commentary on Romans* (London: SCM, 1980); for participation or mysticism, see Albert Schweitzer, *The Mysticism of Paul the Apostle,* orig. 1931 (Baltimore, MD: Johns Hopkins University Press, 1998); E.P. Sanders, *Paul and Palestinian Judaism: A Comparison of Patterns of Religion* (London: SCM, 1977).

6 See Margaret M. Mitchell, *Paul and the Rhetoric of Reconciliation: An Exegetical Investigation of the Language and Composition of 1 Corinthians* (Louisville, KY: Westminster John Knox Press, 1993).

7 Titus Livius (trans. B.O. Foster), *Livy in Fourteen Volumes* vol. 1, Book II, xxxii (Cambridge, MA: Harvard University Press, 1988).

8 Plato, *Phaedrus* 279.

9 This is the so-called North Galatians' hypothesis, rather than the larger Roman province of Galatia that extended further South.

10 Karl P. Donfried (ed.), *The Romans Debate* (rev. and exp. ed.) (Peabody, MA: Hendrickson, 2001).

11 Francis Watson, *Paul, Judaism and the Gentiles. Beyond the New Perspective.* (rev. ed.) (Grand Rapids, MI: Eerdmans, 2007).

12 Hans-Josef Klauck, *Ancient Letters and the New Testament. A Guide*

to *Context and Exegesis* (Waco, TX: Baylor University Press, 2006), pp. 399–406.

13 'The Correspondence of Paul and Seneca, ' in J. K. Elliott (ed.), *The Apocryphal New Testament: a collection of apocryphal Christian literature in an English translation* (Oxford: Clarendon Press, 1993), pp. 547–52.

14 Marianne Bjelland Kartzow, *Gossip and Gender: Othering of speech in the Pastoral Epistles*, BZNW 164 (Berlin: De Gruyter, 2009).

15 1 Cor 1:11; 16:19; Rom 16: 2, 5, 6, 7, 12, Phil 4:1–2.

16 See John H. Elliott, *Home for the Homeless: a Socio-Scientific Criticism of I Peter, Situation and Strategy* (Philadelphia, PA: Fortress, 1990).

CHAPTER 2

1 The following section on orality is based on the works of Werner Kelber and subsequent orality studies (see Further reading). I have also learned much about orality and storytelling from my student Zorodzai Dube and his dissertation, 'Storytelling in Times of Violence: Hearing the Exorcism Stories in Zimbabwe and in Mark's Community', PhD thesis, Faculty of Theology, University of Oslo, 2012.

2 That we may now be in the process of leaving the Gutenberg age for the web age is another matter, one more fully acknowledged in Chapter 5.

3 William V. Harris, *Ancient Literacy* (Cambridge, MA: Harvard University Press, 1989), especially pp. 175–284.

4 We know much about the curriculum and the sequence of subjects: primary (reading, writing, reckoning), secondary (grammar and literature), tertiary (philosophy and rhetoric) but less about the schools and age of students (maybe 7–9, 10–14, 15+). Only elite boys went beyond the primary stage; Teresa Morgan, *Literate education in the Hellenistic and Roman worlds* (Cambridge: Cambridge University Press, 1998).

5 For the following see Richard A. Burridge, *What are the Gospels? A Comparison with Graeco-Roman Biography,* 2nd ed. (Grand Rapids, MI / Cambridge: Eerdmans, 2004).

6 See Richard A. Burridge, *Imitating Jesus. An Inclusive Approach to New Testament Ethics* (Grand Rapids, MI/ Cambridge: Eerdmans, 2007).

7 Later in the Gospel, Mark informs the readers about Jesus' occupation and family, 6:3, and the strained relations between his household of origin and Jesus, 3:20–1, 31–4.

8 James M. Robinson, Paul Hoffmann, John S. Kloppenborg, (eds); Milton C. Moreland (main. ed.), *The Critical edition of Q: a synopsis including the Gospels of Matthew and Luke and Thomas with English,*

German, and French translations of Q and Thomas (Minneapolis, MN: Fortress Press, 2000).

9   Sayings in the Q source are identified with their numbering according to Luke.

10 Leif E. Vaage, *Galilean Upstarts: Jesus' first Followers According to Q* (Valley Forge, PA: Trinity, 1994).

11 The classic study is Raymond E. Brown, *The Birth of the Messiah: A Commentary on the Infancy Narratives in the Gospels of Matthew and Luke* (updated ed.) (New York, NY: Doubleday, 1993).

12 Graham Stanton (M. Bockmuehl and D. Lincicum, eds) *Studies in Matthew and Early Christianity*, WUNT 309 (Tübingen: Mohr Siebeck, 2013), especially pp.105–36; Anthony J. Saldarini, *Matthew's Christian-Jewish Community* (Chicago, IL: University of Chicago Press, 1994).

13 John R. Donahue, *The Gospel in Parable: Metaphor, Narrative, and Theology in the Synoptic Gospels* (Philadelphia, PA: Fortress, 1988).

14 For the position argued here, see Turid Karlsen Seim, *The Double Message: Patterns of Gender in Luke-Acts* (Edinburgh: T & T Clark, 1994).

15 For the following, see R. Alan Culpepper, *The Gospel and Letters of John* (Nashville, TN : Abingdon, 1998), pp. 67–86; and in general, R. Alan Culpepper's groundbreaking study, *Anatomy of the Fourth Gospel. A Study in Literary Design* (Philadelphia, PA: Fortress, 1983).

16 Culpepper, *Gospel and Letters of John,* pp. 72–86.

17 'It is finished', used in most English translations, does not communicate the meaning of fulfilled, accomplished, cf. 4:34. Most German translations have *Es ist vollbracht*.

18 Culpepper, *Anatomy of the Fourth Gospel*, pp. 125–32, and *Gospel and Letters of John*, pp. 291–95.

19 Raymond E. Brown, *The Gospel according to John*, vol 2 (London: Chapman, 1978), pp. lxx–lxxv.

CHAPTER 3

1   See a review of various scholarly opinions on this question in Steve Walton, "The state they were in: Luke's view of the Roman Empire', in Peter Oakes (ed.), *Rome in the Bible and the Early Church* (Grand Rapids, MI: Baker, 2002), pp. 1–41.

2   Werner Georg Kümmel, *Introduction to the New Testament* (London: SCM, 1966), pp. 466–8.

CHAPTER 4

1   Dan Brown, *The Da Vinci Code* (New York, NY: Doubleday, 2003).

2   Especially Bart D. Ehrman, *Lost Christianities. The Battles for Scrip-*

ture and the Faiths We Never Knew (New York, NY: Oxford University Press, 2003), and in several others of his books.

3   Eusebius (trans. G.A. Williamson), *The History of the Church from Christ to Constantine*, rev. with a new introduction by Andrew Louth (Harmondsworth: Penguin Books, 1989).

4   See James M. Robinson (ed.), *The Nag Hammadi Library in English*. 3. rev.ed. (Leiden: Brill, 1988).

5   See especially Michael A. Williams, *Rethinking 'Gnosticism': An Argument for Dismantling a Dubious Category* (Princeton, NJ: Princeton University Press, 1996) and Karen L. King, *What is Gnosticism?* (Cambridge, MA and London: Harvard University Press, 2003).

6   Helmut Koester, *Ancient Christian Gospels: Their History and Development* (London: SCM, 1990), p. 46.

7   See, for example, Robert K Miller (ed), *The Complete Gospels: Annotated Scholars Version* (Sonoma, CA: Polebridge, 1992). The difficulty of giving a fixed number is illustrated by J. K. Elliott, *The Apocryphal New Testament* (Oxford: Clarendon Press, 1993); he divides the apocryphal gospels into five groups: lost gospels; fragments of gospels on papyrus; birth and infancy gospels; gospels of ministry and passions; and the Pilate cycle.

8   For these three groups of apocryphal gospels, see Koester, *Ancient Christian Gospels,* pp. 49–112, 173–200, 303–14.

9   Richard Valantasis, *The Gospel of Thomas* (London: Routledge, 1997), pp. 12–15.

10   The text is taken from Robinson, *Nag Hammadi Library,* pp.126–38.

11   The text is taken from Robinson, *Nag Hammadi Library*, pp. 523–31, and is based on Papyrus Berolinensis 8502, 1, a fifth century Coptic codex.

12   Text in Elliott, *Apocryphal New Testament,* pp. 48–67.

13   See Lee Martin McDonald and James A. Sanders (eds), *The Canon Debate* (Peabody, MA: Hendrickson, 2002), especially Harry Y. Gamble, 'The New Testament Canon: Recent research and the Status Quaestionis', pp. 267–94.

14   See C.E. Hill, *Who Chose the Gospels?: Probing the Great Gospel Conspiracy* (Oxford: Oxford University Press, 2010); pp. 70–5.

15   Hill, *Who Chose the Gospels,* pp. 104–12; Bruce M. Metzger, *The Canon of the New Testament* (Oxford: Clarendon Press, 1987), pp. 114–17.

16   Harry Gamble, *The New Testament Canon: Its Making and Meaning* (Philadelphia, PA: Fortress, 1985), pp. 35–46.

17   Lee Martin McDonald, 'Lists and catalogues of New Testament collections,' in McDonald, *The Canon Debate,* pp. 591–7.

18   The *Wisdom of Solomon* and the *Apocalypse of Peter.*

19   Gamble, *New Testament Canon*, pp. 269–70.
20   Lee Martin McDonald, *The Formation of the Christian Biblical Canon* (Nashville, TN: Abingdon, 1988), pp. 110–16.
21   Metzger, *The Canon,* pp. 201–6; Everett R. Kahlin, 'The New Testament Canon of Eusebius,' in McDonald, *The Canon Debate,* pp. 386–404.
22   L. Papadima, D. Damrosch and T.D'haen (eds.), *The Canonical Debate Today: Crossing Disciplinary and Cultural Boundaries* (Amsterdam: Rodopi, 2011). Quotations from L. Papadima, 'Introduction,' pp. 10–11.

PART 2: RECEPTION OF THE NEW TESTAMENT

1   The Centre for Reception History of the Bible (CRHB) at the University of Oxford (http://www.humanities.ox.ac.uk/research/research_centres/crhb; accessed 7 July 2014); Colloquium on the Reception History of the Bible at Duquesne University.
2   Blackwell Bible commentaries, (Oxford: Blackwell); cf. also a series based on comments from early Christian writers, Thomas C. Oden (ed.), *Ancient Christian commentary on Scripture,* 12 vols.,(Downers Grove, IL; InterVarsity, 1998–2007); and H.-J. Klauck (ed.), *The Encyclopedia of the Bible and Its Reception,* planned 30 vols. (Berlin: Walter de Gruyter, 2009–).
3   Ulrich Luz, *Matthew 1–7: A Commentary* (Minneapolis, MN: Fortress, 2007), German original 1985–2002.
4   See C. Rowland and J. Roberts, *The Bible for Sinners: Interpretation in the Present Time* (London: SPCK, 2008).
5   Luz, *Matthew,* p. 95.
6   Heikki Räisänen, 'The Effective History of the Bible', *Scottish Journal of Theology* 45 (1992), pp. 303–24.

CHAPTER 5

1   Edgar Johnson Goodspeed, *Christianity Goes to Press* (New York, NY: Macmillan, 1940).
2   Larry W. Hurtado and Chris Keith, 'Writing and book production in the Hellenistic and Roman periods', in James Carleton Paget and Joachim Schaper (eds)., *The New Cambridge History of the Bible,* vol. I, *From the Beginnings to 600,* (Cambridge: Cambridge University Press, 2013), pp. 62–80; Robert F. Hull Jr., *The Story of the New Testament Text: Movers, Materialism Motives, Methods, and Models* (Atlanta, GA: Society of Biblical Literature, 2010), pp. 7–17.
3   David C. Parker, *Textual Scholarship and the Making of the New Testament* (Oxford: Oxford University Press, 2012), pp. 62–3.
4   Bart D. Ehrman, *The Orthodox Corruption of Scripture: The Effect*

of Early Christological Controversies on the Text of the New Testament (New York and Oxford: Oxford University Press, 1993).

5   Ehrman, *Orthodox Corruption of Scripture*, pp. 54–7.

6   Larry W. Hurtado, *The Earliest Christian Artifacts: Manuscripts and Christian Origins* (Grand Rapids, MI: Eerdmans, 2006) pp. 209–29.

7   Hurtado, *Earliest Christian Artifacts*, pp. 43–93.

8   See Philip Jenkins, *The Lost History of Christianity* (New York, NY: Harper One, 2008); on the early translations into Latin, Syriac and Coptic, the essays by P.-M. Bougaert, P.J. Williams and W. P. Funk in Paget and Schaper, *New Cambridge History of the Bible*, pp. 505–46.

9   Johann Cochlaeus, *Commentaria de Actis et Scriptis M. Luther,*1522 ; quoted from Phillip Schaff, *The German Reformation* AD.*1517–1530* (Edinburgh: T&T Clark, 1888), p. 350.

10   John N. King and Aaron T. Pratt, 'The materiality of English printed Bibles from the Tyndale New Testament to the King James Bible', in Hannibal Hamlin and Norman W. Jones (eds), *The King James Bible after 400 Years: Literary, Linguistic, and Cultural Influences* (Cambridge: Cambridge University Press, 2010), pp. 61–99.

11   R.S. Sugirtharajah, 'Postcolonial notes on the King James Bible', in Hamlin and Jones, *The King James Bible after 400 Years*, pp. 146–63.

12   Kathleen Cann and John Dean (eds), *Sowing the Word: The Cultural Impact of the British and Foreign Bible Society, 1804–2004* (Sheffield: Sheffield Phoenix Press, 2004).

13   Christopher Anderson, *The Annals of the English Bible*, I (London: Pickering, 1845) x–xi, quoted from R.S. Sugirtharajah, *Postcolonial Criticism and Biblical Interpretation* (Oxford: Oxford University Press, 2002), p. 146.

14   See http://megavoice.com/welcome.html; accessed 9 July 2014.

15   For this section, see Hull Jr., *Story of the New Testament*, pp. 39–150; Bruce M. Metzger and Bart D. Ehrman, *The Text of the New Testament: Its Transmission, Corruption, and Restoration* (New York, NY: Oxford University Press, 2005).

16   See the official website of the Sinaiticus project: http://codexsinaiticus.org/en/codex/history.aspx; accessed 7 July 2014.

17   For a discussion of the principles underpinning the decisions made regarding this text, see Michael W. Holmes, 'Reasoned eclecticism in New Testament textual criticism,' in B.E. Ehrman and M.W. Holmes (eds), *The Text of the New Testament in Contemporary Research*, (Grand Rapids, MI: Eerdmans, 1995), pp. 336–60.

18   For the website of the Institute for New Testament Textual Research (Institut für Neutestamentliche Textforschung, INTF) see http://egora.uni-muenster.de/intf/index_en.shtml; accessed 7 July 2014; for that of

The International Greek New Testament Project (IGNTP) see http://www.igntp.org/; accessed 7th July 2014.

19   George Aichele, 'Electronic culture and the future of the canon of scripture', in R. Boer and E. W. Conrad (eds), *Redirected Travel: Alternative Journeys and Places in Biblical Studies* (Sheffield: Sheffield Academic Press, 2003), pp. 8–23.

CHAPTER 6

1   Cf. Paul Zanker, *The Power of Images in the Age of Augustus* (Ann Arbor, MI : The University of Michigan, 1990).

2   For a history of the painting, see Ross King, *Leonardo and the Last Supper* (London: Bloomsbury, 2012).

3   See some of the other Last Supper frescos in Florence monasteries and convents at http://www.everytrail.com/guide/the-last-supper-fresco-tour; accessed 7 July 2014.

4   See some of his most important paintings at http://www.ibiblio.org/wm/paint/auth/caravaggio; accessed 7 July 2014.

5   For this section, see especially Colin Morris, *The Sepulchre of Christ and the Medieval West: From the Beginning to 1600* (Oxford: Oxford University Press, 2005).

6   *Egeria's Travels to the Holy Land,* (trans. with supporting documentation by John Wilkinson), rev. ed. (Jerusalem: Ariel, 1981).

7   Morris, *Sepulchre of Christ,* pp. 58–77.

8   Ibid., pp. 120–7.

9   Ibid., pp. 230–45.

10   Ibid., pp. 245–52.

11   John Bunyan, *The Pilgrim's Progress* (ed. W. R. Owens; Oxford University Press, 2009), see editorial 'Introduction', pp. i–xxxviii.

12   Bunyan, *Pilgrim's Progress,* p. 92.

13   Moxnes, *Jesus and the Rise of Nationalism,* pp. 39–60.

14   Ernest Renan, *The Life of Jesus* (New York, NY: Modern Library, 1927), p. 61.

15   For the following, see Robin Margaret Jensen, *Understanding Early Christian Art* (London and New York, NY: Routledge, 2000); and Robin Margaret Jensen, *Face to Face: Portraits of the Divine in Early Christianity* (Minneapolis, MN: Fortress, 2005).

16   For a good example, see Antonio Ferrua, *The Unknown Catacomb: A Unique Discovery of Early Christian Art* (New Lanark, Scotland: Geddes & Grosset, 1991).

17   See Jeffrey Spier (ed.), *Picturing the Bible: The Earliest Christian Art* (New Haven, CT: Yale University Press, 2007).

18   Gregory I, *Ep.* 13, quoted in Jensen, *Early Christian Art,* pp. 2–3.

19   *Early Christian Art,* pp. 8–31.

20   For the following, see M. A. Michael, *Stained Glass of Canterbury Cathedral* (London: Scala, 2004); especially pp. 1–29, 46–101.

21   C.M. Kauffmann, *Biblical Imagery in Medieval England 700–1550* (London: Harvey Miller, 2003), pp. 76–84.

22   Michael, *Stained Glass*, pp. 52–5.

23   Kauffmann, *Biblical Imagery*, pp. 205–6.

24   Michael, *Stained Glass*, pp. 86–99.

25   Ål stave church; http://www.kunsthistorie.com/fagwiki/%C3%85l_stavkirke; accessed 7 July 2014; Martin Blindheim, *The stave church paintings: Mediaeval Art from Norway* (London: Collins, 1965).

26   A. Salvesen (trans.) and E. Gunnes (intr.), *Gammalnorsk homiliebok* (Oslo: Oslo University Press, 1971).

27   For the following, see Richard Harries, *The Image of Christ in Modern Art* (Farnham, Surrey: Ashgate, 2013), especially pp. 147–56.

28   Ibid., p. 148.

CHAPTER 7

1   Richard N. Longenecker, *New Testament Social Ethics for Today* (Grand Rapids, MI: Eerdmans, 1984), p. 31.

2   Charles Taylor, *Modern Social Imaginaries* (Durham, NC: Duke University Press, 2004), pp. 23–30; the following quotations are from pp.24, 23, 28.

3   Wayne A. Meeks, 'The Image of the Androgyne: Some uses of a symbol in Earliest Christianity', *History of Religion* 13 (1974), pp. 165–208.

4   Marianne B. Kartzow, *Destabilizing the Margins: An Intersectional Approach to early Christian Memory* (Eugene, OR: Wipf & Stock, 2012).

5   Among the earliest were John Chrysostom (347–407), Jerome (347–420) and Augustine (354–430). See quotations from their comments on Galatians 3:28 in Mark J. Edwards (ed.) *Galatians, Ephesians, Philippians*, Ancient Christian Commentary on Scripture: NT VIII (Downers Grove, IL: InterVarsity, 1999), pp.49–50.

6   See the introduction by Elisabeth Schüssler Fiorenza in Laura Nasrallah and Elisabeth Schüssler Fiorenza (eds), *Prejudice and Christian Beginnings: Investigating Race, Gender, and Ethnicity in early Christian Studies*, (Minneapolis, MN: Fortress, 2009), pp. 9–12.

7   'Blessed is God who has made an Israelite (or a Jew) [...] a free person [...] a human being' in A.-J. Levine and M.Z. Brettler (eds), *The Jewish Annotated New Testament* (New York, NY: Oxford University Press, 2011), p. 339.

8   Pauline Nigh Hogan, *"No longer male and female": interpreting*

Galatians 3.28 in early Christianity', Library of New Testament Studies 380 (London / New York, NY: 2008), pp. 98–105.

9   Denise Kimber Buell, *Why this New Race: Ethnic Reasoning in Early Christianity* (New York, NY: Columbia University Press 2005), pp. 94–115.

10 See Charlotte Klein, *Anti-Judaism in Christian Theology* (Philadelphia, PA: Fortress, 1978).

11 Paula Fredriksen, *Augustine and the Jews: A Christian Defense of Jews and Judaism* (New York, NY: Doubleday, 2008), especially pp. 213–59, 290–302, 315–19.

12 Fredriksen, *Augustine*, pp. 318–19.

13 Jennifer A. Glancy, *Slavery in Early Christianity* (Oxford: Oxford University Press, 2002); J. Albert Harrill, *Slaves in the New Testament: Literary, Social and Moral Dimensions* (Minneapolis, MN: Fortress, 2006); Peter Garnsey, *Ideas of Slavery from Aristotle to Augustine* (Cambridge: Cambridge University Press, 1996). Anders Martinsen, PhD student with a thesis on the parables and slavery at the Faculty of Theology, the University of Oslo, has been an important discussion partner on slavery.

14 'The Martyrdom of Perpetua and Felicitas,' in Herbert Musurillo, (ed.), *The Acts of the Christian Martyrs* (Oxford: Clarendon Press, 1972), pp. 106–31.

15 The longer, fourth century spurious version of Ignatius, *'Epistle to the Philadelphians* 4.10', in A. Roberts and J. Donaldson, (eds), *The Ante-Nicene Fathers*, vol. 1, repr. (Grand Rapids, MI: Eerdmans, 1985), p. 81.

16 Stuart G. Hall (ed.), *Gregory of Nyssa, Homilies on Ecclesiastes*, Proceedings of the Seventh International Colloquium on Gregory of Nyssa, (Berlin: de Gruyter, 1993), pp. 72–5; D. Bentley Hart, 'The "whole humanity": Gregory of Nyssa's critique of slavery in light of his eschatology', *Scottish Journal of Theology* 54 (2001), pp. 51–69.

17 Hans Dieter Betz, *Galatians: A Commentary on Paul's Letter to the Churches in Galatia*, Hermeneia (Philadelphia, PA: Fortress, 1979), pp. 195–6.

18 Thomas Laqueur, *Making Sex: Body and Gender from the Greeks to Freud* (Cambridge: Harvard University Press, 1990).

19 John Chrysostom, *Homily 30 on Romans*.

20 Kari Vogt, '"Becoming male": A gnostic and early Christian metaphor', in Kari E. Børresen (ed.), *The Image of God: Gender Models in Judaeo-Christian Tradition* (Minneapolis, MN: Fortress, 1995), pp. 170–86.

21 Martin Luther, *Lectures on Galatians 1535, Ch. 1–4*; Luther's *Works*, vol. 26 (ed. J. Pelikan; St. Louis: Concordia, 1963), pp. 353–54.

22 The quotations in this section are from Luther, *Lectures on Galatians* pp. 354–6.

23 See the introduction by Brooks Schramm in Brooks Schramm and Kirsi I. Stjerna (eds), *Martin Luther, the Bible, and the Jewish People: A Reader* (Minneapolis, MN: Fortress, 2012), pp. 5–16.

24 Luther, *Lectures on Galatians*, p. 356.

25 W.D.J. Cargill Thompson, *The Political Thought of Martin Luther* (Brighton: Harvester, 1984).

26 John Calvin (trans. Kathy Childress), *Sermons on the Galatians* (Edinburgh: The Banner of Truth Trust, 1997 [1563]), p. 352.

27 http://www.vatican.va/roman_curia/congregations/cfaith/pcb_documents/rc_con_cfaith_doc_20020212_popolo-ebraico_en.html; accessed 7 July 2014.

28 Supercessionism: where the Church has replaced Israel with regard to the promises made by God in the Bible.

29 Along parallel lines, the Commission also recognises Jewish readings of the Bible as possible readings along with Christian (Christ-centred) readings of the Old Testament, § 22.

30 See the comments and criticism from the Catholic theologian Dr. Robert A. Cunningham at, http://www.bc.edu/dam/files/research_sites/cjl/texts/cjrelations/resources/articles/PBC_2001_Summary.htm; accessed 7 July 2014.

31 Cf. the Cambridge Inter-Faith Programme which has the aim of 'promoting high quality engagement between Jews, Christians and Muslims, and deeper understanding of the role that Judaism, Christianity and Islam can play in a complexly religious and secular world.' http://www.interfaith.cam.ac.uk/; accessed 7 July 2014.

32 See Phyllis Trible and Letty M. Russell (eds), *Hagar, Sarah & Their Children: Jewish, Christian & Muslim Perspectives* (Louisville,: Westminster John Knox, 2006).

33 *A Narrative of the Life and Labors of the Rev. G. W. Offley*, Hartford, 1859; quoted from Demetrius K. Williams, 'The Bible and models of liberation in African American experience,' in Randall C. Bailey (ed.), *Yet with a Steady Beat: Contemporary U.S. Afrocentric Biblical Interpretation*, Semeia Studies 42, (Atlanta, GA: Society of Biblical Literature, 2003), p. 51.

34 This section owes much to J. Albert Harrill, 'The Use of the New Testament in the American Slave Controversy' in his *Slaves in the New Testament: Literary, Social and Moral Dimensions* (Minneapolis: Fortress, 2006), pp. 65–92.

35 Both Clarkson and Wilberforce are commemorated in the Anglican church, and Gal 3:28 is part of the readings for the commemoration services.

36   William Wells Brown, *Clotel: Or, The President's Daughter: A narrative of Slave Life in the United States* (London: Partridge & Oakey, 1853).

37   Mary McLeod Bethune (1875–1955), in Demetrius K. Williams, 'The Bible and Models of Liberation in African American Experience,' in *Yet with a Steady Beat: Contemporary U.S. Afrocentre Biblical Interpretation*, Semeia Studies 42, R. C. Bailey (ed.), (Atlanta: Society of Biblical Literature, 2003), p. 52.

38   Harrill, *Slaves in the New Testament*, pp. 193–4.

39   See Bernadette J. Brooten (ed.), with assistance of J. L. Hazelton, *Beyond Slavery: Overcoming its Religious and Sexual Legacies* (New York, NY: Palgrave McMillan, 2010).

40   For the following section, I am indebted to Dale B. Martin, *Sex and the Single Savior: Gender and Sexuality in Biblical Interpretation* (Louisville, KY: Westminster John Knox, 2006).

41   Elizabeth Cady Stanton *The Woman's Bible* (Edinburgh: Polygon, 1895). Strangely enough, the Letter to the Galatians is not included in the book.

42   Elisabeth Schüssler Fiorenza, *In Memory of Her* (London: SCM, 1983).

43   Martin, *Sex and the Single Savior*, pp. 81–2.

44   See especially Lone Fatum, 'Image of God and Glory of Man: Women in the Pauline Congregations', in *The Image of God: Gender Models in Judaeo-Christian Tradition*, Kari E. Børresen, (ed.), (Minneapolis: Fortress, 1995).

45   Marianne Bjelland Kartzow, 'Asking the other question': An intersectional approach to Galatians 3:28 and the Colossian household codes', *Biblical Interpretation* 18 (2010), pp. 364–89.

CHAPTER 8

1   See D. Steinmetz, 'The superiority of pre-critical exegesis', in S.E. Fowl (ed.) *The Theological Interpretation of Scripture. Classic and Contemporary Readings* (Oxford: Blackwell, 1997), pp. 26–38.

2   For medieval exegesis, and the fourfold sense of Scripture, see Steinmetz, 'Superiority of pre-critical exegesis' and James S. Preus, *From Shadow to Promise* (Cambridge, MA: Harvard University Press, 1969), pp. 9–149.

3   See the introduction by Mark S. Burrows, to 'Selections from Martin Luther's Sermons on the Sermon on the Mount', in Stephen E. Fowl (ed.) *The Theological Interpretation of Scripture* (Oxford: Blackwell, 1997), pp. 248–52.

4   Jonathan C.P. Birch, "Enlightenment Messiah, 1627–1778. Jesus in History, Morality and Political Theology". (PhD thesis, University of

Glasgow, 2012), p.84. I am grateful to Jonathan Birch who has made his learned and original study available to me. In the following I draw on his study, with its information about a broad range of literature that otherwise had been unknown to me.

5   Scott W. Hahn and Benjamin Wiker, *Politizing the Bible. The Roots of historical Criticism and the Secularization of Scripture* (New York, NY: Crossroad, 2013), pp. 285–338.

6   Klaus Scholder, *The Birth of Modern Critical Theology: Origins and problems of Biblical Criticism in the Seventeenth Century* (London: SCK, 1990), pp. 138–42; Gregory W. Dawes, *The Historical Jesus Question. The Challenge of History to Religious Authority* (Louisville, KY: Westminster John Knox, 2001); pp. 39–75.

7   John Toland, *Christianity Not Mysterious* (1696); Matthew Tindal, *Christianity as Old as Creation* (1730); Thomas Chubb, *The True Gospel of Jesus Christ Asserted: Wherein is Shown What Is and What is Not that Gospel* (1738).

8   German original published by G. E. Lessing 1774–8; For the English translation, see Hermann Samuel Reimarus, *Fragments*, (ed. Charles H. Talbert; Philadelphia: Fortress, 1970).

9   Thomas A. Howard, *Protestant Theology and the Making of the Modern German University* (Oxford: Oxford University Press, 2006), especially pp. 1–35, 130–77.

10   Maurice Olender, *The Languages of Paradise: Aryans and Semites, A Match made in Heaven* (rev. ed.) (New York, NY: Other, 2002).

11   See their Jesus studies under Further Reading.

12   See editions under Further Reading.

13   H.J. Holtzmann, *Die synoptischen Evangelien: ihr Ursprung und geschichtlicher Charakter* (Leipzig: Engelmann, 1863), See William Baird, *History of New Testament Research 2: From Jonathan Edwards to Rudolf Bultmann* (Minneapolis, MN: Fortress, 2003), pp. 111–17.

14   Dawes, *The Historical Jesus Question*, pp. 76–121, esp. pp. 85–97.

15   Moxnes, *Jesus and the Rise of Nationalism*, pp.100–1.

16   See Further Reading.

17   Dawes, *Historical Jesus Question*, pp. 248–96.

18   Moxnes, *Jesus and the Rise of Nationalism*, pp. 121–47.

19   Edward W. Said, *Orientalism* (London: Penguin, 1978).

20   Renan, *Life of Jesus*, p. 226.

21   For a criticism of modern New Testament studies that continue the paradigm of Orientalism, see R.S. Sugirtharajah, *Exploring Postcolonial Biblical Criticism: History, Method, Practice* (Oxford: Wiley-Blackwell, 2012), pp. 94–122.

22   Susannah Heschel, *The Aryan Jesus: Christianity, Nazis and the Bible* (Princeton, NJ: Princeton University Press, 2007); the most prominent

German scholar was Walter Grundmann, who established The Institute for the Study and Elimination of Jewish Influence on German Church Life, cf. especially Walter Grundmann, *Jesus der Galiläer und das Judentum* (Leipzig: Wigand, 1940).

23 Shawn Kelley, *Racializing Jesus: Race, Ideology and the Formation of Modern Biblical Scholarship* (London and New York, NY: Routledge, 2002).

24 A typical example is Günther Bornkamm, *Jesus of Nazareth* (London: Hodder and Stoughton, 1960[German orig.1956]) where he speaks of Judaism at the time of Jesus as 'an empty void'.

25 E.P. Sanders *Jesus and Judaism* (London: SCM, 1985).

26 See list under Further Reading.

27 John Dominic Crossan, *The Historical Jesus: The Life of a Mediterranean Jewish Peasant* (Edinburgh: T & T Clark, 1991).

28 Sean Freyn, *Jesus, a Jewish Galilean: A New Reading of the Jesus Story* (London: T & T Clark, 2004).

29 Baird, *History of New Testament Research* 2, pp. 269–87.

30 Martin Dibelius, (English trans.) *From Tradition to Gospel* (London: Nicholson and Watson, 1934) For the German original, see Martin Dibelius, *Die Formgeschichte des Evangeliums* (1919); See Baird, *History of New Testament Research* 2, pp. 273–9, especially pp. 275–6.

31 Shailer Mathews, *The Social Teaching of Jesus: An Essay in Christian Sociology* (Philadelphia: Fortress, 1971 (New York: Hodder & Stoughton: G. H. Doran Co., 1897), Shailer Mathews, *Jesus on Social Institutions*, (Ed. Kenneth Cauthen; Philadelphia: Fortress, 1971 (New York: Macmillan, 1928).

32 See Norman Perrin, *What is Redaction Criticism?* (London: S.P.C.K., 1970); Marc Goodacre, 'Redaction criticism', in Paula Gooder (ed.) *Searching for Meaning: An Introduction to Interpreting the New Testament*, (London: SPCK, 2008), pp. 38–44.

33 Günther Bornkamm, 'The stilling of the storm in Matthew', in G. Bornkamm, G. Barth and H.J. Held, *Tradition and Interpretation in Matthew* (Philadelphia, PA: Westminster, 1963 [German orig. 1948]), pp. 52–7.

34 See the books by Culpepper and Rhoads et al. in Further Reading to Chapter 2.

CHAPTER 9

1 H. Zimmermann, *Neutestamentliche Methodenlehre: Darstellung der historisch-kritischen Methode* 2nd ed. (Stuttgart: Katholisches Bibelwerk, 1967).

2 Fernando F. Segovia and Mary Ann Tolbert (eds), *Reading from this Place*, 2 vols (Minneapolis, MN: Fortress Press, 1995).

3   R.S. Sugirtharajah, *Exploring Postcolonial Biblical Criticism: History, Method, Practice* (Oxford: Wiley-Blackwell, 2012), p. 2.

4   S.R.F. Price, *Rituals and Power: The Roman Imperial Cult in Asia Minor* (Cambridge: Cambridge University Press, 1983), pp. 7–19.

5   Krister Stendahl, 'The Apostle Paul and the introspective conscience of the West' *Harvard Theological Review* 56 (1963), pp. 199–215.

6   E.P. Sanders, *Paul and Palestinian Judaism: A Comparison of Patterns of Religion* (London: SCM, 1977).

7   Sanders, *Paul and Palestinian Judaism*, p. 75.

8   'The new perspective on Paul,' *Bulletin of the John Rylands University Library of Manchester* 65 (1983), pp. 95–122.

9   For example L. Gaston and S. Stowers (see Magnus Zetterholm *Approaches to Paul: A Student's Guide to recent Scholarship* (Minneapolis, MN: Fortress, 2009), pp. 127–63.

10 Pamela Eisenbaum, *Paul Was Not a Christian* (San Francisco, CA: HarperOne, 2009).

11 Cf. Stephen Westerholm, *Perspectives Old and New on Paul: the 'Lutheran' Paul and his Critics* (Grand Rapids, MI: Eerdmans, 2004).

12 The first edition, Francis Watson, *Paul, Judaism and the Gentiles: A Sociological Approach,* SNTSMS (Cambridge: Cambridge University Press, 1986), represented Watson's criticism of the 'Lutheran Paul'. The revised edition, subtitled *Beyond the New Perspective* (Grand Rapids, MI: Eerdmans, 2007) pp. 27–56 gives his criticism from 1986; in a new introduction, pp. 1–26, Watson expands his criticism of the 'New Paul'.

13 W.D. Davies, *Paul and Rabbinic Judaism* (London: SPCK, 1948).

14 See Martin Hengel, *Judaism and Hellenism: Studies in their Encounter in Palestine During the Early Hellenistic Period* (London: SCM, 1974).

15 Stanley Stowers, *Letter Writing in Greco-Roman Antiquity* (Philadelphia, PA: Westminster, 1986).

16 J. Paul Sampley and Peter Lampe (eds), *Paul and Rhetoric* (New York, NY: T&T Clark, 2010).

17 Wayne A. Meeks, *The First Urban Christians: The Social World of the Apostle Paul* (New Haven, CT: Yale University Press, 1983).

18 'Social integration and sacramental activity: an analysis of 1 Corinthians 11:17–34' in Gerd Theissen, *The Social Setting of Pauline Christianity: Essays on Corinth* (Philadelphia, PA: Fortress, 1982), pp. 145–74.

19 See Bruce Malina, *The New Testament World: Insights from Cultural Anthropology* (Atlanta, GA: John Knox, 1981).

20 Mary Douglas, *Purity and Danger: An Analysis of the Concepts of Pollution and Taboo* (London: Routledge and Kegan Paul, 1966);

Mary Douglas, *Natural Symbols: Explorations in Cosmology* (New York, NY: Pantheon, 1982).

21   C. Geertz, *Interpretation of Cultures* (New York, NY: Basic, 1973).

22   See an early collected works of the Context Group, Philip F. Esler (ed.), *Modelling Early Christianity: Social-Scientific Studies of the New Testament in its Context* (London: Routledge, 1995).

23   Dietmar Neufeld and Richard E. DeMaris (eds), *Understanding the Social World of the New Testament* (London: Routledge, 2010).

24   Antoinette C. Wire, *The Corinthian Women Prophets: A Reconstruction through Paul's Rhetoric* (Minneapolis, MN: Fortress, 1990); Jorunn Økland, *Women in their Place: Paul and the Corinthian Discourse of Gender and Sanctuary Space* (London: T&T Clark, 2004).

25   Cynthia Briggs Kittredge, 'Feminist approaches: rethinking history and resisting ideologies', in Marchal, *Studying Paul's Letters*, pp. 117–33.

26   See a founding work of post-colonial studies; Bill Ashcroft, Gareth Griffiths and Helen Tiffin, *The Empire Writes Back: Theory and Practice in Post-Colonial Literatures*, 2nd ed. (London: Routledge, 1989/2002).

27   Musa W. Dube, *Postcolonial Feminist Interpretation of the Bible* (St. Louis, MO: Chalice Press, 2000); Fernando F. Segovia, *Decolonizing Biblical Studies: A View from the Margins* (Maryknoll, NY: Orbis, 2000); R.S. Sugirtharajah, *The Bible and the Third World: Precolonial, Colonial and Postcolonial Encounters* (Cambridge: Cambridge University Press, 2001).

28   Neil Elliott, 'The apostle Paul and empire' in Richard A Horsley (ed.), *In the Shadow of Empire* (Louisville, KY: Westminster John Knox, 2008), pp. 98–9.

29   See Warren Carter, and Richar A. Horsley in Further reading.

30   Jeremy Punt, 'Pauline agency in postcolonial perspective: subverter of or agent for empire?' in Christopher D. Stanley (ed.), *The Colonized Apostle: Paul Through Postcolonial Eyes*, (Minneapolis, MN: Fortress, 2011), pp. 53–61.

31   Neil Elliott, *The Arrogance of Nations: Reading Romans in the Shadow of Empire* (Minneapolis, MN: Fortress, 2008), p.15.

32   Paul Zanker *The Power of Images in the Age of Augustus* (Ann Arbor, MI: University of Michigan Press, 1988).

33   See Brigitte Kahe, *Galatians Re-Imagined: Reading with the Eyes of the Vanquished* (Minneapolis, MN: Fortress, 2010).

34   Davina Lopez, *Apostle to the Conquered: Reimagining Paul's Mission* (Minneapolis, MN: Fortress Press, 2008).

35   For the following, see John D. Caputo, 'Postcards from Paul: subtraction versus grafting' in John D. Caputo and Linda Martin Alcoff (eds), *St. Paul Among the Philosophers* (Bloomington, IND: Indiana

University Press, 2009). PhD student Ole Jakob Løland, Faculty of Theology, the University of Oslo, works on a thesis on the philosophers and Paul, and has taught me much about them.

36   Alain Badiou *St. Paul: the Foundation of Universalism* (Stanford, CA: Stanford University Press, 2003).

37   See Caputo and Alcoff, *St. Paul Among the Philosophers*.

CONCLUSION

1   Philip Jenk, *The New Faces of Christianity: Believing the Bible in the Global South* (Oxford: Oxford University Press, 2006).

Index